Fraud Investigation Reports in Practice

Investigation reports are written by fraud examiners after completion of internal reviews in client organizations when there was suspicion of financial wrongdoing. Fraud examiners are expected to answer questions regarding what happened, when it happened, how it happened, and why. This book presents a number of case studies of investigation reports by fraud examiners, offering a framework for studying the report as well as insights into convenience of fraud.

The case studies, including KPMG and PwC, focus on two important subjects. First, convenience themes are identified for each case. Themes derive from the theory of convenience, where fraud is a result of financial motives, organizational opportunities, and personal willingness for deviant behaviors. Second, review maturity is identified for each case. Review maturity derives from a stages-of-growth model, where the investigation is assigned a level of maturity based on explicit criteria. The book provides useful insights towards approaching fraud examinations to enable better understanding of the rational explanations for corporate fraud. The book is framed from the perspective of private policing, which contextualizes how investigation reports are examined.

This book is a valuable resource for scholars and upper-level students researching and studying auditing and investigation work in the corporate and public sectors. Business and management as well as criminal justice scholars and students will learn from the case studies how to frame a white-collar crime incident by application of convenience theory and how to evaluate a completed internal investigation by fraud examiners.

Petter Gottschalk is Professor in the Department of Leadership and Organizational Behavior at BI Norwegian Business School. After two decades in executive positions in business, he joined academics to publish extensively on knowledge management, fraud investigation, white-collar crime, and convenience theory.

Fraud Investigation Reports in Practice

Convenience and Corporate Crime

Petter Gottschalk

Routledge
Taylor & Francis Group
LONDON AND NEW YORK

First published 2023
by Routledge
4 Park Square, Milton Park, Abingdon, Oxon OX14 4RN

and by Routledge
605 Third Avenue, New York, NY 10158

Routledge is an imprint of the Taylor & Francis Group, an informa business

British Library Cataloguing-in-Publication Data
A catalogue record for this book is available from the British Library

Library of Congress Cataloging-in-Publication Data
A catalog record has been requested for this book

ISBN: 978-1-032-30433-5 (hbk)
ISBN: 978-1-032-30434-2 (pbk)
ISBN: 978-1-003-30507-1 (ebk)

DOI: 10.4324/9781003305071

Typeset in Bembo
by Taylor & Francis Books

Contents

Illustrations

Figures

Table

Introduction

Investigation reports are written by fraud examiners after completion of internal reviews in client organizations when there was suspicion of financial wrongdoing. Client organizations hire fraud examiners to reconstruct past events and sequences of events. Fraud examiners are expected to answer questions regarding what happened, when it happened, how it happened, who did what to make it happen or not happen, and why it happened or did not happen.

This book presents a number of case studies of investigation reports by fraud examiners. The case studies focus on two important subjects. First, convenience themes are identified for each case. Themes derive from the theory of convenience, where fraud is a result of financial motives, organizational opportunities, and personal willingness for deviant behaviors. Second, review maturity is identified for each case. Review maturity derives from a stages-of-growth model, where the investigation is assigned a level of maturity based on explicit criteria.

The purpose of this book is to combine insights into convenience of fraud and a following investigation when the offense is detected. Convenience theory is an integrated, deductive, and up-and-down explanation of crime where individual and organizational themes interact with each other. This emerging theory describes crime as a choice, where the relative convenience of legitimate versus illegitimate actions influences the tendency to commit crime. It is the relative extent of convenience that determines whether an offense is attractive. A very conveniently oriented decision-maker may resort to illegal activities when legal activities are slightly more stressful. A less conveniently oriented decision-maker may try intensely to solve problems and explore opportunities without violating the law. The research literature on convenience theory is growing (e.g., Braaten and Vaughn, 2019; Chan and Gibbs, 2020; Dearden and Gottschalk, 2020; Hansen, 2020; Kireenko et al., 2019; Leasure and Zhang, 2018; Otu and Okon, 2019; Reese and McDougal, 2018; Stadler and Gottschalk, 2021; Vasiu and Podgor, 2019).

The research literature focuses on convenience theory applied to white-collar offenders, and so do the case studies in this book. A white-collar offender is a person of respectability and high social status who commits economic crime in the course of occupational activities (Benson and Simpson, 2018; Craig and Piquero, 2017; Gottschalk and Tcherni-Buzzeo, 2017; Holtfreter, 2015; Huisman, 2020;

DOI: 10.4324/9781003305071-1

Logan et al., 2019; Pontell et al., 2014; Schoultz and Flyghed, 2016, 2019, 2020a, 2020b, 2021a, 2021b; Sutherland, 1939, 1983; Wall-Parker, 2020).

Investigation reports by fraud examiners represent the result of private policing, which is provision of policing services such as investigations and detective work other than by public servants (Brooks and Button, 2011; Button, 2020; Button et al., 2007a, 2007b; Button and Gee, 2013; King, 2020a, 2020b; Schneider, 2006; Williams, 2005a, 2005b, 2014). Fraud examiners at local law firms and global auditing firms conduct internal investigations at client organizations such as private enterprises and public authorities. Just like federal and public police investigators (Lee and Cho, 2020), private examiners need knowledge and awareness of typical human error sources such as confirmation traps, tunnel vision, and social stereotypes (Bjerknes and Fahsing, 2018; Goodman-Delahunty and Martschuk, 2020; Lee and Cho, 2020). For example, gender stereotypes distinguishing women and men along traditional thinking can cause investigative errors (Brands and Mehra, 2019).

More than a decade has passed since Schneider (2006) and Williams (2005a, 2005b) emphasized the problematic role of fraud examiners in internal investigations, as examiners conduct private policing of economic crime. In the meantime, however, the business of fraud examinations has grown substantially in forensic departments in auditing firms and in consulting departments in law firms. Examples of auditing firms include Deloitte (2015), Ernst & Young (2020), KPMG (2020), and PwC (2020a, 2020b). Examples of law firms include Plesner (2020), and Wiersholm (2020). This book develops such referenced examples into case studies of internal investigations of economic crime focusing on internal investigations by fraud examiners.

The problematic role of fraud examiners emphasized by Schneider (2006) and Williams (2005a, 2005b) was exemplified more recently by King (2020c: 16) in terms of the transnational nature of many investigations:

> The complexity of financial and corporate crime investigation, coupled with the mix of occupational jurisdictions, raises issues for regulators that may be difficult to overcome, such as creating formal regulatory training programs for private investigative certification. The changing nature of private investigation presents several issues that need resolving, specifically regulation and licensing.

The private forensics business of fraud examinations has expanded rapidly in recent years. One of the reasons is the lack of public police priority to investigate financial crime generally and white-collar crime particularly (Brooks and Button, 2011; Button, 2020; Button and Gee, 2013; Button et al., 2007a, 2007b, 2008, 2009, 2014; Cullen et al., 2020; Gottschalk, 2020a, 2020b; Gottschalk and Gunnesdal, 2018; Lord and Wingerde, 2020; Wood, 2020). Police agencies are not prepared to meet the growing need for policing financial crime, especially crime by white-collar offenders, as public police is finding it difficult to adapt to a rapidly changing landscape (Button et al., 2009; Loveday, 2017). Specially trained detectives for white-collar crime are almost non-existent or incompetent (Skidmore et al., 2018). Public police agencies involved in financial crime investigations concerned with white-collar offenders are typically under-resourced. They lack training, and they perceive that there is a high level of complexity associated with these types of investigations that they do not handle professionally. They do not understand business transactions and offender behaviors, and they may have negative attitudes towards victims (Button et al., 2008; Skidmore et al., 2020). They do not necessarily feel sorry for banks, vendors, shareholders, investors, or employers who suffer from fraud, corruption, or embezzlement. The police duty of care is often neglected or ignored in identifying the need for support of financial crime victims (Button et al., 2009). Furthermore, it is often suggested that fraud victims are largely to blame for their own victimization. Fraud victims are sometimes seen as greedy, opportunistic, and naïve, who lack the necessary skills to control their own activities (Button et al., 2014; Webster and Drew, 2017). For example, if an employee embezzles the employer, it is not obvious that the case is a priority matter for public policing. Rather, an employer is supposed to have control mechanisms to prevent an employee from wrongdoing.

Compared to other types of crime, such as street crime, research has confirmed that governments and law enforcement agencies do not prioritize financial crime (Cullen et al., 2020; Skidmore et al., 2020). Often, police executives do not view financial crime as part of their core duties (Crocker et al., 2017). A lack of competence and apparent disinterest in financial crime in policing persists, despite the growing and overwhelming evidence that financial crime is one of the most commonly experienced crime types (Skidmore et al., 2020) that harm individuals, organizations, as well as society with low detection rates (Andresen and Button, 2019; Gottschalk and Gunnesdal, 2018; Huff et al., 2010), where offenders tend to move under the radar (Williams et al., 2019). Like many other professionals, police officers tend to prefer case work where they understand what is going on, which is typically street crime. Investigations into fraud compete for resources and are generally overshadowed by high-profile crime such as homicide, drugs, and child abuse (Button et al., 2012).

The lack of appropriately trained police investigators increases the volume of undetected and unsolved financial crime cases (Button et al., 2014), which is now partly taken over by the private fraud investigation industry (King, 2020a, 2020b; Wood, 2020). Corporate victims and other stakeholders want to find out what happened, how it happened, when it happened, why it happened, and who did what to make it happen or not happen. An investigation is the information-gathering process aimed to uncover what happened, how the misconduct or offense was committed, by whom, so as successfully to draw conclusions in the reconstruction of past events (Lee and Cho, 2020).

In some countries, organizations are required by law to investigate after whistleblowing of suspected wrongdoing. Organizations typically do not have relevant competence to reconstruct past events. Therefore, they hire private examiners to investigate allegations and accusations that emerge from whistleblower reports. A whistleblower is a person who is or was associated with the organization, who notices deviance, and who reports observations in an acceptable manner to someone who can do something about it. In many countries, you are not a whistleblower if you were a victim of the wrongdoing. Whistleblowing has received increased research interest in recent years (e.g., Alleyne et al., 2013; Andrade, 2015; Bjørkelo et al., 2011; Brown et al., 2016; Bussmann et al., 2018; Culiberg and Mihelic, 2017; Dyck et al., 2010; Gao et al., 2015; Keil et al., 2010; Mesmer-Magnus and Viswesvaran, 2005; Miceli and Near, 2013; Mpho, 2017; Park et al., 2020; Potipiroon and Wongpreedee, 2020; Rehg et al., 2009; Shawver and Clements, 2019; Tankebe, 2019).

Client organizations hire fraud examiners from local law firms and global auditing firms to conduct internal investigations. The result of an examination is a report of investigation that is handed over to the client, and the report becomes the property of the client since the client paid for the investigation. These reports are the subject of study in this book. A typical report is one hundred pages long and presents a mandate, a procedure, and findings. Unfortunately, most clients keep reports secret and confidential (Gottschalk and Tcherni-Buzzeo, 2017; Stenström, 2018). "Typically, corporations tend to take their own measures to resolve instances of fraud without resorting to the police" (King, 2020a: 1). "Corporate clients can effectively choose to sidestep the criminal justice system and not report matters to authorities, propagating debate on the treatment of white-collar criminals compared to others" (King, 2020b: 9). Therefore, only a few investigation reports become available to identify convenience themes and review maturity for research presented in this book.

Beneficiaries of reconstructing past events and sequences of events can range from everyone, as in the case of the criminal justice system, to only those entities that fund private internal investigations. Furthermore, "the public police, as an institution of the criminal justice system, inherently possess a punishment or coercion-based mentality propelled by their authority as agents of the criminal law and their capacity to apply state-sanctioned force" (Wood, 2020: 25). In contrast, private examination of economic crime is consulting work where fraud examiners are supposed to conduct internal investigations to establish facts and advise clients what to do next.

The business of internal investigations by fraud examiners seems to be growing more rapidly than national and international public police organizations to combat fraud (Wood, 2020: 26):

> Determining the ratios of private agents to public agents is invariability hard to do with much accuracy, but it is clear that private policing entities surpass the latter in sheer numbers and to varying degrees across established democracies and countries in transition.

An example of private examination is the investigation of suspected insurance fraud. Stenström (2018: 478) studied the ways private investigation is organized with regard to profitability for insurance firms in Sweden:

> While the literature on private policing has enhanced our understanding of its growth, scope and normative implications, less is known about how "hybrid" policing is conducted to make profit. Informed by 38 qualitative interviews with the seven largest insurance companies in Sweden, the article details how power relations are organized to ensure that the private policing of insurance claims supports and does not pose a threat to profit. Drawing on evidence from the empirical research, a range of issues are discussed, including the relationship between private policing and state power, and the intertwined governance of both claimants and policing actors.

Stenström (2018) found that an investigation has to be profitable, which means that a small claim cannot cause a large investigation effort. A relevant example here from the neighboring country Norway is the insurance company Gjensidige, which has a claim against some Hells Angels members. Since Gjensidige believes there are few valuable assets to be retrieved from the Hells Angels members, the insurance firm is not willing to spend resources investigating them. While the perspective of corporate social responsibility might imply that the insurance firm should nevertheless investigate and thus help Norwegian police investigate organized criminals such as Hells Angels, the insurance firm is reluctant to do it (Gottschalk, 2013). The perspective of internal investigations by fraud examiners being profitable is relevant for this book, as a fraud examination effort can be considered an investment, where benefits can exceed costs of the investigation. King (2020a) argues that nine attributes are critical for the corporate investigator's inquiry success: communication, motivation, industry experience, qualifications, police or regulatory experience, business acumen, conceptual thinking, resilience, and rapport building.

The purpose of this book is to study cases of internal investigations by fraud examiners. The book presents two frameworks to study investigation reports by fraud examiners. First, a structural model is introduced to identify convenience themes in each case study. Second, a stage model is introduced to identify maturity level in each case study.

The emerging theory of convenience for white-collar crime is concerned with financial possibilities and threats, organizational opportunity to commit and conceal financial crime, as well as personal willingness for deviant behavior. The research literature on convenience theory is growing (e.g., Braaten and Vaughn, 2019; Chan and Gibbs, 2020; Dearden and Gottschalk, 2020; Gottschalk, 2020b; Hansen, 2020; Kireenko et al., 2019; Leasure and Zhang, 2018; Otu and Okon, 2019; Reese and McDougal, 2018; Vasiu and Podgor, 2019).

White-collar offenders commit financial crime during their occupations (Craig, 2019; Craig and Piquero, 2016; Dearden, 2016, 2017, 2019; Jordanoska, 2018; Klenowski et al., 2011; Onna, 2020; Onna and Denkers, 2019). Convenience theory suggests that the financial motive in white-collar crime is to explore possibilities and avoid threats; the organizational opportunity is to commit as well as conceal crime, while the willingness is deviant behavior by justification and neutralization (Vasiu and Podgor, 2019). The theory of convenience is an integrated and deductive perspective based on the synthesis of individual-level, group-level, and nation-level themes (Chan and Gibbs, 2020; Gottschalk, 2020b). Convenience theory builds on previous theoretical perspectives on fraud, such as the fraud triangle, the fraud scale, the fraud diamond, the MICE model, and the ABC model (Desai, 2016), as well as general theoretical perspectives on economic crime.

Convenience is the state of being able to proceed with something with little effort or difficulty, avoiding pain and strain (Mai and Olsen, 2016). Convenience is savings in time and effort (Farquhar and Rowley, 2009), as well as avoidance of pain and obstacles (Higgins, 1997). Convenience is a relative concept concerned with efficiency in time and effort as well as reduction in pain and solution to problems (Engdahl, 2015). Convenience is an advantage in favor of a specific action to the detriment of alternative actions. White-collar offenders choose the most convenient path to reach their goals.

White-collar crime results from delinquent behavior by individuals in competent positions (Piquero, 2018). White-collar offenders commit and conceal their crime in a professional setting (Gottschalk, 2020a, 2020b) where they have legitimate access to premises, resources, and systems (Logan et al., 2019). The benefit from white-collar crime might be financial gain, personal adventure, or some other desired outcome (Craig and Piquero, 2017; Jordanoska, 2018; Sutherland, 1939, 1983; Williams et al., 2019).

Figure 0.1 illustrates the structure of white-collar convenience as derived from the research literature within criminology, sociology, psychology, and management (Gottschalk, 2020b). The extent of white-collar crime convenience manifests itself by motive, opportunity, and willingness. The motive is either occupational crime to benefit the individual or corporate crime to benefit the organization because of possibilities or threats (Alalehto, 2020). The ability of white-collar offenders to commit and conceal crime links to their privileged position, the social structure, and their orientation to legitimate and respectable careers (Friedrichs et al., 2018).

The personal willingness for deviant behavior manifests itself by offender choice and perceived innocence. The choice of crime can be caused by deviant identity, rational consideration, or learning from others. Social identity is an individual's self-concept as an organizational member (Piening et al., 2020). The perceived innocence at crime manifests itself by justification and neutralization (Schoultz and Flyghed, 2020a). Identity, rationality, learning, justification, neutralization, and lack of self-control all contribute to making white-collar crime action a convenient behavior for offenders (Craig and Piquero, 2017; Engdahl, 2015; Holtfreter et al., 2010; Sutherland, 1983; Sykes and Matza, 1957).

In criminology, the conceptualization of deviant behavior is implicitly negative actions that lack conformity to norms (Sykes and Matza, 1957). Deviant behavior typically causes harm to victims. Offenders depart from norms in destructive ways. In our context, deviance is negative departure from norms by white-collar offenders.

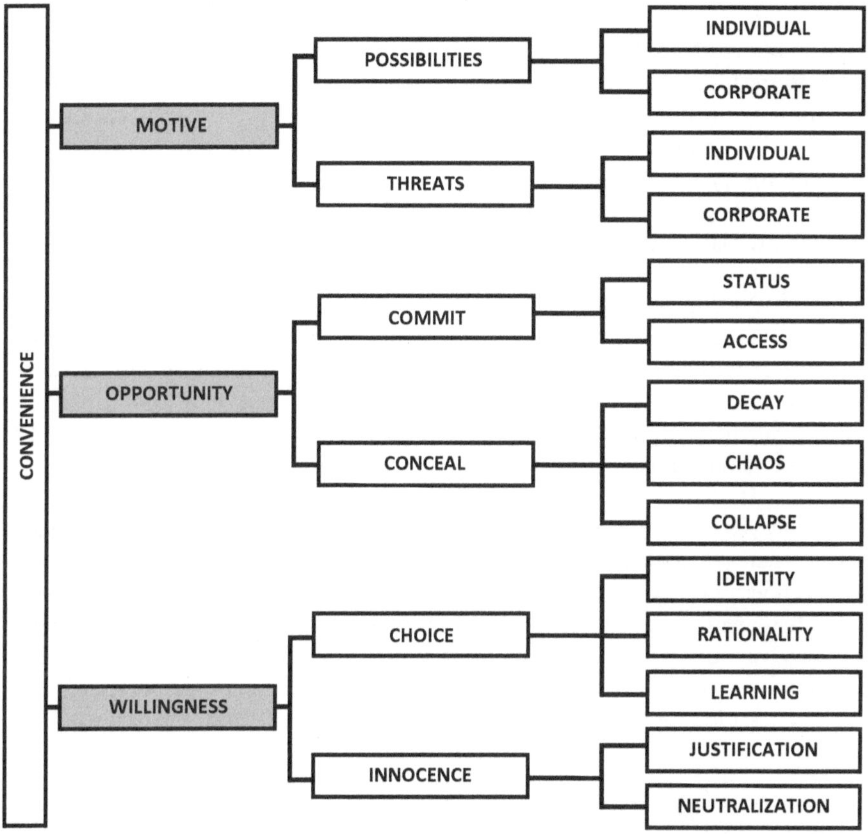

Figure 0.1 Structural model of convenience theory for white-collar crime

In white-collar research, there are different kinds of conception and operationalization of the construct of white-collar crime. Even though Sutherland (1939) coined the term more than eight decades ago, white-collar research remains preoccupied with definition. While many still engage in agitation and dispute about the white-collar crime concept, as exemplified by Galvin (2020), this research simply applies the basic characteristics of the offender, which include status, trust, and access.

Each case study in this book applies the described structural model for convenience theory in Figure 0.1. Each case study also applies the maturity model for private investigations in Figure 0.2.

Stages of growth models for maturity levels help to assess and evaluate a variety of phenomena (e.g., Masood et al., 2020; Röglinger et al., 2012; Solli-Sæther and Gottschalk, 2015). Stage models predict the development or evolution of investigative maturity from basic performance to superior results (Iannacci et al., 2019: 310).

They also suggest that this development is progressive (i.e., each successive stage is better than the previous one), stepwise (i.e., each step is a necessary prerequisite for the following step in the sequence), and prescriptive (i.e., each step must occur in a prescribed order in accordance with a pre-existing plan or vision), thus emphasizing the chain of successful events rather than the mechanisms by which subsequent stages come about.

Here we apply the concept of stages in terms of maturity levels to evaluate private internal investigations (Brooks and Button, 2011; Button and Gee, 2013; Button et al., 2007a, 2007b; King, 2020a, 2020b; Schneider, 2006; Williams, 2005a, 2005b). The purpose is to develop characteristics of investigations at different maturity levels. Based on previous studies of investigation reports (Gottschalk, 2020a), we present a five-stage model as illustrated in Figure 0.2.

The four maturity levels in the stage model for fraud examinations have the following descriptions:

1 *Activity-oriented investigation: The examination is a chaos.* The investigation focuses on activities that may have been carried out in a reprehensible manner. The examiners look for activities and prepare descriptions of these. Then examiners make up their minds whether the activities were reprehensible or not. Here it is often auditors and others with financial knowledge. They are to assess financial transactions and management of assets. The investigation at level 1 is often passive, fruitless, and characterized by

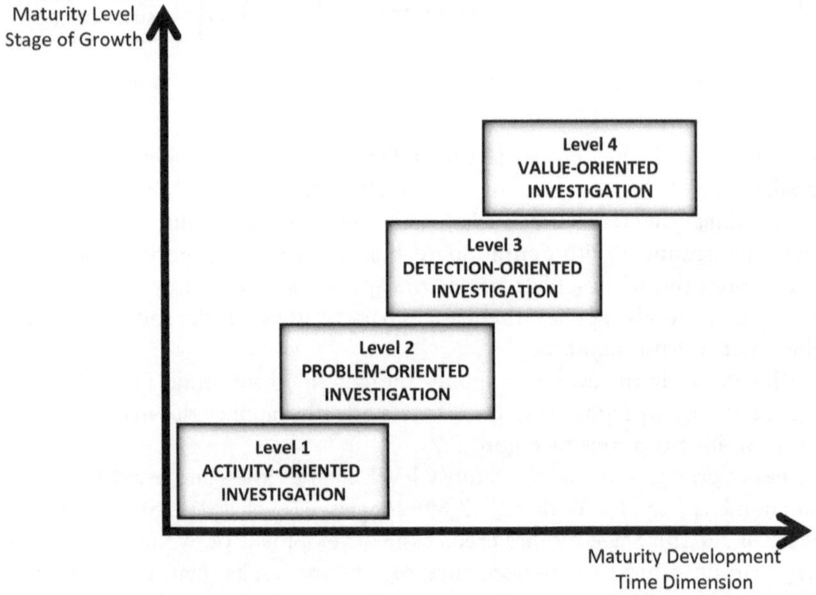

Figure 0.2 Maturity model for internal private investigations with four stages

unnecessary use of resources. At this lowest maturity level, investigators typically attempt to find an answer to the question: What happened?

2 The investigation might cause more confusion than before the examination was initiated. The investigation is typically insufficient, inadequate, surface-oriented, a waste of time, useless, passive, unprofessional, worthless, immature, unacceptable, bad, meaningless, fruitless, awful, and chaotic. The investigation is often a failure and a disaster. The investigation lacks useful results and has little or no value. Investigators typically look where it is easy to find something, rather than searching for relevant information to solve the case. This stage might deserve the following label: Waste of time.

3 *Problem-oriented investigation: The examination is a mess.* The investigation focuses on an issue that needs clarification. Examiners are looking for answers. Once examiners believe they have found answers, the investigation is terminated. It is important to spend as little resources as possible on the investigation, which should take the shortest possible time. Delamination and management are important for success. The client had an unresolved problem, and the client regulates premises for the investigation. There is no room for investigators to pursue other paths than those that address the predefined problem. Here it is often lawyers and others with legal knowledge. They are to map the facts. At this second maturity level, investigators typically attempt to find an answer to the question: How did it happen?

4 Often, little or nothing comes out of the investigation. The investigation is typically random, amateurish, formalities-focused, somewhat beneficial, but not enough, mainly descriptive, problem-oriented, neutral, unsystematic, inadequate, activity-oriented, shortsighted, fruitless, deviations-oriented, reactive, questions-oriented, and messy. The investigation tends to lack scrutiny, is a collection of information without analysis, and has too many assumptions that make conclusions less valid or invalid. The investigation is superficial and very limited. This stage might deserve the following label: Wishful thinking.

5 *Detection-oriented investigation: The examination is a disclosure.* The investigation focuses on something being hidden, which should be revealed. Investigators choose their tactics to succeed in exposing possible misconduct and perhaps even financial crime. Investigative steps are adapted to the terrain, where different sources of information and methods are used to get as many facts on the table as possible. Here it is often police-trained investigators and other private detectives. They are to uncover possible crime. While level 1 and level 2 are focused on suspicions of financial crime, level 3 is focused on suspicions against potential financial criminals. There are always criminals who commit crime. Level 3 has a focus on individuals, while level 2 has a focus on activities. Level 3 is characterized by the search for responsible persons who may have abused their positions for personal or corporate gain. This is a more demanding examination, because suspicions and suspects must be handled in a responsible manner in relation to the rule of law and human rights. Level 3 investigations are active with significant breakthroughs in the examinations.

Investigation projects are carried out in a professional and efficient manner. At this third maturity level, investigators typically attempt to find an answer to the question: Why did it happen?

6 Examiners are successful in identifying and documenting some new facts. The investigation has a clear perspective. It is competence-oriented, average, biased, targeted, systematized, integrated, moderate, indifferent, standard, competent, cause-based, revealing, and disclosure-oriented. The investigation is problem-oriented and limited by the mandate. The investigation is reflective, yet only slightly above average. This stage might deserve the following label: Better luck next time.

7 *Value-oriented investigation: The examination is a clarification.* The investigation focuses on value created by the examination, where the investigation is an investment by the client with an expectation of benefits exceeding costs. The ambition of the investigation is that the result will be valuable to the client. The value can lie in clean-up, change, simplification, renewal, and other measures for the future. The investigation also focuses on being justifiable. A number of explicit considerations are identified and practiced throughout the inquiry. In addition, the investigation has a focus on explicit decisions regarding information strategy, method strategy, configuration strategy, and system strategy. By explicit strategic choices, the investigation becomes transparent and understandable to the parties involved and affected. It is often examiners in interdisciplinary teams who are to contribute to value creation for the client. Level 4 investigations are characterized by the active use of strategies, with significant and decisive breakthroughs in the inquiries, which lay the foundation for learning and value creation in the client's organization. The value may, for example, be that detected deviations and wrongdoings become sanctioned and corrected in a satisfactory manner. At level 4, detection, disclosure, clarification, and solution are seen in context. There will be less to detect in the future if prevention is strengthened. It will be better in the future if the case is completely resolved. The examiners create value by proper investigation. Value is created before, during, and after the investigation. Before the investigation, risk understanding and prioritization are developed. During the investigation, method understanding is developed. After the investigation, barriers are built against fraud, holes are closed, routines are developed and practiced, and evaluation is established on a continuous basis. At this top maturity level, investigators try to find the answer to the questions: What went wrong, what can the client learn, and how can wrongdoing be prevented from happening again in the future?

8 Examiners at level 4 are able to reconstruct past events and sequences of events. The investigation is responsible, detailed, conscientious, enough, professional, neutral, unprejudiced, integrated, proactive, preventive, mature, competent, systematic, professional, explorative, immaculate, expedient, truth seeking, facts-based, complete, independent, and clarifying. The investigation adds value. The investigation is thorough and works well. This stage might deserve the following label: Time well spent.

9 The investigation is an investment. The investigation makes a valuable contribution to the client organization, where investigation benefits exceed investigation costs. The investigation is optimal, innovative, profitable, strategic, extraordinary, outstanding, provident, value-oriented, advanced, learning-focused, valuable, irreversible, truth-based, socially responsible, exceptional, excellent, perfect, exemplary, and a profitable investment. The investigation is a masterpiece and enrichment for the client and society. The investigation is complete and influential. The investigation is strategically a success. This stage might deserve the following label as well as the first-mentioned label: Here's my money.

Fraud examination strategies influence the level of maturity, where Gottschalk (2020a) makes distinctions between five strategies. First, knowledge strategy defines the areas of expertise that fraud examiners must apply to the task of reconstructing past events and sequences of events, where knowledge sharing from different professionals is required (Muhammed and Zaim, 2020). Very often, knowledge of the law is the dominating expertise applied, while there is a lack of organizational and accounting knowledge in the investigation. Next, information strategy defines sources of information that contribute to reconstructing past events and sequences of events. Very often, formal documents such as minutes of meetings are the dominating source applied, while there is a lack of investigative interviewing and visits to potential crime scenes. Third, value configuration strategy defines the primary activities in the investigation. Very often, the value chain is the dominating configuration, where tasks follow in a sequential manner, while the alternative of the value shop is a more relevant configuration, where tasks follow each other iteratively by returning to earlier tasks. Fourth, systems strategy defines the application of information technology and digitalization in the investigation. Very often, simple search words are used in digital queries that provide few and inconclusive instances of suspicious activities. Finally, methods strategy defines the overall approach and perspectives in the investigation. Very often, fraud examiners conduct interviews in a confrontational rather than cooperative manner. Very often, examiners have a thinking style of systematic analysis rather than the challenge style or the risk style of investigative thinking.

Each case study in this book applies the described model of maturity in fraud investigations. Each case study also applies the structural model of convenience theory as illustrated in Figure 0.1. The emerging theory of convenience for white-collar crime is concerned with financial possibilities and threats, organizational opportunity to commit and conceal financial crime, as well as personal willingness for deviant behavior.

The methodology applied to investigation reports in this book is content analysis (Bell et al., 2018; Braaten and Vaughn, 2019; Saunders et al., 2007). Content analysis is any methodology or procedure that works to identify characteristics within texts attempting to make valid inferences (Krippendorff, 1980; Patrucco et al., 2017). Content analysis assumes that language reflects both how people understand their surroundings and their cognitive processes. Therefore, content analysis makes it possible to identify and determine relevant text in a context (McClelland et al., 2010).

Chapter 1 presents the core of convenience theory in terms of convenience themes in the opportunity structure for misconduct and crime. Convenience themes include high social status in privileged positions, legitimate access to crime resources, disorganized institutional deterioration, lack of oversight and guardianship, and crime market structures. Such themes contribute to the convenience of offending by privileged individuals.

In the following nine chapters, case studies are presented to identify specific convenience themes as well as to assess review maturity of investigation reports. Chapter 2 analyzes the case of a publicly funded entity where whistleblowers had presented allegations of fraud that were then investigated by audit firm Ernst & Young. Chapter 3 analyzes the case of a Danish bank where bank customers perceived illegitimately being denied funds that was investigated by law firm Plesner. Chapter 4 analyzes the case of an energy company where large-scale spending occurred in the United States that was investigated by audit firm PwC. Chapter 5 analyzes a Norwegian cruise line that seemed to ignore a Covid-19 outbreak for financial reasons, which was then investigated by law firm Wiersholm. Chapter 6 analyzes the case of funds that never arrived at the correct destination of Cambodia, but rather disappeared, where the disappearance was investigated by audit firm PwC.

Chapter 7 analyzes the case of executives who allegedly provided illegitimate preference to an entrepreneur, which was then investigated by audit firm KPMG. Chapter 8 analyzes the case of alleged corruption from an Icelandic seafood company to Namibian ministers to gain access to fishing rights that were then investigated by law firm Wikborg Rein. Chapter 9 analyzes a German financial institution that was accused of accounting manipulation, which was investigated by audit firm KPMG.

The final Chapter 10 is a different case study of a convicted white-collar criminal in the United States who recently wrote his autobiography. Based on his book, it is possible to identify his convenience themes when committing fraud.

References

Alalehto, T. (2020). Corporate crime: A logical misconception, but with one analytical point, *Journal of Financial Crime*, published online doi:10.1108/JFC-04-2020-0063.

Alleyne, P., Hudaib, M. and Pike, R. (2013). Towards a conceptual model of whistle-blowing intentions among external auditors, *The British Accounting Review*, 45 (1), 10–23.

Andrade, J. (2015). Reconceptualising whistleblowing in a complex world, *Journal of Business Ethics*, 128 (2), 321–335.

Andresen, M.S. and Button, M. (2019). The profile and detection of bribery in Norway and England & Wales: A comparative study, *European Journal of Criminology*, 16 (1), 18–40.

Bell, E., Bryman, A. and Harley, B. (2018). *Business Research Methods*, 2nd edition, New York, NY: Oxford University Press.

Benson, M.L. and Simpson, S.S. (2018). *Understanding White-Collar Crime – An Opportunity Perspective*, 2nd edition, New York, NY: Routledge.

Bjerknes, O.T. and Fahsing, I.A. (2018). *Etterforskning – Prinsipper, metoder og praksis (Investigation – Principles, Methods, and Practice)*, Bergen, Norway: Fagbokforlaget publishing house.

Bjørkelo, B., Einarsen, S., Nielsen, M.B. and Matthiesen, S.B. (2011). Silence is golden? Characteristics and experiences of self-reported whistleblowers, *European Journal of Work and Organizational Psychology*, 20 (2), 206–238.

Braaten, C.N. and Vaughn, M.S. (2019). Convenience theory of cryptocurrency crime: A content analysis of U.S. federal court decisions, *Deviant Behavior*, published online doi:10.1080/01639625.2019.1706706.

Brands, R.A. and Mehra, A. (2019). Gender, brokerage, and performance: A construal approach, *Academy of Management Journal*, 62 (1), 196–219.

Brooks, G. and Button, M. (2011). The police and fraud investigation and the case for a nationalized solution in the United Kingdom, *The Police Journal*, 84, 305–319.

Brown, J.O., Hays, J. and Stuebs, M.T. (2016). Modeling accountant whistleblowing intentions: Applying the theory of planned behavior and the fraud triangle, *Accounting and the Public Interest*, 16 (1), 28–56.

Bussmann, K.D., Niemeczek, A. and Vockrodt, M. (2018). Company culture and prevention of corruption in Germany, China and Russia, *European Journal of Criminology*, 15 (3), 255–277.

Button, M. (2020). The "new" private security industry, the private policing of cyberspace and the regulatory questions, *Journal of Contemporary Criminal Justice*, 36 (1), 39–55.

Button, M. and Gee, J. (2013). *Countering Fraud for Competitive Advantage – The Professional Approach to Reducing the Last Great Hidden Cost*, Chichester, UK: John Wiley & Sons.

Button, M., Frimpong, K., Smith, G. and Johnston, L. (2007a). Professionalizing counter fraud specialists in the UK: assessing progress and recommendations for reform, *Crime Prevention and Community Safety*, 9, 92–101.

Button, M., Johnston, L., Frimpong, K. and Smith, G. (2007b). New directions in policing fraud: The emergence of the counter fraud specialists in the United Kingdom, *International Journal of the Sociology of Law*, 35, 192–208.

Button, M., Johnston, L. and Frimpong, K. (2008). The fraud review and the policing of fraud: Laying the foundations for a centralized fraud police or counter fraud executive? *Policing: A Journal of Policy and Practice*, 2 (2), 241–250.

Button, M., Lewis, C. and Tapley, J. (2009). *A Better Deal for Fraud Victims: Research into Victim's Needs and Experiences*, London, UK: National Fraud Authority (NFA), Office of Fair Trading.

Button, M., Lewis, C., Shepherd, D., Brooks, G. and Wakefield, A. (2012). *Fraud and Punishment: Enhancing Deterrence through more Effective Sanctions*, Technical Report, Portsmouth, UK: University of Portsmouth.

Button, M., Blackbourn, D. and Tunley, M. (2014). 'The not so thin blue line after all?' Investigative resources dedicated to fighting fraud/economic crime in the United Kingdom, *Policing: A Journal of Policy and Practice*, 9 (2), 129–142.

Chan, F. and Gibbs, C. (2020). Integrated theories of white-collar and corporate crime, in: Rorie, M.L. (editor), *The Handbook of White-Collar Crime*, Hoboken, NJ: Wiley & Sons, chapter 13, pages 191–208.

Craig, J.M. (2019). Extending situational action theory to white-collar crime, *Deviant Behavior*, 40 (2), 171–186.

Craig, J.M. and Piquero, N.L. (2016). The effects of low self-control and desire-for-control on white-collar offending: A replication, *Deviant Behavior*, 37 (11), 1308–1324.

Craig, J.M. and Piquero, N.L. (2017). Sensational offending: An application of sensation seeking to white-collar and conventional crimes, *Crime & Delinquency*, 63 (11), 1363–1382.

Crocker, R., Webb, S., Garner, S., Skidmore, M., Gill, M. and Graham, J. (2017). *The Impact of Organized Crime in Local Communities*, London, UK: The Police Foundation / Perpetuity Research.

Culiberg, B. and Mihelic, K.K. (2017). The evolution of whistleblowing studies: A critical review and research agenda, *Journal of Business Ethics*, 146 (4), 787–803.

Cullen, F.T., Chouhy, C. and Jonson, C.L. (2020). Public opinion about white-collar crime, in: Rorie, M.L. (editor), *The Handbook of White-Collar Crime*, Hoboken, NJ: Wiley & Sons, chapter 14, pages 211–228.

Dearden, T.E. (2016). Trust: the unwritten cost of white-collar crime, *Journal of Financial Crime*, 23 (1), 87–101.

Dearden, T.E. (2017). An assessment of adults' views on white-collar crime, *Journal of Financial Crime*, 24 (2), 309–321.

Dearden, T.E. (2019). How modern psychology can help us understand white-collar criminals, *Journal of Financial Crime*, 26 (1), 61–73.

Dearden, T.E. and Gottschalk, P. (2020). Gender and white-collar crime: Convenience in target selection, *Deviant Behavior*, published online doi:10.1080/01639625.2020.1756428.

Deloitte (2015). *Investigation Report, Summary Version, Independent Investigation Committee for Toshiba Corporation*, report of investigation, audit firm Deloitte Tohmatsu, Tokyo, Japan.

Desai, V.M. (2016). Under the radar: Regulatory collaborations and their selective use to facilitate organizational compliance, *Academy of Management Journal*, 59 (2), 636–657.

Dyck, A., Morse, A. and Zingales, L. (2010). Who blows the whistle on corporate fraud? *The Journal of Finance*, 65 (6), 2213–2253.

Engdahl, O. (2015). White-collar crime and first-time adult-onset offending: Explorations in the concept of negative life events as turning points, *International Journal of Law, Crime and Justice*, 43 (1), 1–16.

Ernst & Young (2020). *Notat vedrørende undersøkelser utført for IMDi (Report concerning investigation conducted for IMDi)*, report of investigation, audit firm Ernst & Young, Oslo, Norway, September 18, 36 pages.

Farquhar, J.D. and Rowley, J. (2009). Convenience: a services perspective, *Marketing Theory*, 9 (4), 425–438.

Friedrichs, D.O., Schoultz, I. and Jordanoska, A. (2018). *Edwin H. Sutherland, Routledge Key Thinkers in Criminology*, London, UK: Routledge.

Galvin, M.A. (2020). Gender and white-collar crime – Theoretical issues, *Criminal Justice Studies*, published online, doi:10.1080/1478601X.2020.1709954.

Gao, J., Greenberg, R. and Wong-On-Wing, B. (2015). Whistleblowing intentions of lower-level employees: The effect of reporting channel, bystanders, and wrongdoing, *Journal of Business Ethics*, 126 (1), 85–99.

Goodman-Delahunty, J. and Martschuk, N. (2020). Securing reliable information in investigative interviews: Coercive and noncoercive strategies preceding turning points, *Police Practice and Research*, 21 (2), 152–171.

Gottschalk, P. (2013). Limits to corporate social responsibility: The case of Gjensidige Insurance Company and Hells Angels Motorcycle Club, *Corporate Reputation Review*, 16 (3), 177–186.

Gottschalk, P. (2020a). *The Privatization of Fraud Investigation: Internal Investigation by Fraud Examiners*, Abingdon, UK: Routledge.

Gottschalk, P. (2020b). *Convenience Dynamics and White-Collar Crime*, Abingdon, UK: Routledge.

Gottschalk, P. and Gunnesdal, L. (2018). *White-Collar Crime in the Shadow Economy: Lack of Detection, Investigation, and Conviction compared to Social Security Fraud*, London, UK: Palgrave Pivot, Palgrave Macmillan, Springer Publishing.

Gottschalk, P. and Tcherni-Buzzeo, M. (2017). Reasons for gaps in crime reporting: The case of white-collar criminals investigated by private fraud examiners in Norway, *Deviant Behavior*, 38 (3), 267–281.

Hansen, L.L. (2020). Review of the book "Convenience Triangle in White-Collar Crime: Case Studies of Fraud Examinations", *ChoiceConnect*, vol. 57, no. 5, Middletown, CT: Association of College and Research Libraries.

Higgins, E.T. (1997). Beyond pleasure and pain, *American Psychologist*, 52, 1280–1300.

Holtfreter, K. (2015). General theory, gender-specific theory, and white-collar crime, *Journal of Financial Crime*, 22 (4), 422–431.

Holtfreter, K., Beaver, K.M., Reisig, M.D. and Pratt, T.C. (2010). Low self-control and fraud offending, *Journal of Financial Crime*, 17 (3), 295–307.

Huff, R., Desilets, K. and Kane, J. (2010). *The National Public Survey on White Collar Crime*, West Virginia: National White Collar Crime Center, Fairmont, www.nw3c.org.

Huisman, W. (2020). Blurred lines: Collusions between legitimate and illegitimate organizations, in: Rorie, M.L. (editor), *The Handbook of White-Collar Crime*, Hoboken, NJ: Wiley & Sons, chapter 10, pages 139–158.

Iannacci, F., Seepma, A.P., Blok, C. and Resca, A. (2019). Reappraising maturity models in e-government research: The trajectory-turning point theory, *Journal of Strategic Information Systems*, 28, 310–329.

Jordanoska, A. (2018). The social ecology of white-collar crime: Applying situational action theory to white-collar offending, *Deviant Behavior*, 39 (11), 1427–1449.

Keil, M., Tiwana, A., Sainsbury, R. and Sneha, S. (2010). Toward a theory of whistleblowing intentions: A benefit-cost differential perspective, *Decision Sciences*, 41 (4), 787–812.

King, M. (2020a). What makes a successful corporate investigator – An exploration of private investigators attributes, *Journal of Financial Crime*, published online doi:10.1108/JFC-02-2020-0019.

King, M. (2020b). Out of obscurity: The contemporary private investigator in Australia, *International Journal of Police Science and Management*, published online doi:10.1177/1461355720931887.

King, M. (2020c). Private investigation into economic crime: Regulation of a multidisciplinary field, *Journal of Applied Security Research*, published online doi:10.1080/19361610.2020.1832018.

Kireenko, A.P., Nevzorova, E.N. and Fedotov, D.Y. (2019). Sector-specific characteristics of tax crime in Russia, *Journal of Tax Reform*, 5 (3), 249–264.

Klenowski, P.M., Copes, H. and Mullins, C.W. (2011). Gender, identity, and accounts: How white collar offenders do gender when making sense of their crimes, *Justice Quarterly*, 28 (1), 46–69.

KPMG (2020). *Report Concerning the Independent Special Investigation at Wirecard AG*, April 27, audit firm KPMG, Munich, Germany, 74 pages.

Krippendorff, K. (1980). *Content Analysis: An Introduction to its Methodology*, Beverly Hills, CA: Sage.

Leasure, P. and Zhang, G. (2018). "That's how they taught us to do it": Learned deviance and inadequate deterrents in retail banking, *Deviant Behavior*, 39 (5), 603–616.

Lee, Y.H. and Cho, S. (2020). The different crime solving styles of police agencies across the United States: A latent class analysis of criminal investigation goals, *American Journal of Criminal Justice*, published online doi:10.1007/s12103-0200-09558-w.

Logan, M.W., Morgan, M.A., Benson, M.L. and Cullen, F.T. (2019). Coping with imprisonment: Testing the special sensitivity hypothesis for white-collar offenders, *Justice Quarterly*, 36 (2), 225–254.

Lord, N. and Wingerde, K. (2020). Preventing and intervening in white-collar crimes: The role of law enforcement, in: Rorie, M.L. (editor), *The Handbook of White-Collar Crime*, Hoboken, NJ: Wiley & Sons, chapter 16, 246–261.

Loveday, B. (2017). Still plodding along? The police response to the changing profile of crime in England and Wales, *International Journal of Police Science and Management*, 19 (2), 101–109.

Mai, H.T.X. and Olsen, S.O. (2016). Consumer participation in self-production: The role of control mechanisms, convenience orientation, and moral obligation, *Journal of Marketing Theory and Practice*, 24 (2), 209–223.

Masood, T., Cherifi, C.B. and Moalla, N. (2020). A machine learning approach for performance-oriented decision support in service-oriented architecture, *Journal of Intelligent Information Systems*, published online doi:10.1007/s10844-020-00617-6.

McClelland, P.L., Liang, X. and Barker, V.L. (2010). CEO commitment to the status quo: Replication and extension using content analysis, *Journal of Management*, 36 (5), 1251–1277.

Mesmer-Magnus, J.R. and Viswesvaran, C. (2005). Whistleblowing in an organization: An examination of correlates of whistleblowing intentions, actions, and retaliation, *Journal of Business Ethics*, 62 (3), 266–297.

Miceli, M.P. and Near, J.P. (2013). An international comparison of the incidence of public sector whistle-blowing and the prediction of retaliation: Australia, Norway, and the US, *Australian Journal of Public Administration*, 72 (4), 433–446.

Mpho, B. (2017). Whistleblowing: What do contemporary ethical theories say? *Studies in Business and Economics*, 12 (1), 19–28.

Muhammed, S. and Zaim, H. (2020). Peer knowledge sharing and organizational performance: The role of leadership support and knowledge management success, *Journal of Knowledge Management*, published online doi:10.1108/JKM-03-2020-0227.

Onna, J.H.R. (2020). From the avalanche to the game: White-collar offenders on crime, bonds, and morality, *Crime, Law and Social Change*, published online doi:10.1007/s10611-020-09899-x.

Onna, J.H.R. and Denkers, A.J.M. (2019). Social bonds and white-collar crime: A two-study assessment of informal social controls in white-collar offenders, *Deviant Behavior*, 40 (10), 1206–1225.

Otu, S.E. and Okon, O.N. (2019). Participation in fraud/cheat in the buying and selling of meats without legal metrology: A theoretical and empirical investigation, *Deviant Behavior*, 40 (2), 205–224.

Park, H., Bjørkelo, B. and Blenkinsopp, J. (2020). External whistleblowers' experiences of workplace bullying by superiors and colleagues, *Journal of Business Ethics*, 161, 591–601.

Patrucco, A.S., Luzzini, D. and Ronchi, S. (2017). Research perspectives on public procurement: Content analysis of 14 years of publications in the Journal of Public Procurement, *Journal of Public Procurement*, 16 (2), 229–269.

Piening, E.P., Salge, T.O., Antons, D. and Kreiner, G.E. (2020). Standing together or falling apart? Understanding employees' responses to organizational identity threats, *Academy of Management Review*, 45 (2), 325–351.

Piquero, N.L. (2018). White-collar crime is crime: Victims hurt just the same, *Criminology & Public Policy*, 17 (3), 595–600.

Plesner (2020). *Response to DFSA-letter: Anmodning om redegørelse om Danske Bank A/S' gældsinddrivelsessystem (Response to DFSA letter: Request for account concerning Danske Bank*

Inc.'s debt collection system), investigation report by Danske Bank, law firm Plesner, Copenhagen, Denmark, 120 pages.

Pontell, H.N., Black, W.K. and Geis, G. (2014). Too big to fail, too powerful to jail? On the absence of criminal prosecutions after the 2008 financial meltdown, *Crime, Law and Social Change*, 61 (1), 1–13.

Potipiroon, W. and Wongpreedee, A. (2020). Ethical climate and whistleblowing intentions: Testing the mediating roles of public service motivation and psychological safety among local government employees, *Public Personnel Management*, published online doi:10.1177/0091026020944547.

PwC (2020a). *Independent assessment of the LOLC incident: Report developed for Norfund, report of investigation*, June 30, 34 pages, Oslo, Norway: PricewaterhouseCoopers.

PwC (2020b). *Equinor in the USA: Review of Equinor's US onshore activities and learnings for the future*, preparet for Equinor ASA's board of directors, October 9, 53 pages, Oslo, Norway: PricewaterhouseCoopers.

Reese, B. and McDougal, M.K. (2018). Gender, status, and tax offenses, *Deviant Behavior*, 39 (12), 1647–1657.

Rehg, M.T., Miceli, M.P., Near, J.P. and Scotter, J.R.V. (2009). Antecedents and outcomes of retaliation against whistleblowers: Gender differences and power relationships, *Organization Science*, 19 (2), 221–240.

Röglinger, M., Pöppelbuss, J. and Becker, J. (2012). Maturity model in business process management, *Business Process Management Journal*, 18 (2), 328–346.

Saunders, M., Lewis, P. and Thornhill, A. (2007). *Research Methods for Business Students*, 5th edition, London, UK: Pearson Education.

Schneider, S. (2006). Privatizing economic crime enforcement: Exploring the role of private sector investigative agencies in combating money laundering, *Policing & Society*, 16 (3), 285–312.

Schoultz, I. and Flyghed, J. (2016). Doing business for a 'higher loyalty' How Swedish transnational corporations neutralize allegations of crime, *Crime, Law and Social Change*, 66 (2), 183–198.

Schoultz, I. and Flyghed, J. (2019). From "we didn't do it" to "we've learned our lesson": Development of a typology of neutralizations of corporate crime, *Critical Criminology*, published online doi:10.1007/s10612–10019–09483–09483.

Schoultz, I. and Flyghed, J. (2020a). Denials and confessions: An analysis of the temporalization of neutralizations of corporate crime, *International Journal of Law, Crime and Justice*, published online doi:10.1016/j.ijlcj.2020.100389.

Schoultz, I. and Flyghed, J. (2020b). "We have been thrown under the bus": Corporate versus individual defense mechanisms against transnational corporate bribery charges, *Journal of White Collar and Corporate Crime*, published online doi:10.1177/2631309x20911883.

Schoultz, I. and Flyghed, J. (2021a). "We have been thrown under the bus": Corporate versus individual defense mechanisms against transnational corporate bribery charges, *Journal of White Collar and Corporate Crime*, 2 (1), 24–35.

Schoultz, I. and Flyghed, J. (2021b). Performing unbelonging in court: Observations from a transnational corporate bribery trial – A dramaturgical approach, *Crime, Law and Social Change*, published online doi:10.1007/s10611-021-09990-x.

Shawver, T. and Clements, L.H. (2019). The impact of value preferences on whistleblowing intentions of accounting professionals, *Journal of Forensic and Investigative Accounting*, 11 (2), 232–247.

Skidmore, M., Ramm, J., Goldstraw-White, J., Barrett, C., Barleaza, S., Muir, R. and Gill, M. (2018). *More Than Just a Number: Improving the Police Response to Victims of Fraud*, London, UK: The Police Foundation / Perpetuity Research.

Skidmore, M., Goldstraw-White, J. and Gill, M. (2020). Understanding the police response to fraud: The challenges in configuring a response to a low-priority crime on the rise, *Public Money & Management*, 40 (5), 369–379.

Solli-Sæther, H. and Gottschalk, P. (2015). Stages-of-growth in outsourcing, offshoring and backsourcing: Back to the future? *Journal of Computer Information Systems*, 55 (2), 88–94.

Stadler, W.A. and Gottschalk, P. (2021). Testing convenience theory for white-collar crime: Perceptions of potential offenders and non-offenders, *Deviant Behavior*, published online doi:10.1080/01639625.2021.1919037.

Stenström, A. (2018). The private policing of insurance claims: Power, profit and private justice, *British Journal of Criminology*, 58 (2), 478–496.

Sutherland, E.H. (1939). White-collar criminality, *American Sociological Review*, 5, 1–12.

Sutherland, E.H. (1983). *White Collar Crime – The Uncut Version*, New Haven, CT: Yale University Press.

Sykes, G. and Matza, D. (1957). Techniques of neutralization: A theory of delinquency, *American Sociological Review*, 22 (6), 664–670.

Tankebe, J. (2019). Cooperation with the police against corruption: Exploring the roles of legitimacy, deterrence and collective action theories, *British Journal of Criminology*, 59, 1390–1410.

Vasiu, V.I. and Podgor, E.S. (2019). Organizational opportunity and deviant behavior: Convenience in white-collar crime, *Criminal Law and Criminal Justice Books*, Rutgers, the State University of New Jersey, July, www.clcjbooks.rutgers.edu.

Wall-Parker, A. (2020). Measuring white collar crime, in: Rorie, M.L. (editor), *The Handbook of White-Collar Crime*, Hoboken, NJ: John Wiley & Sons, chapter 3, pages 32–44.

Webster, J. and Drew, J.M. (2017). Policing advance fee fraud (AFF): Experiences of fraud detectives using a victim-focused approach, *International Journal of Police Science and Management*, 19 (1), 39–53.

Wiersholm (2020). *Granskningsrapport: Utbrudd av covid-19 på Hurtigruten-skipet MS Roald Amundsen 17.-31. juli 2020 (Investigation Report: Outbreak of Covid-19 on the Hurtigruten ship MS Roald Amundsen July 17 to 31)*, Norwegian law firm Wiersholm, Oslo, Norway, 49 pages.

Williams, J.W. (2005a). Reflections on the private versus public policing of economic crime, *British Journal of Criminology*, 45, 316–339.

Williams, J.W. (2005b). Governability matters: The private policing of economic crime and the challenge of democratic governance, *Policing & Society* 15 (2), 187–211.

Williams, J.W. (2014). The Private Eyes of Corporate Culture: The Forensic Accounting and Corporate Investigation Industry and the Production of Corporate Financial Security, in: Walby, K. and Lippert, R.K. (editors), *Corporate Security in the 21st Century – Theory and Practice in International Perspective*, Hampshire: Palgrave Macmillan, pages 56–77.

Williams, M.L., Levi, M., Burnap, P. and Gundur, R.V. (2019). Under the corporate radar: Examining insider business cybercrime victimization through an application of routine activities theory, *Deviant Behavior*, 40 (9), 1119–1131.

Wood, J.D. (2020). Private policing and public health: A neglected relationship, *Journal of Contemporary Criminal Justice*, 36 (1), 19–38.

1 Convenient Organizational Opportunity

This chapter addresses the opportunity side of white-collar crime. White-collar offenders are individuals with high social status in privileged positions, which they abuse to commit financial crime. Offenders have legitimate access to resources that make it convenient to commit and conceal crime. Crime convenience increases when disorganized institutional deterioration occurs. Crime convenience can be excellent for offenders when there is a lack of oversight and guardianship. Some industries have criminal market structures, where an organization simply adapts to illegitimate practices.

The organizational opportunity is concerned with illegal profit that seem more conveniently achieved in an organizational setting where the offender can enjoy power and influence based on position and trust. Opportunity suggests the ability to commit wrongdoing with the expectation that nobody will detect or report it, and the offender will not be punished (Schnatterly et al., 2018). The organizational dimension sets white-collar criminals apart from other financial criminals. White-collar crime can be distinguished from ordinary crime ("street crime") based on the status of the offenders, their access to legitimate occupations, the common presence of an organizational form, and the extent of the costs and harmfulness of such crime. Sutherland (1983) specifically focused on emphasizing the respectability of white-collar offenders, stating that persons of the upper socio-economic class commit all kinds of financial crime. The ability of white-collar offenders to commit and conceal crime links to their privileged position, the social structure, and their orientation to legitimate and respectable careers (Friedrichs et al., 2018).

The opportunity perspective suggests that many white-collar offences manifest the following opportunity properties: (1) the offender has legitimate access to the location in which the crime is committed; (2) the offender is spatially separate from the victim; and (3) the offender's actions have a superficial appearance of legitimacy (Benson and Simpson, 2018).

Coleman (1987: 424) suggests that an opportunity's attractiveness is determined by four factors:

> The first is the actor's perception of how great a gain he or she might expect to reap from the opportunity. Second is the perception of potential

DOI: 10.4324/9781003305071-2

> risks, such as the likelihood that a criminal act will be detected and the severity of the sanctions that would be invoked if detection indeed occurs. The third factor is the compatibility of the opportunity with the ideas, rationalizations, and beliefs the individual actor already has. Finally, the evaluation of an illicit opportunity is made in comparison with the other opportunities of which the actor is aware and is therefore influenced by the actor's entire opportunity structure.

Opportunity is a distinct characteristic of fraud and corruption by white-collar offenders and varies depending on the kinds of criminals involved. An opportunity is attractive as a means of responding to desires, wishes, and ambitions. The organizational dimension provides the white-collar criminal an opportunity to commit financial crime and conceal it in legal organizational activities as seemingly legitimate. Aguilera and Vadera (2008: 434) describe a criminal opportunity as "the presence of a favorable combination of circumstances that renders a possible course of action relevant". Opportunity arises when individuals or groups can engage in illegal and unethical behavior and expect, with reasonable confidence, to avoid detection and punishment. It is convenient for the offender to conceal crime and give it an appearance of outward acceptability.

As suggested by Coleman (1987: 424), "a decrease in the availability or attractiveness of legitimate opportunities will normally increase the attractiveness of illegal opportunities". This is in line with the convenience perspective, where the relative convenience of legal versus illegal opportunities influences decision-making. White-collar offenses are the result of crime-as-a-choice thinking, where the relative attractiveness determines future actions.

The theory of convenience is a crime-as-a-choice theory where offenders have the option to choose legitimate rather than illegitimate paths to solve problems and gain from possibilities. Grabosky and Shover (2010) discuss how crime as a choice can receive less attention because of lower relative attractiveness compared to alternative paths. They suggest that three target areas for policy initiatives stand out: (1) reducing the supply of lure, (2) increasing prevailing estimates of the credibility of external oversight, and (3) increasing the use of effective systems of internal oversight and self-restraint. In convenience terminology, all of these initiatives relate to the organizational dimension: (1) less attractive opportunities for illegal gain, (2) increased risk of detection from outside the organization, and (3) increased risk of detection from inside the organization.

High Social Status in Privileged Positions

Some members of the elite are simply too powerful to blame. Pontell et al. (2014) found that the financial crisis obviously had its cause in mismanagement in the financial sector, but all in the financial sector avoided serious blame. Status-related factors such as influential positions, upper-class family ties, and community roles often preclude perceptions of blameworthiness (Slyke and

Bales, 2013). Blameworthiness is the extent to which it is clear that an individual is engaged in a questionable act (Dewan and Jensen, 2020).

Evidence of the perspective of too powerful to blame is the observation of the absence of prosecution after the disclosure of crime because authorities consider the organization too big to fail, and authorities consider executives too powerful to jail. In their classical article on the absence of failure prosecution after the 2008 financial meltdown, Pontell et al. (2014: 1) suggest that some were too big to fail and too powerful to jail:

> These companies had balance sheets that were saturated with securities containing toxic subprime mortgages. They collapsed, were bought by competitors, or were bailed out by the federal government with huge infusions of taxpayer money. For most onlookers, including criminologists and the public in general, the corporate actions represented intricate and arcane business practices that were difficult to understand fully and to portray as sound bites – and therefore tended to become trivialized in regard to their failure components.

One of the companies mentioned in their article is Lehman Brothers that went bankrupt. A private internal report of 2208 pages written by fraud examiner Jenner Block (2010: 16) concluded with innocence for the powerful executives who drove the bank into bankruptcy: "The business decisions that brought Lehman to its crisis of confidence may have been in error but were largely within the business judgment rule". Some years later, Crosina and Pratt (2019) studied organizational mourning among former Lehman Brothers bankers.

Pontell et al. (2014: 10) argue that the financial meltdown points to the need to unpack the concept of status when examining white-collar and corporate offenses:

> The high standing of those involved in the current scandal has acted as a significant shield to accusations of criminal wrongdoing in at least three ways. First, the legal resources that offenders can bring to bear on any case made against them are significant. This would give pause to any prosecutor, regardless of the evidence that exists. Second, their place in the organizations assures that the many below them will be held more directly responsible for the more readily detected offenses. The downward focus on white-collar and corporate crimes is partly a function of the visibility of the offense and the ease with which it can be officially pursued. Third, the political power of large financial institutions allows for effective lobbying that both distances them from the criminal law and prevents the government from restricting them from receiving taxpayer money when they get into trouble.

Pontell et al. (2014) mention criminal wrongdoing, where wrongdoing generally is a behavior that a social-control agent judges to transgress a line separating right from wrong, where such a line can separate legal, ethical, and socially responsible behavior from its antithesis (Schnatterly et al., 2018).

High social status in privileged positions is sometimes associated with entrepreneurship, where an entrepreneurial individual can create opportunities for deviant behavior (Ramoglou and Tsang, 2016). The entrepreneurship perspective emphasizes that entrepreneurs discover and create innovative and changing opportunities.

However, Ramoglou and Tsang (2017: 738) argue that opportunities are not the result of innovation, discovery, or creation: "They are objectively existing propensities to be creatively actualized". Criminal entrepreneurs thus actualize illegal opportunities in the shadow economy (McElwee and Smith, 2015). Criminal entrepreneurship represents the dark side of entrepreneurialism. To understand entrepreneurial behavior by white-collar criminals, important behavioral areas include "modus essendi", "modus operandi", and "modus vivendi". Modus essendi is a philosophical term relating to modes of being. Modus operandi is a method of operating, which is an accepted criminological concept for classifying generic human actions from their visible and consequential manifestations. Modus vivendi represents the shared symbiotic relationship between different entrepreneurial directions (Smith, 2009). Entrepreneurs are often important economic agents, driving forward employment, opportunities, and economic development. Entrepreneurship is associated with innovation, adaptation, change and dynamism, hard work, willpower, and overcoming challenges and struggles. According to Welter et al. (2017), entrepreneurship is a broadly available social technology for creating organizations that may pursue a myriad of goals. Tonoyan et al. (2010) found that viewing illegal business activities as a widespread business practice provides the rationale for entrepreneurs to justify their own corrupt activities. Peixoto et al. (2021: 2) focused on entrepreneurial startups as a breeding ground for unethical behavior:

> It should be emphasized that accessing external funding is critical for entrepreneurs and their startups' birth and survival; however, getting it is often challenging. Since the startups' financial history and the necessary information to establish a reputation is usually nonexistent, investors cannot readily observe venture quality. They may thus be reluctant to provide funding. Given these struggles, the entrepreneurial ecosystem appears as a propitious breeding ground for unethical behaviors, high-lighting the importance of assessing entrepreneurs' ethical standards to, eventually, help predict and prevent these types of behaviors and consequent social and economic damages.

While it might seem reasonable that individual corporate officers could be found guilty of violating laws without exhibiting any unlawful intent, negligence or knowledge, as long as they hold a position of responsibility, this is not the case in most legislations. Even if it is obvious that they could prevent the violation or fail to prevent it, they will never become a target for prosecution and possible incarceration. There is little or no support for the responsible corporate officer doctrine (Müller, 2018). Rather, the worst that can happen as a consequence of corporate crime is that the business organization has to pay a fine that in some countries can be a substantial amount.

Individuals with high social status in privileged positions sometimes use language that people simply do not understand. Executives and others in the elite may use language that followers do not necessarily understand – however, nevertheless, they trust executive messages (Ferraro et al., 2005). Cryptology is concerned with techniques for secure communication in the presence of third parties called adversaries. Cryptology is about constructing and analyzing protocols that prevent third parties or the public from understanding messages. In an organizational context, executive communication applies a management language that few others understand.

According to Ferraro et al. (2005), language affects what people see or don't see; how they see it; and the social categories and descriptors that they use to interpret their reality. Language shapes what people notice and ignore, and what they believe is and is not important. Reality is socially constructed, and language plays an important role in such constructions. Srivastava and Goldberg (2017) argue that language is a window into culture. Subcultures develop in the organization, where the language is different from other parts of the organization. The language through which people in the elite communicate with colleagues on the job illustrates how people fit into an organization's culture or subculture. Language use can predict an individual's influence and adaption on the job and can reveal distinct linguistic patterns for executives involved in misconduct and crime.

Making sense of executive language, attorney language and other professionals' languages is difficult for outsiders (Weick, 1995). People tend to trust what they do not understand based on the authority positions occupied by senders of messages. Sense making links to crime signal detection by the challenge of perceiving and understanding a crime signal, as discussed later. The sense-making perspective consists of both the interpretation of information and generating results from interpretations (Huff and Bodner, 2013). People give meaning to experiences by the sense-making process. Since most people have little or no experience with fraud and corruption, they will not understand crime signals related to financial crime. People without experience are not able to make sense of weak crime signals from white-collar offenders. They are unable to frame or categorize through words what the signal is about (Holt and Cornelissen, 2014). Thus, even if a signal of fraud or corruption is present, colleagues and subordinates are unable to make sense of it since they lack experience. Only experience can help to give meaning. Without experience in the organization, a white-collar offender can feel quite safe, as nobody will be able to make sense of crime signals.

Deviant individuals with high social status in privileged positions might not only use language that simply does not make sense to people. White-collar offenders can also use humor to distract attention from their crime. Offender humor distraction, as suggested by Yam et al. (2018), implies that potential white-collar offenders can influence the organizational opportunity structure by aggressive humor. Aggressive humor is a negatively directed style of humor that an individual carries out at the expense and detriment of one's relationships with others. It can be teasing with a humorous undertone, or it can be victimization of the receiver. It can be the opposite of self-irony, where the offender makes jokes about others and makes them look ridiculous. The more aggressive an offender's style, the more a sense of humor will signal acceptability of norm violations for the offender. Aggressive humor is a form of hostile behavior.

Aggressive leader humor expands the organizational opportunity for white-collar crime, and it influences the willingness of victims of such humor (Yam et al., 2018: 349): "The more aggressive a leader's style, the more a sense of humor will signal acceptability of norm violations, which will be positively associated with deviance."

Aggressive humor refers to a specific style of humor aimed at teasing or ridiculing. It may include sarcasm humorously to convey disapproving information to followers. Aggressive humor may signal to followers that the accepted social norm of being respectful towards others is not important. It signals that violating norms of human decency is acceptable.

The leader humor perspective suggests that the leader's sense of humor is positively associated with followers' perceived acceptability of norm violations. When leaders display humor and, as a result, violate norms, followers will likely perceive that it is socially acceptable to violate norms in the organization for two reasons (Yam et al., 2018: 352):

> First, leaders' formal position makes them strong sources of normative expectations. Leaders, as role models, are more likely to be observed by followers who are scanning the environment for information on how to behave in the work context. In other words, leaders who make light of norm violations in order to produce humor are likely to imply to followers that mild norm violations in the organizations are generally acceptable. Second, when a leader acts in a humorous manner, others will likely react with laughter and amusement, an implicit signal of approval. Followers will be likely to interpret this social information as signaling the acceptability of norm violations. When a norm violation is enacted – and interpreted by others – in a playful, humorous way, it also signals to followers that violations need not be taken seriously or scrutinized.

Aggressive leader humor might cause fear among subordinates that prevent them from intervening or in any visible way reacting when the deviant leader is into wrongdoing and misconduct (Dion, 2020: 1032):

> Machiavelli asserted that wise leaders want to be liked and feared by people. They can be benevolent toward their friends and cruel toward their enemies. People harm others either by fear or by hatred. An excess of fear is always better than an excess of love, since it allows the leader to keep his power and influence. The leader could lose power and influence

> if people do not fear his cruelty. However, people's fear must be accompanied by an absence of hatred. The balance between fear and love could allow the leader to safeguard his political stability.

Some followers can attempt to restore the feeling of equity by committing crime (Zhong and Robinson, 2021: 1441):

> We found a collection of studies showing beneficial consequences after specific types of harmful behavior. More specifically, when actors experience or witness injustice, mistreatment, or wrongdoing by others, such as after witnessing others' transgressions, responding to it with negative acts can lead to emotional benefits. This benefit may not necessarily come from conducting behavior that is negative per se but may emerge from any behavior that regulates the emotion via righting a wrong or restoring a sense of equity.

High social status in privileged positions creates power inequality compared to those without any status in their positions. The perspective of power inequality suggests that, for example, family members in family firms wield significant influence in their firms (Patel and Cooper, 2014). Family members often have legitimate access to firm resources that nonfamily executives in the firm cannot question.

Individuals with high social status in privileged positions can cooperate to create a business climate of "organized irresponsibility" (Berghoff, 2018: 425): "The term implies that management had conspired to prevent efficient controls and therefore facilitated and promoted corruption."

Leaders reinforce a culture of financial crime by ignoring criminal actions and otherwise facilitate unethical behavior. At the same time, they try to distance themselves from criminal actions (Pontell et al., 2021: 9): "High status corporate criminals often go to great lengths to distance themselves from the crimes committed by their subordinates and to hide any incriminating evidence of their role in the decisions that authorized those criminal acts."

Dewan and Jensen (2020) studied high social status individuals in times of scandals that can change the role of status from being an asset to being a liability. They defined scandal as the disruptive publicity of misconduct, that is, a situation after detection and disclosure to the public. While the importance of status in convenience theory is related to prevention of blame before disclosure, Dewan and Jensen's (2020: 1657) research was concerned with status after disclosure:

> Because scandal diminishes the effectiveness of factors that make status an asset, status offers less protection during a scandal. At the same time that scandal decreases the protective benefits of status; the factors that make status a liability remain or are augmented.

Status can thus be a liability in the context of blaming, shaming, and labeling of misconduct and crime. High status creates high expectations that are seriously violated in a scandal. The disappointment causes an expectation of consequence for the person responsible for the disappointment.

The status of individuals may vary with a number of factors. In the United States, researchers have emphasized race as a determining factor for the status of individuals. For example, Sohoni and Rorie (2021: 66) found that many middle- and upper-class US whites live in environments of relative social isolation:

> When this social isolation is combined with financial advantage, it serves to block the development of empathy toward outgroups and increases feelings of individual entitlement, which leads to the formation of crime-specific cultural frames that include neutralizations and justifications for elite white-collar crime. We argue that whiteness plays a role that is independent from (but exacerbated by) socioeconomic status, and is an important contributor to the generative worlds from which many white-collar criminals emanate.

Similarly, Benson et al. (2021: 10) found that status makes white dominate the arena of white-collar crime, although some changes have occurred:

> Since the mid-1970s, the percentage of non-white people convicted of white-collar crimes in the federal judicial system has been growing steadily. In 2015, non-whites accounted for more than half of all convictions for certain white-collar type crimes, but the increase in non-white participation has not occurred evenly across all race and ethnic groups. Asians and Latinos have increased their participation in white-collar crime more so than Blacks.

In Europe, researchers have emphasized gender as a determining factor for the status of individuals. For example, Benson and Gottschalk (2015) found very limited support for the emancipation hypothesis as they compared Norway with the United States, where the Norwegian gender gap is much smaller than the US gender gap. Even though gender inequality is much lower in Norway than in the United States, the gender gap in Norwegian white-collar crime appears to be nearly identical to that observed in the United States. The emancipation hypothesis suggests that incidents of women in white-collar crime will increase as access to opportunities increase (Lutz, 2019). The gendered focal concern hypothesis contradicts the emancipation hypothesis as it suggests that women socialize into accepting nurturing role obligations that emphasize the importance of social relationships and communalistic orientation towards others. Through the assimilation of these obligations, women develop identities as caregivers (Steffensmeier et al., 2013).

Gender can influence the type of financial crime committed, where white-collar crime encompasses many types of offenses (Poehlinng and Bolton, 2021). Women comprised close to half of the bank embezzlement offenders, but only 5% of the antitrust, securities, tax, and bribery offenders in the United States, while no convicted female offenders in Norway were involved in corruption

(Benson and Gottschalk, 2015). The lack of involvement of women in corruption might be explained by their status.

High social status in privileged positions might have the convenient benefit of neutralization techniques applied by in-group members. In-group members may defend their leaders against charges of misconduct. Sims and Barreto (2021) found that in-group members use neutralizing techniques to defend their leaders in the same way they would defend themselves. Group membership has important implications for how individuals perceive and respond to allegations of leader misconduct. They may rally to defend their leaders in both word and deed on multiple occasions. The defense of their leaders might be explained by social identity, where group membership is an important part of an individual's identity. Perceptions, behaviors, and attitudes can sometimes be less associated with the individual and more associated with the in-group when the in-group is salient.

Legitimate Access to Crime Resources

A white-collar offender has typically legitimate access to resources to commit and conceal crime (Williams et al., 2019). A resource is an enabler applied and used to satisfy human and organizational needs. A resource has utility and limited availability. A white-collar offender has usually access to resources that are valuable (application of the resource provides desired outcome), unique (very few have access to the resource), not imitable (resource cannot be copied), not transferrable (resource cannot be released from context), combinable with other resources (results in better outcome), exploitable (possible to apply in criminal activities), and not substitutable (cannot be replaced by a different resource). According to Petrocelli et al. (2003), access to resources equates access to power. Others are losers in the competition for resources (Wheelock et al., 2011). In the conflict perspective suggested by Petrocelli et al. (2003), the upper class in society exercises its power and controls the resources.

Opportunity is dependent on social capital available to the criminal. The structure and quality of social ties in hierarchical and transactional relationships shape opportunity structures. Social capital is the sum of actual or potential resources accruing to the criminal by virtue of his or her position in a hierarchy and in a network. Social capital accumulated by the individual in terms of actual and potential resources, which are accessible because of profession and position, creates a larger space for individual behavior and actions that others can hardly observe. Many initiatives by trusted persons in the elite are unknown and unfamiliar to others in the organization. Therefore, white-collar criminals do not expect consequences for themselves.

Berghoff and Spiekermann (2018: 291) argue that all economic transactions depend on a certain degree of trust, without which transaction costs would simply be too high for economic activity: "White-collar criminals abuse the good faith of various stakeholders, from customers to the general public, from shareholders to the authorities. Therefore, white-collar crime often coincides with the breach of trust."

Offenders take advantage of their positions of power with almost unlimited authority in the opportunity structure (Kempa, 2010), because they have legitimate and often privileged access to physical and virtual locations in which crime is committed, are totally in charge of resource allocations and transactions, and are successful in concealment based on key resources used to hide their crime. Offenders have an economic motivation and opportunity (Huisman and Erp, 2013); linked to an organizational platform and availability, and in a setting of people who do not know, do not care, or do not reveal the individual(s) with behavioral traits who commit crime. Opportunity includes people who are loyal to the criminal either as a follower or as a silent partner, for example, when the follower perceives ambitious goals as invariable.

The resource-based perspective postulates that differences in individuals' opportunities find explanation in the extent of resource access and the ability to combine and exploit those resources. Executives and other members of the elite are potential offenders that are able to commit financial crime to the extent that they have convenient access to resources suitable for illegal actions. Access to resources in the organizational dimension makes it more relevant and attractive to explore possibilities and avoid threats using financial crime. The willingness to exploit a resource for fraud and corruption increases when a potential offender has a perception of relative convenience. Criminal acts disappear from easy detection in a multitude of legal transactions in different contexts and different locations performed by different people. The organizational affiliation makes crime look like ordinary business. Offenders conceal economic crime among apparently legal activity. Offenders leverage resources that make it convenient to conceal crime among regular business transactions. In particular, businesses that practice secrecy rather than transparency enable convenient concealment of financial crime (Transparency, 2018). Chasing profits leaves people more creative in finding ways to make more legal as well as illegal profits for themselves and the organization, and people become more creative in concealing crime in various ways (Füss and Hecker, 2008). Offenders carry out crime in such a way that the risk of detection is minimal and even microscopic (Pratt and Cullen, 2005).

As suggested by Berghoff and Spiekermann (2018: 290), sophisticated concealment is an important factor in white-collar crime:

> The privileged position of white-collar criminals is the result of several factors. Their offences are especially difficult to prosecute because the perpetrators use sophisticated means to conceal them. They can also often afford the best lawyers and have the political clout to influence the legislative process to their advantage and, if need be, to bribe prosecutors and judges. Additionally, the class bias of the courts works to their benefit. The law is often seen as not binding, at least not for and by economic elites.

White-collar offenders have legitimate access to premises (Benson and Simpson, 2018; Williams et al., 2019), and they have specialized access in routine activities (Cohen and Felson, 1979). The routine activity perspective suggests three conditions for crime to occur: a motivated offender, an opportunity in terms of a suitable target, and the absence of a capable or moral guardian. The existence or absence of a likely guardian represents an inhibitor or facilitator for crime. The premise of the routine activity perspective is that crime is to a minor extent affected by social causes such as poverty, inequality, and unemployment. Motivated offenders are individuals who are not only capable of committing criminal activity but are willing to do so. Suitable targets are financial sources that offenders consider particularly attractive. Lack of guardians is not only lack of protective rules and regulations, audits and controls, but also lack of mental models in the minds of potential offenders that reduce self-control against attraction from criminal acts. Both Reyns (2013) and Tientcheu (2021) expanded the routine activity perspective into online routines where insider business cybercrime occurs without direct manual contact.

Corruption is a typical crime category among white-collar offenses. Lange (2008) defines organizational corruption as the pursuit of individual interests by one or more organizational actors through the intentional misdirection of organizational resources or perversion of organizational routines. Pinto et al. (2008) makes a distinction between corrupt organizations and organizations of corrupt individuals. A corrupt organization is usually a top-down phenomenon in which a group of organizational members – typically, the dominant coalition, organizational elites, or top management team – undertakes corrupt actions. An organization of corrupt individuals is an emergent, bottom-up phenomenon in which informal processes facilitate personally corrupt behaviors that cross a critical threshold such that the organization deserves the characteristic of being corrupt.

In the rare case of detection of possible crime, the potential offender has access not only to better defense as a strategic resource, but also often access to an alternative avenue of private investigation. When suspicion of misconduct and crime emerges, then the organization may hire a fraud examiner to conduct a private investigation into the matter. The enterprise takes control of suspicions by implementing an internal investigation (Friedrich, 2021). An external law firm or auditing firm is engaged to reconstruct past events and sequence of events. Typically, the resulting investigation report points to misconduct, while at the same time concluding that there have been no criminal offenses. The police will monitor the internal investigation and await its conclusion. When the conclusion states that there may be misconduct, but no crime, then the police and prosecution tend to settle down with it (Brooks and Button, 2011; Button and Gee, 2013; Button et al., 2007a, 2007b; King, 2020a, 2020b; Schneider, 2006; Williams, 2005a, 2005b, 2008, 2014).

Legitimate access to crime resources can be illustrated by the case of a chairman of the board who published his autobiography (Olav, 2014, 2015). The chairman used a tax haven where he had an account when he ran business through another company there (Bjørklund, 2018; Oslo tingrett, 2015). A tax haven is a country or place with very low or no rates of taxation for foreign investors, where foreigners enjoy complete secrecy about their investments. Money laundering of proceeds from criminal activity is an attractive opportunity in tax havens. On the legitimate side, the use of tax havens enables transfer-pricing strategies to lower overall tax burdens for multinational corporations. Subsidiaries located in tax havens serve multinationals to avoid taxes by shifting income from high-tax countries to low-tax countries. Firms also use tax havens in strategies that involve inter-company debt or leasing arrangements to shift income across jurisdictions. Tax authorities in various countries attempt to challenge this kind of tax evasion (Dyreng et al., 2019; Guenther et al., 2019).

Disorganized Institutional Deterioration

An institution is a system of interrelated formal and informal elements – rules, guidelines, norms, traditions, beliefs – governing relationships between institutional members within which members pursue their mutual interests (Gyõry, 2020). Institutional deterioration can occur conveniently as a result of external legitimacy where deviance is the norm (Rodriguez et al., 2005). Executive deviance enacted at institutional deterioration is dependent on a number of factors. For example, in the case of government corruption for multinational enterprises in host countries, both pervasiveness and arbitrariness are important factors. Pervasiveness is the average firm's likelihood of encountering bribery, while arbitrariness is the inherent degree of ambiguity associated with corrupt transactions in a given nation or state (Rodriguez et al., 2005). Pinto et al. (2008: 686) define the beneficiary of corruption as the actor deriving direct and primary benefit from the action: "For example, even if individuals can benefit financially from corruption on behalf of the organization (e.g., through bonuses or high prices for their stocks), the organization is still the primary and direct financial beneficiary".

It becomes more convenient to commit financial crime by white-collar offenders in organizations characterized by moral deterioration and collapse. The institutional perspective of moral deterioration suggests that opportunities improve for white-collar criminals. For example, Bradshaw (2015) found criminogenic industry structures in the offshore oil industry.

The institutional perspective contributes an understanding of organizational behavior that experiences influence from individuals, groups, other organizations, as well as the larger society of which they are a part. The perspective emphasizes how organizational structure and organizational culture derive from norms, attitudes, and rules, which are common to most organizations in society. While organizational structure is characterized by design of positions in terms of job specialization, behavioral formalization, unit grouping, and unit size (Donk and Molloy, 2008), organizational culture is characterized by accepted practices, rules, and principles of conduct that are applied to a variety of situations and that define appropriate attitudes and behaviors for organizational members, as well as generalized rationales and beliefs (Barton, 2004). Guiso et al. (2015) found that organizational cultures which promote low levels of integrity are associated with negative business outcomes such as low employee productivity and corporate profitability. Integrity is the quality of acting in accordance with the moral values, norms, and rules that are considered valid and relevant within the context in which the actor operates (Loyens et al., 2021).

Berghoff and Spiekermann (2018: 291) found that white-collar crime is often systemic and part of a culture, either of a corporate culture inside the firm or of a culture in the firm's environment:

> In the first case, the corporation's control mechanisms are typically weak, intentionally or unintentionally, which is an obstacle to the prevention and the investigation of economic crimes. Individual responsibility is therefore hard to ascertain. Defendants routinely deny responsibility and point to their superiors who made them commit crimes, or to their inferiors who engaged in shady practices without their knowledge or authorization.

The institutional perspective applied to white-collar crime means that white-collar offenders find opportunity for and acceptance of illegal behaviors because of moral collapse generally in their organizations. The institutional perspective argues that business enterprises are much more than simple tools and instruments to achieve financial goals and ambitions. The perspective says that organizations are adaptable systems that recognize and learn from the environment by mirroring values in society. This reasoning is relevant to explain why business organizations tend to be similar in the same industry and the same nation and region (Kostova et al., 2008).

Moral collapse happens when organizations are unable to see that bright line between right and wrong. Seven signs of ethical collapse can become visible: (i) pressure to maintain those numbers; (ii) fear and silence antidotes to openness; (iii) young ones and a bigger-than-life CEO; (iv) a weak board; (v) conflicts; (vi) innovation like no other; and (vii) goodness in some areas atones for evil in others.

Shadnam and Lawrence (2011: 379) apply the institutional perspective to explain moral decline and potential crime in organizations:

> Our theory of moral collapse has two main elements. First, we argue that morality in organizations is embedded in nested systems of individuals, organizations and moral communities in which ideology and regulation flow "down" from moral communities through organizations to individuals, and moral ideas and influence flow "upward" from individuals through organizations to moral communities. Second, we argue that moral collapse is associated with breakdowns in these flows and explore conditions under which such breakdowns are likely to occur.

Shadnam and Lawrence (2011: 393) formulated several research hypotheses, which imply that the likelihood of moral decline will vary depending on a number of circumstances:

- Moral collapse is more likely to happen in organizations that operate in moral communities in which flows of corporate ideology and culture disappear. Either it can happen through a lack of commitment to formal communication mechanisms by community leaders, or it can happen through the disruption of informal communication networks by high rates of membership turnover.
- Moral collapse is more likely to happen in organizations in which structures and practices diminish the organization's capacity to absorb and incorporate morally charged institutions from the organization's moral community, because the organization monopolizes the attention of its members and/or because the organization delegitimizes the morally charged institutions rooted in the moral community.
- Moral collapse is more likely to happen in organizations in which accusing individuals of misconduct creates significant social and economic costs for the organization or the moral community within which it operates.
- Moral collapse is more likely to occur in organizations to the degree that employment conditions undermine disclosure and/or work arrangements diminish the effectiveness of surveillance.

The institutional perspective is mainly a sociological and public policy perspective on organizational studies. The perspective sheds light on normative structures and activities. The institutional perspective in public policy emphasizes the formal and legal aspects of government structures. Signs from organizations represent observations as indications of values in organizational members. When activities occur repetitively in the same way and within the same structure, then those activities become part of the institution itself, as the sum of activities based on shared perceptions of reality are an institution.

The institutional perspective considers the processes by which structures, including schemes; rules; norms; and routines become established as authoritative guidelines for social behavior. Triggers of institutional adaption include political, cultural, and social influences. Behavioral patterns supported by norms, values, and expectations lead to cultural influence. A desire to equal others implies social influence. Normative institutional pressure is concerned with conformity, where deviance is disliked, disapproved, or even dismissed (Witt et al., 2021).

The institutional perspective is in line with the dysfunctional network perspective, in that organizations tend to mirror the basic elements of their environments. The largest business corporations can more easily absorb the negative impact of legal sanctions that certain governmental or regulatory agencies might impose on them. The largest business enterprises might have better lawyers and other resources, so that they are able to contend with legal pursuits in more effective and efficient ways. Microsoft versus the United States and Microsoft versus the European Union are typical examples. Therefore, laws and regulations tend to have less deterrent effect in the case of large business organizations (Dion, 2008).

Institutional deterioration often occurs at the same time as social disorganization, which further improves the opportunity structure for white-collar crime. The disorganization perspective argues that structural conditions lead to higher levels of social disorganization – especially of weak social controls – in organizations and between organizations, which in turn results in higher rates of crime (Pratt and Cullen, 2005). Of course, rates of financial crime vary across time and space in the private and public sectors with different motivational bases (Kjeldsen and Jacobsen, 2013; Miceli and Near, 2013; Perry et al., 2010; Wright, 2007).

Social disorganization increases offenders' opportunities to commit financial crime without any likelihood of detection. Offenders have unrestricted and legitimate access to the location in which the crime is committed without any kinds of controls (Williams et al., 2019). Offenders' actions have a superficial appearance of legitimacy also internally, since both legal and illegal actions in the organization occur in a manner characterized by disorganization (Benson and Simpson, 2018).

The social disorganization perspective argues that crime is a function of people dynamics in the organization and between organizations, and not necessarily a function of each individual within such organizations. Business enterprises experiencing rapid changes in their social and economic structures that are in a zone of transition will experience higher crime rates. Management mobility is another structural factor or antecedent that can produce organizations that develop into socially disorganized entities. Conventional mechanisms of social control are weak and unable to regulate the behavior within organizations (Pratt and Cullen, 2005).

Especially in knowledge organizations where the hierarchical structure tends to be weak, social controls among colleagues are of importance to prevent financial crime. An unstable and disorganized unit will suffer from lack of knowledge exchange and collaboration to prevent and detect white-collar crime (Swart and Kinnie, 2003).

Structural antecedents include not only management instability and rapid organizational changes, but also external factors such as family disruptions and no intelligence about life outside work. Social disorganization may well occur at the very top of organizations, where chief executives have created large business space for themselves without access for others. The board of directors is incapable of controlling chief executive activities (Ghannam et al., 2019).

Rivalry among members of the top management group, sometimes incorrectly labeled a team, can create silos of allies and enemies in the organization that hardly communicate honestly with each other. There are no ties allowing others to act collectively to fight problems (Pratt and Cullen, 2005). Corporate disorganization weakens the ability of social bonds to circumscribe delinquent behavior. In enterprises characterized by instability and heterogeneity, there is reduced likelihood of effective socialization and supervision. The impact of social bonds varies by type of organization, and disorganized units negatively affect the ability of social bonds to reduce delinquent behavior (Hoffmann, 2002; Onna and Denkers, 2019).

Concerted ignorance can occur in deteriorated organizations, where the normalization of deviant thinking and behavior in organizations develops. Employees slowly adapt to organizations' deviant norms and values that become dominant due to the higher authority of deviating individuals (Katz, 1979). For example, Shichor and Heeren (2021: 99) described concerted ignorance at Wells Fargo:

> Management expectations of making profits through lower level employees, without being interested in how the results are achieved can be characterized as "concerted ignorance" which is a general way of covering up when open discussion of certain practices or policies would threaten the solidarity and cohesion in an organization.

Shichor and Heeren (2021) found that concerted ignorance was created by an organizational emphasis on decentralization. Concerted ignorance was promoted by the common interest of limiting the knowledge each member of the organization obtains about other members of the organization.

The essence of a deteriorated institution is that its norms, behaviors, and ways of thinking are rooted in its deviant culture. For example, Campbell and Göritz (2014) identified corrupt organizations as enterprises that systematically receive bribes or provide bribes that lead to advantages in competitions. Executives who facilitate corruption either on the bribed or bribing side harm other companies for the advantage of their own organizations. In corrupt organizations, executives perceive corrupt behavior as appropriate.

Disorganized institutional deterioration can cause potential whistleblowers to become reluctant to blow the whistle on observed wrongdoings. Potential whistleblowers can fear organizational death and job loss, in addition to reprisals and retaliation. They may feel strongly for their organization, and they may be dependent on the income from their jobs. As argued by Crosina and Pratt (2019), organizations can foster deep bonds among their members, whether in the form of person-organization fit, organizational commitment, organizational identification, or some other type of attachment. A potential scandal from exposure of white-collar crime suspicion can threaten members' bonds to the organization. Organizational failure and closure can lead to organizational mourning, which Crosina and Pratt (2019: 67) define as "the thoughts, feelings, and actions that individual members undergo when processing and responding to the loss of their organization". The threat of organizational collapse is a stressor that can prevent attention to possible crime, which can create a scandal. Job loss because of a corporate scandal is detrimental to individuals' needs, desires, and goals. Job loss in conjunction to organizational death results in a large number of people entering the stage of organizational mourning that they all would like to avoid.

An element of disorganized institutional deterioration is the opportunity of fraudulent misreporting in accounting (Qiu and Slezak, 2019). Lack of transparency makes concealment in accounting convenient (Goncharov and Peter,

2019; Mehrpouya and Salles-Djelic, 2019). Elite members can withhold bad news by accounting misrepresentation (Bao et al., 2019). Balakrishnan et al. (2019) found that reduced corporate transparency is associated with increased corporate tax aggressiveness.

Disorganized institutional deterioration in combination with lack of corporate social responsibility cause both internal and external collapse. Executives in the organization do not care about the community, the environment, or product safety (Davidson et al., 2019).

Lack of government and governance is another enabler of disorganized institutional deterioration. The last decades have seen a shift of regulatory authority of business conduct from governments to the private sector. Self-regulation and self-policing have become the norm rather than the exception when it comes to white-collar crime suspicions (Kourula et al., 2019).

Kourula et al. (2019: 1103) define government as those public actors that have exclusive authority over legitimate force in a specific territory:

> In our contemporary world, governments defined in this way are generally coextensive with nation-states. By virtue of this unique mode of authority, the "sine qua non" of state power, governments have the capacity, within their jurisdictions, to impose legally binding constraints and sanctions over non-governmental actors, whether in politics, society, or markets.

When there is suspicion of corporate white-collar crime, the government branch typically involved is the national criminal justice system. The police have the task of investigating suspicions by reconstructing past events and sequences of events. If the police find sufficient evidence of law violation, then the case moves to the prosecution. The defendant faces the prosecutor in court, where a jury or a judge decides whether the suspected criminal is guilty of law violation.

Kourula et al. (2019: 1104) define governance as those private actors, which direct behaviors in business conduct by rulemaking, enforcement, and sanctioning: "By 'governance' we refer not to corporate governance, but to the wider concept of societal governance, that of the collective means to give 'direction to society' which we take to include direction to society's politics and markets."

When there is suspicion of corporate white-collar crime, the governance branch typically involved should be the compliance function, potentially cooperating with internal and external auditors as well as various controllers. Internal or external fraud examiners have the task of investigating suspicions by reconstructing past events and sequences of events. If fraud examiners find sufficient evidence of law violation, then the case stops, moves internally or moves externally to the national criminal justice system. If secrecy to protect corporate reputation is the main concern, then the case typically stops and remains internal. However, organizations with inefficient or non-existing compliance functions or governance branch generally, contribute to disorganized institutional deterioration.

Lack of Oversight and Guardianship

The perspective of principal and agent suggests that when a principal delegates tasks to an agent, the principal is often unable to control what the agent is doing. Agency problems occur when principal and agent have different risk willingness and different preferences, and knowledge asymmetry regarding tasks exists (Eisenhardt, 1989). The principal-agent perspective (or simply agency perspective) can illuminate fraud and corruption in an organizational context. The principal may be a board of a company that leaves the corporate management to the chief executive officer (CEO). The CEO is then the agent in the relationship. The CEO in turn may entrust tasks to other executives, where the CEO becomes the principal, while people in positions such as chief financial officer (CFO), chief operating officer (COO), and chief technology officer (CTO) are agents. Agents perform tasks on behalf of principals. A CEO may cheat and defraud owners (Khanna et al., 2015; Zahra et al., 2005; Williams, 2008), and a purchasing manager can fool the CEO when selecting vendors (Chrisman et al., 2007) by taking bribes that can cause the company to pay more for inferior quality, for instance. The agency perspective assumes narrow self-interest among both principals and agents. The interests of principal and agent tend to diverge, and the principal has imperfect information about the agent's contribution (Bosse and Phillips, 2016). According to principal-agent analysis, exchanges can encourage illegal private gain for both principal and agent (Pillay and Kluvers, 2014). Managers are viewed as opportunistic agents motivated by individual utility maximization. Taking an economic model of man that treats human beings as rational actors seeking to maximize individual utility – when given the opportunity – then executives and other members of the elite will maximize their own utilities at the expense of shareholders and others.

As evidenced by many internal investigation reports by fraud examiners after white-collar crime scandals, internal auditors, external auditors, compliance committees, and other internal and external control units do not function properly (e.g., Bruun Hjejle, 2018; Clifford Chance, 2020; Deloitte, 2015; Mannheimer Swartling, 2016; Shearman Sterling, 2017). Oversight and control functions tend to be formal units without any insights into the substance of business activities. They tend to review procedures rather than transactions within procedures. Therefore, ineffective control functions are often an important part of the opportunity structure for white-collar crime. For example, at Toshiba Corporation, lack of controls was an important element of the opportunity structure (Deloitte, 2015). Fraud examiners emphasized lack of internal controls by accounting and auditing functions, as well as lack of finance control in each corporate division. At Wells Fargo, corporate control functions were constrained by the decentralized organizational structure (Shearman Sterling, 2017; Shichor and Heeren, 2021). Fraud examiners excused corporate control functions since they suffered from harm by the decentralized organizational structure and a culture of substantial independence for business units. At Fuji Xerox, CEO Whittaker had gained control over reporting lines to manipulate accounting. At Danske Bank where money laundering occurred in their Estonian branch, corporate control functions did not work because the branch operated computer systems different from computer systems at the headquarter (Bruun Hjejle, 2018). Telenor executives ignored corruption rumors at VimpelCom since the chief compliance officer and chief legal officer did not know how to handle whistleblowing (Deloitte, 2016).

Lack of oversight and guardianship becomes even worse when auditors slide over on the wrong side of the law. Mohliver (2019: 310) found that some auditors prioritize their clients' interests over their legal obligation by recommending client malfeasance, for example in terms of illegal stock option backdating: "The findings suggest that professional experts' involvement in the diffusion of liminal practices is highly responsive to the institutional environment."

Auditors are supposed to serve as gatekeepers to protect shareholders and report directly to shareholder representatives on the board of directors, but auditors become surprisingly often hired by corporate management to whom they are loyal (Hurley et al., 2019). Reporting fraud to public authorities will also harm auditors (Mohliver, 2019: 316):

> As organizations, audit firms are often severely penalized for client malfeasance. Yet the individual auditors working for these firms are susceptible to "motivated blindness" stemming from conflicts of interest that bias their moral judgment toward choices that help their clients.

Mohliver (2019) found that auditor bias towards accepting deviant financial reports increased when there is ambiguity about the appropriateness of a course of action. Financial misreporting that is viewed favorably by the client organization can be recommended by external auditors on the grounds that such reporting is already adopted among companies served by the same auditing firm.

Lack of whistleblowing is an important part of the opportunity structure for white-collar crime. When people notice wrongdoing in the organization, they are reluctant to report it because of perceived retaliation threats. As argued by Keil et al. (2010), costs tend to exceed benefits for individual whistleblowers. In addition, as argued by Bussmann et al. (2018), employees in societies characterized by collectivist values are reluctant to blow the whistle on others.

Whistleblowing is the disclosure by an individual in an organization or in society of deviant practices to someone who can do something about it (Bjørkelo et al., 2011). Whistleblowing is an action by employees who believe that their business or colleague(s) are involved in activities of misconduct or crime, cause unnecessary harm, violate human rights, or contribute to otherwise immoral offenses (Mpho, 2017). Whistleblowing is the disclosure by an organizational member of deviant practices to someone who can do something about it. Whistleblowers stand out as a group of reporters who have made observations and who are willing to disclose what they have observed. However, executives may try to withhold bad news (Bao et al., 2019) and punish whistleblowers by reprisals and retaliation.

A potential whistleblower might thus be afraid of retaliation. Retaliation makes informants reluctant to blow the whistle. Reprisal and retaliation against a whistleblower represent an outcome between an organization and its employee, in which members of the organization attempt to control the employee by threatening to take, or actually taking, an action that is detrimental to the well-being of the employee (Mesmer-Magnus and Viswesvaran, 2005; Rehg et al., 2009).

If someone blows the whistle on observed wrongdoing, it is not at all sure that the receiver of the message will react by following it up. Kaplan et al. (2020) found that anonymous reports by whistleblowers are perceived as less credible and follow-up intentions are weaker. Perceived credibility seems to mediate the relationship between whistleblowing reports and follow-up intentions. Previous confrontation is not significantly associated with either perceived credibility or follow-up intentions.

The lack of whistleblowing is an organizational inhibitor in relation to addressing white-collar crime and thus an enabler of wrongdoing. Shepherd and Button (2019) suggest that a range of avoidant rationalizations constructed by observers justify not noticing, reporting, or tackling white-collar crime. These rationalizations and justifications for disregard of observed wrongdoing can be similar to those rationalizations applied by offenders when committing crime, such as denial of victim and denial of damage (Kaptein and Helvoort, 2019).

Guardianship, oversight, and control become more difficult in times of wrongdoing by misleading attributions. The attribution perspective implies that white-collar offenders are able to attribute causes of crime to everyone else but themselves in the organization. Attribution theory is about identifying causality predicated on internal and external circumstances (Eberly et al., 2011). External attributions place the cause of a negative event on external factors, absolving the account giver and the privileged individual from personal responsibility. Innocent subordinates receive blame for crime committed by elite members (Lee and Robinson, 2000). According to Sonnier et al. (2015: 10), affective reactions influence blame attribution directly and indirectly by altering structural linkage assessments: "For example, a negative affective reaction can influence the assessment of causation by reducing the evidential standards required to attribute blame or by increasing the standards of care by which an act is judged."

When the Siemens corruption scandal emerged in the public, top management attempted to blame lower-level managers (Berghoff, 2018: 423): "At first the company defended itself with set phrases like 'mishaps of individuals' and isolated offenses committed by a 'gang' of criminals, or 'This is not Siemens'."

Status-related factors such as influential positions, upper-class family ties, and community roles often preclude perceptions of blameworthiness (Slyke and Bales, 2013). According to the attribution perspective, parties involved in a personal conflict or crime suspicion will naturally wonder "Why is this happening?" in the hope that if they understand the negative event, they might be able to predict its cause. The cause can be either individual behavior (personal attribution) or organizational behavior (system attribution). The attribution perspective suggests that, all else being equal, the odds are in favor of making a personal attribution (Keaveney, 2008). If a white-collar offender fails to attribute crime to another individual, then there is the alternative of blaming the system.

Attribution theory explains individuals attribute responsibility for both own and others' behavior. The central premise is that attributions of responsibility depend on whether individuals view the causes of behavior as a result of internal or external factors. If individuals determine that a behavior results from internal factors in terms of actor personality characteristics and actor disposition, then they typically will attribute the behavior to the actor. Alternatively, individuals can attribute the behavior to other people or the situation such as social structure or organizational context. The strength of attribution in terms of responsibility can depend on a number of factors such as causality, knowledge, intentions, and seriousness (Gailey and Lee, 2005).

Control functions in charge of crime signal detection have to make decisions when there is a new signal. The perspective of crime signal detection suggests that there is often too much interference and noise for white-collar crime to reach the attention of observers. The issue of signal detection reflects the challenging task of detecting a given signal against a background of noise that reflects a situation of uncertainty (Manning and Kowalska, 2021). There are four possibilities in the decision matrix of the observer of potential misconduct and crime (Karim and Siegel, 1998: 368):

- The observer notices a noise when it is a signal (called a miss).
- The observer notices a signal when it is a signal (called a hit).
- The observer notices a noise when it is a noise (called a correct identification).
- The observer notices a signal when it is a noise (called a false alarm).

The observer needs to decide concerning the event and classify it as either a signal or a noise. In an organizational context, where less powerful individuals may suspect powerful individuals, the less powerful will conveniently prefer to think of the event as a noise signal rather than as a crime signal. The perspective of crime signal detection holds that the observation of a stimulus depends on both the intensity of the stimulus and the physical and psychological state of the observer. An observer's ability or likelihood to detect some stimulus depends on the intensity of the stimulus as well as the extent of alertness of the observer. Perceptual sensitivity depends upon the perceptual ability of the observer to detect a signal or target or to discriminate signal from non-signal events (Szalma and Hancock, 2013). Furthermore, detecting persons may have varying ability to discern between information-bearing recognition (called pattern) and random patterns that distracts from information (called noise), as illustrated by the four possibilities in the decision alternatives earlier. Lack of oversight and guardianship can thus be the result of failed crime signal detection versus noise signal detection.

The ethical climate can be another element of the opportunity structure for white-collar crime. The ethical climate perspective defines five distinct climate types within organizations: instrumental, caring, independence, rules, and law and code. A work climate is the sum of perceptions that provide meaningful insights into the working environment, which people can agree characterize an organization's values, practices, and procedures. The instrumental climate is the climate in which Murphy and Free (2015) believe fraud is most likely to occur. Instrumental means that executives and others in the organization tend to prioritize decisions that either provide personal benefits or serve the organization's interests with little regard for ethical considerations. There is an association between instrumental climate and workplace deviance extending to fraud. Workplace deviance is voluntary behavior that violates significant organizational norms and in so doing threatens the well-being of an organization, its members, or both. However, fraud and corruption can be a consequence of following, rather than violating, an organizational norm. For example, a case against Siemens in Germany alleged that Siemens executives abroad routinely bribed foreign officials as part of an overall pattern of corporate conduct in marketing. The climate encouraged corruption and fraudulent behavior as normal and acceptable (Murphy and Dacin, 2011).

Lack of oversight and guardianship was obvious in the Siemens corruption scandal, as phrased by the judge in the German court (Berghoff, 2018: 430): "He compared the Siemens compliance department with 'fire fighters, who were equipped with a toothbrush mug to extinguish major fires'."

Lack of control is both a formal and social phenomenon. Social control agents can have the legitimate authority to define specific conduct as right and wrong. When social control agents are missing or not functioning then executives have no way of reacting on deviance and misconduct by other executives. An example of managerial misconduct occurs when management intentionally misleads investors or when shareholders become injured as result of management's disclosure decisions (Jennings, 2019).

Criminal Market Structures

As mentioned earlier in this book, Sutherland (1983) emphasized attitudes in society where people consider white-collar crime as less serious than traditional street crime. While convenience theory so far emphasizes factors at the individual and organizational level, Sutherland (1983) emphasized hypotheses at the community level. In its earlier version, convenience theory was lacking explicit representations of community-level factors such as criminal market structures including competition-avoiding cartels (Goncharov and Peter, 2019) and corruption networks (Nielsen, 2003).

In its current version, convenience theory applies three levels of analysis. In addition to the individual and the organization as units of analysis, the community is the unit of analysis mainly in an opportunity perspective. Community-level factors such as corruption networks enable individuals and organizations to commit and conceal white-collar crime. At the community level, the focus is not on the isolated individual act of providing a bribe or receiving a bribe, but rather "the systematic, pervasive sub-system of bribery that can and has existed across historical periods, geographic areas, and political-economic systems" (Nielsen, 2003: 125). If the third level of criminal market structures is defined as the individual perceptions of structures rather than the actual structures, then the extent of criminal market structures can vary with white-collar offenders.

While cartels can represent painful corporate economic threats as discussed earlier in the economical dimension of convenience theory, a cartel can represent an opportunity for those enterprises that have joined the cartel. In many markets, there are cartels that regulate the supply side. Cartel members agree not only on market division but also on prices to various customers (Goncharov and Peter, 2019).

The social exchange perspective aids explanations of how power structures in cartels and corruption networks develop and institutionalize through relationship building and social exchanges among participating enterprises. The perspective suggests that organizational activities are contingent on the actions of other organizations. The successful cartels and networks are dependent on generation of obligations and fulfillment of rewards. Relational efforts in an industry or in a community lead to repeated patterns of interactions that may develop into durable institutions of interdependencies in cartels and networks (Cropanzano and Mitchell, 2005; Lawler and Hipp, 2010).

Cartels and corruption networks are important to many global business enterprises. When the corruption case at Siemens became public, Murphy and Dacin (2011) found that the business climate encouraged corruption and fraudulent behavior as normal and acceptable. To cope with the scandal, Siemens replaced its management board (Berghoff, 2018: 423):

> Siemens is one of the world's leading electrical engineering corporations. In 2006, a massive corruption scandal erupted, concluded in 2008 with a record fine. For Siemens the largest risk was being barred from government contracts. As a consequence, it replaced virtually its entire managing board, an unprecedented procedure in the history of the company.

However, the criminal market structures did not change. Siemens thus "thrived in the cozy world of national monopolies and cartels, which guaranteed high margins and no worries about rivals" (Berghoff, 2018: 425). While the new management at Siemens attempted trust repair among stakeholders by introducing updates on rules and guidelines, Eberl et al. (2015: 1205) found that the new rules were paradoxical in nature and thus difficult to implement in practice:

> Our findings suggest that tightening organizational rules is an appropriate signal of trustworthiness for external stakeholders to demonstrate that the organization seriously intends to prevent integrity violations in the future. However, such rule adjustments were the source of dissatisfaction among employees since the new rules were difficult to implement in practice. We

> argue that these different impacts of organizational rules result from their inherent paradoxical nature.

After a white-collar scandal, many companies attempt window dressing by introducing new rules for their employees. However, the new rules do not necessarily apply to those levels in the organization where you find the criminals. For example, when top executives at the Norwegian company Yara were charged with corruption, and one of them ended up in prison, the company introduced new anti-corruption rules that did not apply to the top executives. They continued to enjoy the freedom of choice in their business decisions. The chief compliance officer continued to report to an executive whose predecessor in the position ended up in jail.

Interactions between Crime Enablers

This chapter has presented a number of organizational enablers of white-collar crime. Some of these factors can interact with each other. For example, principal-agent misfit can interact with institutional pressure as suggested by Aguilera et al. (2018). While the principal-agent misfit is an internal contributor to the organizational opportunity structure, institutional pressure is an external contributor. External institutional forces can influence organizational agency to create an improved opportunity structure for convenient white-collar crime.

Furthermore, the factors that can explain organizational opportunity as presented earlier can find their foundation in the situational action perspective, as the factors represent an inviting environment for an individual to commit crime. The situational action perspective is concerned with crime causation (Wikstrom et al., 2018: 12):

> It analyses crime as acts of rule-breaking and stresses the importance of the person-environment interaction and the need to properly understand and explicate the action mechanism that links people and their immediate environments to their actions, such as acts of crime.

The situational action perspective insists that people are the source of their actions, but that the causes of their actions are situational. This is in line with the theory of convenience since people's particular perception of action alternatives determines the choice between legal or illegal actions. The processes of choice and execution of action are a result of a person–environment interaction, where the individual chooses the most attractive avenue. The situation is not so much the immediate environment but more the particular perception of action alternatives. The factors listed earlier represent a setting's particular criminogenic inducement that makes white-collar crime more convenient.

There is a strong interaction between crime signal detection and whistleblowing intentions among potential whistleblowers. A low uncertainty that there is a crime signal will relate positively to whistleblowing intentions. If the signal is weak and confused by noise, whistleblowing intentions are likely to deteriorate as the potential whistleblower considers risk for him or her (Brown et al., 2016). It is convenient for an offender to know that even though others in the organization may develop suspicions, they will not notify others about what they have observed. They are not sure if something wrong has occurred, they are not sure who to notify, and they are not sure if any whistleblowing may have consequences for themselves in the form of reprisals. That is why many people are reluctant to report suspicion of misconduct and crime, even when they feel quite certain that something wrong has happened. Many who have cast light on critical conditions have experienced unwillingness, and they have been isolated and considered less attractive in the labor market afterwards (Rehg et al., 2009). According to Shawver and Clements (2019), potential whistleblowers often decide not to report ethical wrongdoing because of the likelihood of retaliation.

Interactions between crime enablers occur in the organizational opportunity dimension of convenience theory. Interactions can also occur across dimensions, which we return to in the description of the crime convenience triangle later in this book.

In summary, this chapter has described how elements of individual position, organizational culture, and market conditions all contribute to convenient opportunity structures for financial crime by white-collar offenders. White-collar criminals can be distinguished from other financial criminals in their ability to abuse their positions of trust. Even when others observe and notice misconduct, very few subordinates or colleagues might be willing to blow the whistle on white-collar offenders in fear of retaliation and reprisals.

References

Aguilera, R.V. and Vadera, A.K. (2008). The dark side of authority: Antecedents, mechanisms, and outcomes of organizational corruption, *Journal of Business Ethics*, 77, 431–449.

Aguilera, R.V., Judge, W.Q. and Terjesen, S.A. (2018). Corporate governance deviance, *Academy of Management Review*, 43 (1), 87–109.

Balakrishnan, K., Blouin, J.L. and Guay, W.R. (2019). Tax aggressiveness and corporate transparency, *The Accounting Review*, 94 (1), 45–69.

Bao, D., Kim, Y., Mian, G.M. and Su, L. (2019). Do managers disclose or withhold bad news? Evidence from short interest, *The Accounting Review*, 94 (3), 1–26.

Barton, H. (2004). Cultural reformation: a case for intervention within the police service, *International Journal of Human Resources Development and Management*, 4 (2), 191–199.

Benson, M.L. and Gottschalk, P. (2015). Gender and white-collar crime in Norway: An empirical study of media reports, *International Journal of Law, Crime and Justice*, 43 (4), 535–552.

Benson, M.L. and Simpson, S.S. (2018). *Understanding White-Collar Crime – An Opportunity Perspective*, 2nd edition, New York, NY: Routledge.

Benson, M.L., Feldmeyer, B., Gabbidon, S.L. and Chio, H.L. (2021). Race, ethnicity, and social change: The democratization of middle-class crime, *Criminology*, 59 (1), 10–41.

Berghoff, H. (2018). "Organised irresponsibility?" The Siemens corruption scandal of the 1990s and 2000s, *Business History*, 60 (3), 423–445.

Berghoff, H. and Spiekermann, U. (2018). Shady business: On the history of white-collar crime, *Business History*, 60 (3), 289–304.

Bjørkelo, B., Einarsen, S., Nielsen, M.B. and Matthiesen, S.B. (2011). Silence is golden? Characteristics and experiences of self-reported whistleblowers, *European Journal of Work and Organizational Psychology*, 20 (2), 206–238.

Bjørklund, I. (2018). *MÅ betale over 137 mill I erstatning (Must pay over 137 million in compensation), daily Norwegian business newspaper Dagens Næringsliv*, www.dn.no, published January 19.

Bosse, D.A. and Phillips, R.A. (2016). Agency theory and bounded self-interest, *Academy of Management Review*, 41 (2), 276–297.

Bradshaw, E.A. (2015). "Obviously, we're all oil industry": The criminogenic structure of the offshore oil industry, *Theoretical Criminology*, 19 (3), 376–395.

Brooks, G. and Button, M. (2011). The police and fraud investigation and the case for a nationalized solution in the United Kingdom, *The Police Journal*, 84, 305–319.

Brown, J.O., Hays, J. and Stuebs, M.T. (2016). Modeling accountant whistleblowing intentions: Applying the theory of planned behavior and the fraud triangle, *Accounting and the Public Interest*, 16 (1), 28–56.

Bruun Hjejle (2018). *Report on the Non-Resident Portfolio at Danske Bank's Estonian branch*, report of investigation, 87 pages, law firm Bruun Hjejle, Copenhagen, Denmark.

Bussmann, K.D., Niemeczek, A. and Vockrodt, M. (2018). Company culture and prevention of corruption in Germany, China and Russia, *European Journal of Criminology*, 15 (3), 255–277.

Button, M. and Gee, J. (2013). *Countering Fraud for Competitive Advantage – The Professional Approach to Reducing the Last Great Hidden Cost*, Chichester, UK: John Wiley & Sons.

Button, M., Frimpong, K., Smith, G. and Johnston, L. (2007a). Professionalizing counter fraud specialists in the UK: assessing progress and recommendations for reform, *Crime Prevention and Community Safety*, 9, 92–101.

Button, M., Johnston, L., Frimpong, K. and Smith, G. (2007b). New directions in policing fraud: The emergence of the counter fraud specialists in the United Kingdom, *International Journal of the Sociology of Law*, 35, 192–208.

Campbell, J.L. and Göritz, A.S. (2014). Culture corrupts! A qualitative study of organizational culture in corrupt organizations, *Journal of Business Ethics*, 120 (3), 291–311.

Chrisman, J.J., Chua, J.H., Kellermanns, F.W. and Chang, E.P.C. (2007). Are family managers agents or stewards? An exploratory study in privately held family firms, *Journal of Business Research*, 60 (10), 1030–1038.

Clifford Chance (2020). *Report of Investigation on Swedbank*, report of investigation, 218 pages, law firm Clifford Chance, Washington, DC, USA.

Cohen, L.E. and Felson, M. (1979). Social change and crime rate trends: A routine activity approach. *American Sociological Review*, 44, 588–608.

Coleman, J. (1987). Toward an integrated theory of white-collar crime, *American Journal of Sociology*, 93 (2), 406–439.

Cropanzano, R. and Mitchell, M.S. (2005). Social exchange theory: An interdisciplinary review, *Journal of Management*, 31 (6), 874–900.

Crosina, E. and Pratt, M.G. (2019). Toward a model of organizational mourning: The case of former Lehman Brothers bankers, *Academy of Management Journal*, 62 (1), 66–98.

Davidson, R.H., Dey, A. and Smith, A.J. (2019). CEO materialism and corporate social responsibility, *The Accounting Review*, 94 (1), 101–126.

Deloitte (2015). *Investigation Report, Summary Version, Independent Investigation Committee for Toshiba Corporation*, report of investigation, audit firm Deloitte Tohmatsu, Tokyo, Japan.

Deloitte (2016). *Review – Ownership VimpelCom Telenor*, report of investigation, 54 pages, audit firm Deloitte, Oslo, Norway.

Dewan, Y. and Jensen, M. (2020). Catching the big fish: The role of scandals in making status a liability, *Academy of Management Journal*, 63 (5), 1652–1678.

Dion, M. (2008). Ethical leadership and crime prevention in the organizational setting, *Journal of Financial Crime*, 15 (3), 308–319.

Dion, M. (2020). Bribery, extortion and "morally ambiguous" leadership in organizations, *Journal of Financial Crime*, 27 (4), 1027–1046.

Donk, D.P. and Molloy, E. (2008). From organizing as projects, to projects as organizations, *International Journal of Project Management*, 26, 129–137.

Dyreng, S.D., Hanlon, M. and Maydew, E.L. (2019). When does tax avoidance result in tax uncertainty? *The Accounting Review*, 94 (2), 179–203.

Eberl, P., Geiger, D. and Assländer, M.S. (2015). Repairing trust in an organization after integrity violations. The ambivalence of organizational rule adjustments, *Organization Studies*, 36 (9), 1205–1235.

Eberly, M.B., Holley, E.C., Johnson, M.D. and Mitchell, T.R. (2011). Beyond internal and external: A dyadic theory of relational attributions, *Academy of Management Review*, 36 (4), 731–753.

Eisenhardt, K.M. (1989). Agency theory: An assessment and review, *Academy of Management Review*, 14 (1), 57–74.

Ferraro, F., Pfeffer, J. and Sutton, R.I. (2005). Economics language and assumptions: How theories can become self-fulfilling, *Academy of Management Review*, 30 (1), 8–24.

Friedrich, C. (2021). *Corporate Misconduct and the Impact of Market Forces, Regulatory Change, and Auditor-Provided Services*, Doctoral dissertation, Technical University of Darmstadt, Germany.

Friedrichs, D.O., Schoultz, I. and Jordanoska, A. (2018). *Edwin H. Sutherland, Routledge Key Thinkers in Criminology*, London, UK: Routledge.

Füss, R. and Hecker, A. (2008). Profiling white-collar crime. Evidence from German-speaking countries, *Corporate Ownership & Control*, 5 (4), 149–161.

Gailey, J.A. and Lee, M.T. (2005). An integrated model of attribution of responsibility for wrongdoing in organizations, *Social Psychology Quarterly*, 68, 338–358.

Ghannam, S., Bugeja, M., Matolcsy, Z.P. and Spiropoulos, H. (2019). Are qualified and experienced outside directors willing to join fraudulent firms and if so, why? *The Accounting Review*, 94 (2), 205–227.

Goncharov, I. and Peter, C.D. (2019). Does reporting transparency affect industry coordination? Evidence from the duration of international cartels, *The Accounting Review*, 94 (3), 149–175.

Grabosky, P. and Shover, N. (2010). Forestalling the next epidemic of white-collar crime, *Criminology & Public Policy*, 9 (3), 641–654.

Guenther, D.A., Wilson, R.J. and Wu, K. (2019). Tax uncertainty and incremental tax avoidance, *The Accounting Review*, 94 (2), 229–247.

Guiso, L., Sapienza, P. and Zingales, L. (2015). The value of corporate culture, *Journal of Financial Economics*, 117, 60–76.

Gyõry, C. (2020). The institutional context of financial fraud in a post-transition economy: The Quaestor scandal, *European Journal of Criminology*, 17 (1), 31–49.

Hoffmann, J.P. (2002). A contextual analysis of differential association, social control, and strain theories of delinquency, *Social Forces*, 81 (3), 753–785.

Holt, R. and Cornelissen, J. (2014). Sensemaking revisited, *Management Learning*, 45 (5), 525–539.

Huff, M.J. and Bodner, G.E. (2013). When does memory monitoring succeed versus fail? Comparing item-specific and relational encoding in the DRM paradigm, *Journal of Experimental Psychology: Learning, Memory, and Cognition*, 39 (4), 1246–1256.

Huisman, W. and Erp, J. (2013). Opportunities for environmental crime, *British Journal of Criminology*, 53, 1178–1200.

Hurley, P.J., Mayhew, B.W. and Obermire, K.M. (2019). Realigning auditors' accountability: Experimental evidence, *The Accounting Review*, 94 (3), 233–250.

Jenner Block (2010). *United States Bankruptcy Court, Southern District of New York, in regard Lehman Brothers Holdings*, law firm Jenner Block, Chicago, IL, USA, 239 pages.

Jennings, J. (2019). The role of sell-side analysts after accusations of managerial misconduct, *The Accounting Review*, 94 (1), 183–203.

Kaplan, S.E., Lanier, D., Pope, K.R. and Samuels, J.A. (2020). External investigators' follow-up intentions when whistleblowers report healthcare fraud: The effects of report anonymity and previous confrontation, *Behavioral Research in Accounting*, 32 (2), 91–101.

Kaptein, M. and Helvoort, M. (2019). A model of neutralization techniques, *Deviant Behavior*, 40 (10), 1260–1285.

Karim, K.E. and Siegel, P.H. (1998). A signal detection theory approach to analyzing the efficiency and effectiveness of auditing to detect management fraud, *Managerial Auditing Journal*, 13 (6), 367–375.

Katz, J. (1979). Concerted ignorance: The social construction of cover-up, *Urban Life*, 8 (3), 295–316.

Keaveney, S.M. (2008). The blame game: An attribution theory approach to marketer-engineer conflict in high-technology companies, *Industrial Marketing Management*, 37, 653–663.

Keil, M., Mann, J. and Rai, A. (2000). Why software projects escalate: An empirical analysis and test of four theoretical models, *MIS Quarterly*, 24 (4), 631–664.

Keil, M., Tiwana, A., Sainsbury, R. and Sneha, S. (2010). Toward a theory of whistleblowing intentions: A benefit-cost differential perspective, *Decision Sciences*, 41 (4), 787–812.

Kempa, M. (2010). Combating white-collar crime in Canada: Serving victim needs and market integrity, *Journal of Financial Crime*, 17 (2), 251–264.

Khanna, V., Kim, E.H. and Lu, Y. (2015). CEO connectedness and corporate fraud, *The Journal of Finance*, 70, 1203–1252.

King, M. (2020a). What makes a successful corporate investigator – An exploration of private investigators attributes, *Journal of Financial Crime*, published online doi:10.1108/JFC-02-2020-0019.

King, M. (2020b). Out of obscurity: The contemporary private investigator in Australia, *International Journal of Police Science and Management*, published online doi:10.1177/1461355720931887.

Kjeldsen, A.M. and Jacobsen, C.B. (2013). Public service motivation and employment sector: Attraction or socialization? *Journal of Public Administration Research and Theory*, 23 (4), 899–926.

Kostova, T., Roth, K. and Dacin, M.T. (2008). Institutional theory in the study of multinational corporations: A critique and new directions, *Academy of Management Review*, 33 (4), 994–1006.

Kourula, A., Moon, J., Salles-Djelic, M.L. and Wicker, C. (2019). New roles of government in the governance of business conduct: Implications for management and organizational research, *Organization Studies*, 40 (8), 1101–1123.

Lange, D. (2008). A multidimensional conceptualization of organizational corruption control, *Academy of Management Journal*, 33 (3), 710–729.

Lawler, E.J. and Hipp, L. (2010). Corruption as social exchange, *Advances in Group Processes*, 27, 269–296.

Lee, F. and Robinson, R.J. (2000). An attributional analysis of social accounts: Implications of playing the blame game, *Journal of Applied Social Psychology*, 30 (9), 1853–1879.

Loyens, K., Claringbould, I., Heres-van Rossem, L. and van Eekeren, F. (2021). The social construction of integrity: A qualitative case study in Dutch football, *Sports in Society*, published online doi:10.1080/17430437.2021.1877661.

Lutz, J.R. (2019). Pink-collar crime, in Bernat, F.P. and Frailing, K. (editors), *The Encyclopedia of Women and Crime*, New York, NY: John Wiley and Sons, pages 791–796.

Mannheimer Swartling (2016). *Report on Investigation of Nordea Private Banking in Relation to Offshore Structures*, law firm Mannheimer Swartling, Stockholm, Sweden, 42 pages.

Manning, L. and Kowalska, A. (2021). Illicit alcohol: Health risk of methanol poisoning and policy mitigation strategies, *Foods*, 2021, 10, 1625, doi:10.3390/foods10071625.

McElwee, G. and Smith, R. (2015). Towards a nuanced typology of illegal entrepreneurship: A theoretical and conceptual overview, in: McElwee, G. and Smith, R. (editors), *Exploring Criminal and Illegal Enterprise: New Perspectives on Research, Policy & Practice: Contemporary Issues in Entrepreneurship Research* Volume 5, Bingley, UK: Emerald Group Publishing.

Mehrpouya, A. and Salles-Djelic, M.L. (2019). Seeing like the market; Exploring the mutual rise of transparency and accounting in transnational economic and market governance, *Accounting, Organizations and Society*, 76, 12–31.

Mesmer-Magnus, J.R. and Viswesvaran, C. (2005). Whistleblowing in an organization: An examination of correlates of whistleblowing intentions, actions, and retaliation, *Journal of Business Ethics*, 62 (3), 266–297.

Miceli, M.P. and Near, J.P. (2013). An international comparison of the incidence of public sector whistle-blowing and the prediction of retaliation: Australia, Norway, and the US, *Australian Journal of Public Administration*, 72 (4), 433–446.

Mohliver, A. (2019). How misconduct spreads: Auditors' role in the diffusion of stock-option backdating, *Administrative Science Quarterly*, 64 (2), 310–336.

Mpho, B. (2017). Whistleblowing: What do contemporary ethical theories say? *Studies in Business and Economics*, 12 (1), 19–28.

Murphy, P.R. and Dacin, M.T (2011). Psychological pathways to fraud: Understanding and preventing fraud in organizations, *Journal of Business Ethics*, 101, 601–618.

Murphy, P.R. and Free, C. (2015). Broadening the fraud triangle: Instrumental climate and fraud, *Behavioral Research in Accounting*, 28 (1), 41–56.

Müller, S.M. (2018). Corporate behavior and ecological disaster: Dow Chemical and the Great Lakes mercury crisis, 1970–1972, *Business History*, 60 (3), 399–422.

Nielsen, R.P. (2003). Corruption networks and implications for ethical corruption reform, *Journal of Business Ethics*, 42 (2), 125–149.

Olav, H.E. (2014). *Det store selvbedraget: Hvordan statsmakt ødelegger menneskeverd og velferd (The grand self-deception: How state power harms human dignity and welfare)*, Kolofon publishing, Oslo, Norway.

Olav, H.E. (2015). *The Grand Self-Deception: A Libertarian Manifesto Against the Deep State – The Failed Welfare-Taxation Model of Norway*, Kindle Edition, printed in Great Britain by Amazon.

Onna, J.H.R. and Denkers, A.J.M. (2019). Social bonds and white-collar crime: A two-study assessment of informal social controls in white-collar offenders, *Deviant Behavior*, 40 (10), 1206–1225.

Oslo tingrett (2015). Verdict 14–067448MED-OTIR/06, judge Bjørn Feyling, *Oslo tingrett* (Oslo district court), January 12.

Patel, P.C. and Cooper, D. (2014). Structural power equality between family and nonfamily TMT members and the performance of family firms, *Academy of Management Journal*, 57 (6), 1624–1649.

Peixoto, A., Gouveia, T., Sousa, P., Faria, R. and Almeida, P.R. (2021). Dark personality traits and tolerance towards unethical behaviors on entrepreneurship: A comparison between entrepreneurs and non-entrepreneurs, *Journal of White Collar and Corporate Crime*, published online doi:10.1177/2631309X211029877, 9 pages.

Perry, J., Hondeghem, A. and Wise, L. (2010). Revisiting the motivational bases of public service, *Public Administration Review*, 70 (5), 681–690.

Petrocelli, M., Piquero, A.R. and Smith, M.R. (2003). Conflict theory and racial profiling: An empirical analysis of police traffic stop data, *Journal of Criminal Justice*, 31 (1), 1–11.

Pillay, S. and Kluvers, R. (2014). An institutional theory perspective on corruption: The case of a developing democracy, *Financial Accountability & Management*, 30 (1), 95–119.

Pinto, J., Leana, C.R. and Pil, F.K. (2008). Corrupt organizations or organizations of corrupt individuals? Two types of organization-level corruption, *Academy of Management Review*, 33 (3), 685–709.

Poehlinng, H. and Bolton, S. (2021). A reflection on the link between gender and white-collar crime, *British Journal of Criminology, Law & Justice*, 1 (1), 15–24.

Pontell, H.N., Black, W.K. and Geis, G. (2014). Too big to fail, too powerful to jail? On the absence of criminal prosecutions after the 2008 financial meltdown, *Crime, Law and Social Change*, 61 (1), 1–13.

Pontell, H.N., Ghazi-Tehrani, A.K. and Burton, B. (2020). White-collar and corporate crime in China, in: Rorie, M.L. (editor), *The Handbook of White-Collar Crime*, Hoboken, NJ: Wiley & Sons, chapter 22, pages 347–362.

Pontell, H.N., Tillman, R. and Ghazi-Tehrani, A.K. (2021). In-your-face Watergate: Neutralizing government lawbreaking and the war against white-collar crime, *Crime, Law and Social Change*, published online doi:10.1007/s10611-021-09954-1, 19 pages.

Pratt, T.C. and Cullen, F.T. (2005). Assessing macro-level predictors and theories of crime: A meta-analysis, *Crime and Justice*, 32, 373–450.

Qiu, B. and Slezak, S.L. (2019). The equilibrium relationships between performance-based pay, performance, and the commission and detection of fraudulent misreporting, *The Accounting Review*, 94 (2), 325–356.

Ramoglou, S. and Tsang, E.W.K. (2017). In defence of common sense in entrepreneurship theory: Beyond philosophical extremities and linguistic abuses, *Academy of Management Review*, 42 (4), 736–744.

Rehg, M.T., Miceli, M.P., Near, J.P. and Scotter, J.R.V. (2009). Antecedents and outcomes of retaliation against whistleblowers: Gender differences and power relationships, *Organization Science*, 19 (2), 221–240.

Reyns, B.W. (2013). Online routines and identity theft victimization: Further expanding routine activity theory beyond direct-contact offenses, *Journal of Research in Crime and Delinquency*, 50, 216–238.

Rodriguez, P., Uhlenbruck, K. and Eden, L. (2005). Government corruption and the entry strategies of multinationals, *Academy of Management Review*, 30 (2), 383–396.

Schnatterly, K., Gangloff, K.A. and Tuschke, A. (2018). CEO wrongdoing: A review of pressure, opportunity, and rationalization, *Journal of Management*, 44 (6), 2405–2432.

Schneider, S. (2006). Privatizing economic crime enforcement: Exploring the role of private sector investigative agencies in combating money laundering, *Policing & Society*, 16 (3), 285–312.

Shadnam, M. and Lawrence, T.B. (2011). Understanding widespread misconduct in organizations: An institutional theory of moral collapse, *Business Ethics Quarterly*, 21 (3), 379–407.

Shawver, T. and Clements, L.H. (2019). The impact of value preferences on whistleblowing intentions of accounting professionals, *Journal of Forensic and Investigative Accounting*, 11 (2), 232–247.

Shearman Sterling (2017). *Independent Directors of the Board of Wells Fargo & Company: Sales Practices Investigation Report*, law firm Shearman Sterling, New York, NY, 113 pages.

Shepherd, D. and Button, M. (2019). Organizational inhibitions to addressing occupational fraud: A theory of differential rationalization, *Deviant Behavior*, 40 (8), 971–991.

Shichor, D. and Heeren, J.W. (2021). Reflecting on corporate crime and control: The Wells Fargo banking saga, *Journal of White Collar and Corporate Crime*, 2 (2), 97–108.

Sims, R.L. and Barreto, T.S. (2021). In defense of leader misconduct: The use of neutralization techniques by ingroup members, *The Journal of Social Psychology*, published online doi:10.1080/00224545.2021.1944033.

Slyke, S.R.V. and Bales, W.D. (2013). Gender dynamics in the sentencing of white-collar offenders, *Criminal Justice Studies*, 26 (2), 168–196.

Smith, R. (2009). Understanding entrepreneurial behavior in organized criminals, *Journal of Enterprising Communities: People and Places in the Global Economy*, 3 (3), 256–268.

Sohoni, T. and Rorie, M. (2021). The whiteness of white-collar crime in the United States: Examining the role of race in a culture of elite white-collar offending, *Theoretical Criminology*, 25 (1), 66–87.

Sonnier, B.M., Lassar, W.M. and Lassar, S.S. (2015). The influence of source credibility and attribution of blame on juror evaluation of liability of industry specialist auditors, *Journal of Forensic & Investigative Accounting*, 7 (1), 1–37.

Srivastava, S.B. and Goldberg, A. (2017). Language as a window into culture, *California Management Review*, 60 (1), 56–69.

Steffensmeier, D. and Allan, E. (1996). Gender and crime: Toward a gendered theory of female offending. *Annual Review of Sociology*, 22, 459–487.

Steffensmeier, D., Schwartz, J., and Roche, M. (2013). Gender and twenty-first-century corporate crime: Female involvement and the gender gap in Enron-era corporate frauds, *American Sociological Review*, 78 (3), 448–476.

Sutherland, E.H. (1983). *White Collar Crime – The Uncut Version*, New Haven, CT: Yale University Press.

Swart, J. and Kinnie, N. (2003). Sharing knowledge in knowledge-intensive firms, *Human Resource Management Journal*, 13 (2), 60–75.

Szalma, J.L. and Hancock, P.A. (2013) A signal improvement to signal detection analysis: Fuzzy SDT on the ROCs, *Journal of Experimental Psychology: Human Perception and Performance*, 39 (6), 1741–1762.

Tientcheu, P.P. (2021). *Security Awareness Strategies Used in the Prevention of Cybercrimes by Cybercriminals*, doctoral dissertation, Walden University.

Tonoyan, V., Strohmeyer, R., Habib, M. and Perlitz, M. (2010). Corruption and entrepreneurship: How formal and informal institutions shape small firm behavior in transition and mature market economies, *Entrepreneurship: Theory & Practice*, 34 (5), 803–831.

Transparency (2018). Corruption perceptions index 2018, *Transparency International*, www.transparency.org/cpi2018.

Weick, K.E. (1995). What theory is not, theorizing is, *Administrative Science Quarterly*, 40, 385–390.

Welter, F., Baker, T., Audretsch, D.B. and Gartner, W.B. (2017). Everyday entrepreneurship: A call for entrepreneurship research to embrace entrepreneurial diversity, *Entrepreneurship: Theory and Practice*, 41 (3), 323–347.

Wheelock, D., Semukhina, O. and Demidov, N.N. (2011). Perceived group threat and punitive attitudes in Russia and the United States, *British Journal of Criminology*, 51, 937–959.

Wikstrom, P.O.H., Mann, R.P. and Hardie, B. (2018). Young people's differential vulnerability to criminogenic exposure: Bridging the gap between people- and place-oriented approaches in the study of crime causation, *European Journal of Criminology*, 15 (1), 10–31.

Williams, J.W. (2005a). Reflections on the private versus public policing of economic crime, *British Journal of Criminology*, 45, 316–339.

Williams, J.W. (2005b). Governability matters: The private policing of economic crime and the challenge of democratic governance, *Policing & Society*, 15 (2), 187–211.

Williams, J.W. (2008). The lessons of 'Enron' – Media accounts, corporate crimes, and financial markets, *Theoretical Criminology*, 12 (4), 471–499.

Williams, J.W. (2014). The private eyes of corporate culture: The forensic accounting and corporate investigation industry and the production of corporate financial security, in: Walby, K. and Lippert, R.K. (editors), *Corporate Security in the 21st Century – Theory and Practice in International Perspective*, Hampshire, UK: Palgrave Macmillan, pages 56–77.

Williams, M.L., Levi, M., Burnap, P. and Gundur, R.V. (2019). Under the corporate radar: Examining insider business cybercrime victimization through an application of routine activities theory, *Deviant Behavior*, 40 (9), 1119–1131.

Witt, M.A., Fainshmidt, S. and Aguilera, R.V. (2021). Our board, our rules: Nonconformity to global corporate governance norms, *Administrative Science Quarterly*, published online doi:10.1177/00018392211022726, pages 1–36.

Wright, B.E. (2007). Public service and motivation: Does mission matter? *Public Administration Review*, 67 (1), 54–64.

Yam, K.C., Christian, M.S., Wei, W., Liao, Z. and Nai, J. (2018). The mixed blessing of leader sense of humor: Examining costs and benefits, *Academy of Management Journal*, 61 (1), 348–369.

Zahra, S.A., Priem, R.L. and Rasheed, A.A. (2005). The antecedents and consequences of top management fraud, *Journal of Management*, 31, 803–828.

Zhong, R. and Robinson, S.L. (2021). What happens to bad actors in organizations? A review of actor-centric outcomes of negative behavior, *Journal of Management*, 47 (6), 1430–1467.

2 Born Free by Ernst & Young

The Norwegian government published the following press release on its website Regjeringen.no on September 21, 2020:

> The organization Born Free has used part of the state support they received for purposes other than those for which they received the funds and lacks good financial management, shows a report from Ernst & Young. According to the review published September 18, 2020, some of the funds may also have been used for private purposes. On the basis of a whistleblowing, the directorate commissioned Ernst & Young to investigate, among other things, the financial management of the foundation Born Free.
>
> - The report shows that publicly allocated funds have not been used in line with the purpose, and this is very serious. We expect organizations who receive state support to use the money for what they have been given and to have control of the finances. In this case, we will follow the directorate's recommendation, and we will not continue to support Born Free in 2021. The directorate will also withhold payments for the rest of this year, says state secretary with responsibility for integration matters in the Ministry of Education, Grunde Almeland (…)
> - Based on the findings in the report from Ernst & Young, our assessment is that the conditions for the grant, as they appear in our grant letters, have not been met. The directorate considers it to be sufficiently substantiated that the financial management of the foundation is not good, and that parts of the grants are not considered to have been used in line with the purpose of the grant scheme, says director of the directorate, Libe Rieber-Mohn.

One of the five whistleblowers was Laial Janet Ayoub. She claimed that the foundation had a waste culture and that Rehman did not focus on the mandate for the foundation (Buggeland et al., 2020). Another whistleblower was Rania Al-Nahi. She claimed that as a believing Muslim it became impossible to work for Born Free (Brandvold, 2020).

DOI: 10.4324/9781003305071-3

A trip to London, where people went to a concert and a show, and stayed at a spa hotel, is an example of expenses charged to the foundation that seems private (Ernst & Young, 2020).

The comedian, writer, and speaker Shabana Rehman was the founder of Born Free. She was born in Karachi, Pakistan in 1976, and her parents immigrated with the family to Norway in 1977 (Bai, 2020). The purpose of the foundation was to work for the individual's freedom and common equality goals regardless of faith, orientation, gender, or ethnicity (www.fodtfri.no). Born Free (Født Fri) was a voice for everyone who became persecuted because of their different identity. The foundation was established in the autumn of 2017 as a movement with the goal of working against negative social control and equality across gender, faith, and ethnicity. Since 2017, the organization has received just over NOK (Norwegian kroner) 15 million (USD 1.5 million) in grants from the state budget and through grant schemes managed by the directorate for integration and diversity (IMDi), including as a national resource center (Ruud, 2020; Slettholm, 2020a, 2020b).

Reactions from the Accused

When the government published its press release and opened access to the report by Ernst & Young (EY) on September 18, 2020, Shabana Rehman said to the press: "This is simply not true" (Johnsen, 2020a):

> Shabana Rehman says that the report about her foundation having used public funds for private purposes is full of errors.
>
> (I) I have read the entire report now. Ernst & Young try to protect themselves by saying that they are not responsible for potentially incorrect information from people and documents, and that Born Free did not respond to any of the allegations when we were given a response deadline. This is not true. Our lawyer has demonstrably answered them, writes Shabana Rehman in a text message to the newspaper.
>
> She also specifically mentions the seminar, which according to the report also included a "day package" at the spa, which she says is an inaccurate rendering.
>
> - This had nothing to do with the spa. We rented a meeting room to work with the script for the Stovner school show. The manuscripts are dated, and statements submitted. The perspective on this is deliberately turned towards making professionally serious work appear like extravagant luxury. The rest of EY's report is constructed in the same way, she writes.

It was one month earlier that IMDi received a warning from a whistleblower about Born Free (Lindvåg, 2020a, 2020b). The notice included allegations that state grants had not been used for the purpose of the funding, or in line with the purpose of the foundation.

Not only founder and general secretary Rehman was upset with the report by Ernst & Young (2020). Also the chairperson at the foundation and the attorney for the foundation expressed their anger (Johnsen, 2020a):

> The chairperson of the board at Born Free, Jan Sverre Asker, says the following to the newspaper:
>
> - It is shocking that IMDi has issued this report before we have had access to it. It seems that they have not taken our response into account. I will discuss every single item with IMDi and the government before I discuss it in the media, Asker says to the newspaper.
>
> Attorney for Born Free, Harald F. Strandenæs, tells the newspaper that they are surprised by the outcome of the investigation. He has forwarded to the newspaper his letter that he sent to Ernst & Young as a contradiction to statements in the draft report.
>
> - It is much unexpected conclusion that IMDi draws on the basis of what appears in the report itself. We find that the entire process of the investigation has been very unsatisfactory, partly due to the haste the work is characterized by, the attorney tells the newspaper.

As described by Østrem (2020a), the start-up of an ideal organization such as the foundation Born Free was chaotic. Much enthusiasm resulted in lack of administrative procedures. However, there is a long way to go from mess, confusion, and chaos to accusations of wrongdoing, misconduct, and crime, as emphasized by attorney Strandenæs (2020a).

The accused asked to get access to accusations reported by whistleblowers, but they were denied insight into the notices to protect whistleblowers. This is an interesting dilemma between the accuser and the accused that both need protection in a whistleblowing situation. Traditionally, whistleblowing has been ignored, and whistleblowers have suffered retaliation and reprisals, while the accused has been protected (Mesmer-Magnus and Viswesvaran, 2005; Rehg et al., 2009). More recently, whistleblowers are protected and trusted, often at the expense of the accused.

Whistleblowing is the disclosure by an individual in an organization or in society of deviant practices to someone who can do something about it (Bjørkelo et al., 2011). Whistleblowing is an action by former or current employees who believe that their business or colleague(s) are involved in activities of misconduct or crime, cause unnecessary harm, violate human rights, or contribute to otherwise immoral offenses (Mpho, 2017). Whistleblowing is the disclosure by an organizational member of deviant practices to someone who can do something about it. Whistleblowers stand out as a group of reporters who have made observations and who are willing to disclose what they have observed. However, managers as accused may try to withhold bad news (Bao et al., 2019).

In the case of Foundation Born Free, the issues raised by whistleblowers were relevant to the extent that the foundation needed to change its practice, but not necessarily to the extent that they would lose government funding (Reymert, 2020a, 2020b).

Offender Convenience Themes

Assuming that the accusations of fraud are correct and evidenced, convenience themes can be identified by application of the structural model in Figure 2.1. The possibilities to abuse government funds benefited both individuals and the foundation. Shabana Rehman already enjoyed fame as a public speaker and comedian before she founded Born Free. Maybe she then suffered from a

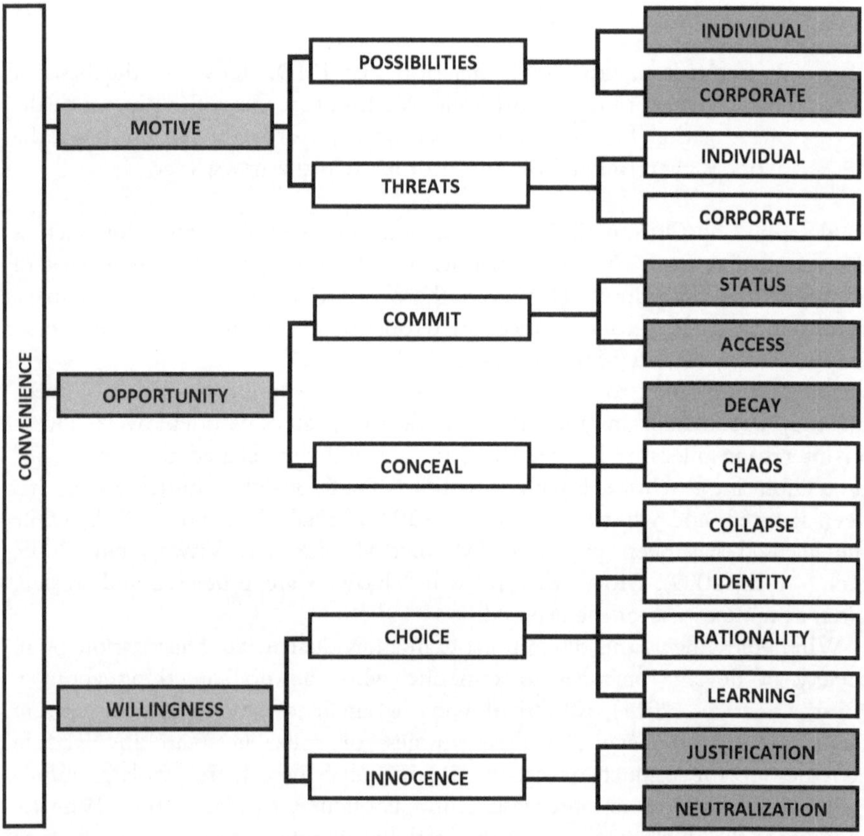

Figure 2.1 Convenience themes in the case of Foundation Born Free

desire to satisfy the need for acclaim as a narcissist (Chatterjee and Pollock, 2017). Her main motive for involvement was the fight against negative control, especially among minorities in Norway, where she wanted to satisfy her own desire to help others as social concern (Agnew, 2014). At the organizational level, the motive was to reach ambitious objectives for the foundation, where goals can justify means (Jonnergård et al., 2010).

The opportunity structure can be found in the status of Shabana Rehman as general secretary and as a well-known comedian and writer in Norway. Status is an individual's social rank within a formal or informal hierarchy, or the person's relative standing along a valued social dimension. Status is the extent to which an individual is respected and admired by others, and status is the outcome of a subjective assessment process (McClean et al., 2018). High-status individuals enjoy greater respect and deference from, as well as power and influence over, those who are positioned lower in the social hierarchy (Kakkar et al., 2020: 532):

> Status is a property that rests in the eyes of others and is conferred to individuals who are deemed to have a higher rank or social standing in a pecking order based on a mutually valued set of social attributes. Higher social status or rank grants its holder a host of tangible benefits in both professional and personal domains. For instance, high-status actors are sought by groups for advice, are paid higher, receive unsolicited help, and are credited disproportionately in joint tasks. In innumerable ways, our social ecosystem consistently rewards those with high status.

She had legitimate access to all accounts and vendors, which she handled on her own. A white-collar offender has typically legitimate and convenient access to resources to commit crime (Adler and Kwon, 2002; Füss and Hecker, 2008; Huisman and Erp, 2013; Lange, 2008; Pinto et al., 2008; Reyns, 2013). A resource is an enabler applied and used to satisfy human and organizational needs. A resource has utility and limited availability. According to Petrocelli et al. (2003), access to resources equates access to power. Other organizational members are losers in the competition for resources (Wheelock et al., 2011).

The lack of guardianship caused decay that improved the opportunity structure for offenses at the Foundation Born Free. The agency perspective suggests that a principal is often unable to control an agent who does work for the principal. The agency perspective assumes narrow self-interest among both principals and agents. The interests of principal and agent tend to diverge, they may have different risk willingness or risk aversion, there is knowledge asymmetry between the two parties, and the principal has imperfect information about the agent's contribution (Bosse and Phillips, 2016; Chrisman et al., 2007; Pillay and Kluvers, 2014; Williams, 2008). In this case, Born Free is the agent, while IMDi is the principal.

The foundation had numerous successful activities to help individuals gain freedom and common equality regardless of faith, orientation, gender, or ethnicity. The success made it easy for Foundation Born Free to justify deviant behavior and to neutralize any potential guilt feelings. Justification (Schnatterly et al., 2018; Chen and Moosmayer, 2020) and neutralization (Sykes and Matza, 1957; Schoultz and Flyghed, 2016, 2019, 2020a, 2020b) are applied to reduce and remove feelings of guilt. An important neutralization technique was to blame rule complexity (Lehman et al., 2019), where it is not at all obvious what is right and what is wrong when spending funds from the government.

Fraud Investigation Outcome

Fraud examiners reviewed the warnings from the whistleblowers about Born Free. The report of investigation reveals shortcomings in the foundation's financial management, and that parts of the funds have not been used in accordance with the guidelines for the grant scheme.

In addition, the review reveals economic activity and transactions that indicate that the organization's funds have financed activities that were not reported. The review also refers to expenses of a private nature and procurements from a supplier closely related to Shabana Rehman at Born Free.

Concerning lack of financial management, Ernst & Young (2020: 4) found that

> The secretary general has mainly alone approved and been responsible for procurement of goods and services for the foundation. The review has revealed shortcomings in the Foundation Born Free's routines for financial management. For example, the foundation does not have

- Established authorization limits that specify amounts for procurements
- Established control routines for approval and payment upon procurements
- Established controls in the selection of suppliers or relevance control of procurements made by the secretary general, for example in connection with procurements from related parties.

Concerning suspicion of funds spent outside the purpose, Ernst & Young (2020: 4) found that:

> EY's factual survey provides a basis for being able to claim that the foundation Born Free has used funds from IMDi for purposes other than as described as the purpose for allocating funds from IMDi or with the foundation's business purpose.

Ernst & Young is also skeptical towards the extensive hiring of friends and procurement of services from relatives and friends. For example, the firm responsible for accounting at Born Free was also responsible for accounting at Shabana Rehman's personal enterprise Wanted Production Norway.

In the report, Ernst & Young (2020: 36) recommend that IMDi consider reporting the incidents described in the report to the police in order to obtain an assessment of whether there has been a violation of the penal code or other laws and regulations

> EY's inquiries have shown that the foundation Born Free has used funds received from IMDi for purposes other than as described in the award letter from IMDi to the foundation. In EY's opinion, the financial management of the foundation has not been satisfactory and in accordance with requirements for good financial management. It is recommended to make a legal assessment of whether the foundation's use of the funds from IMDi has resulted in a breach of the basic conditions for allocations to the foundation for the years 2018, 2019, and 2020. It is further recommended that, based on the results of the above, consider reporting the incidents described in this report to the police in order to obtain an assessment of whether the circumstances may have led to a breach of the penal code or other legislation.

Investigation Report Maturity

It is a very serious matter to recommend police reporting. The evidence should be obvious regarding both misconduct and monitoring. Misconduct in this case might include embezzlement and other forms of fraud committed mainly by the founder and general secretary at the foundation Born Free, Shabana Rehman. Monitoring in this case implies that the directorate has done what is required to provide guidelines for the establishment of Born Free, and not just financial funding. As the funding body, IMDi carries responsibility for guiding and helping Born Free in a principal-agent relationship. This aspect seems completely ignored by the fraud examiners from Ernst and Young (2020).

In a principal-agent relationship, IMDi carries responsibility as the agent to stay informed about activities carried out by Born Free as the agent. Principal is a term for the body leaving work to an agent. The agent carries out work for the principal (Pillay and Kluvers, 2014). The interests of the principal and the agent may diverge, and the principal has imperfect information about the agent's contribution (Bosse and Phillips, 2016). Since IMDi paid for the investigation, fraud examiners did not review IMDi's potential lack of guardianship in the Born Free scandal. As argued by Ruud (2020: 8) the directorate has the responsibility "to ensure that regulations for the allocation are followed".

Attribution of guilt is thus obvious in the investigation report. Shabana Rehman was handling most financial transactions on her own, where grant money covered expenses that seemed to have private rather than foundation purposes. Examples include hotel and restaurant bills. Furthermore, she employed friends who were not necessarily the most competent people she could find. Therefore, she receives blame in the report. However, some of the blame attributions can be misleading (Cianci et al., 2019; Eberly et al., 2011).

The ignorance of fraud examiners to review the role of IMDi can be derived from the mandate. The ignorance is nevertheless unfortunate. For example, rule complexity might explain some of the deviance at Born Free. Rule complexity is a common phenomenon in the public sector. For outsiders receiving funding, it might seem impossible to understand what is right and what is wrong. Some laws, rules, and regulations are so complex that compliance becomes random, where compliance is the action of complying with laws, rules, and regulations. The regulatory legal environment is supposed to define the boundaries of appropriate organizational conduct. However, legal complexity is often so extreme that even specialist compliance officers struggle to understand what to recommend to business executives in the organizations (Lehman et al., 2019).

Fraud examiners seem to suffer from uncritical tunnel view when interpreting findings. In police investigations, the term tunnel vision implies that you only see the light at the end of the tunnel and nothing outside and around the tunnel (Bjerknes and Fahsing, 2018). For example, the manuscript work session at a hotel was interpreted by Ernst & Young (2020: 28) as private since it took place during the weekend:

> That the trip took place on a weekend as well as the choice of hotel with access to spa facilities (day package) indicates that the purpose of the trip may have been of a private nature. Furthermore, the cost level exceeds what can be considered reasonable for business-related purposes.

Fraud examiners deny responsibility for the quality of information on which they base their conclusions and recommendations (Ernst & Young, 2020: 2): "EY disclaims any responsibility for possible errors or omissions as a result of EY having received incorrect and/or incomplete information and documentation."

This statement deserves criticism, as examiners are to conduct triangulation when they are in doubt about information sources and information correctness. Triangulation implies that examiners find other documents, other witnesses or communication excerpts that either confirm or disconfirm information already obtained.

The investigation team at Ernst & Young included Ole Jacob Øglænd, Eivind Buajordet Bøe, Cecilie Lunde Antzee, and Frode Krabbesund. Øglænd was director and head of investigation services at Ernst & Young in Oslo, which was part of forensic and integrity services. Krabbesund was partner and head of forensic and integrity services. The report by the investigation team was published on September 18. The previous day, September 17, the examiners received a letter from attorney Harald Strandenæs on behalf of chair Jan Asker and general secretary Shabana Rehman at Born Free as the contradiction to the draft report. The attorney emphasized a number of shortcomings in the draft report such as (Strandenæs, 2020b: 2):

> The report writer has completely failed to accept explanations and documentation that the foundation is largely based on voluntary contributions

> with no or low pay, where meeting food and the social environment contribute to the necessary motivation and are the foundation's operational basis.

All contradictions points were ignored by the examiners as they published their report the following day with the Strandenæs letter as a listed but not included appendix.

Despite all the investigative shortcomings discussed earlier, the task of identifying some questionable transactions was successfully completed by fraud examiners. Nevertheless, the investigation is allocated at maturity level 1 in Figure 2.2. The investigation focused on activities that may have been carried out in a reprehensible manner. The examiners looked for activities and prepared descriptions of these. Then examiners made up their minds whether the activities were reprehensible or not. The examiners found several minor activities that indicate wrongdoing.

However, the examiners' interpretations of activities tell more about the forensic accountants' lack of insights into the cultural sector in society than about actual misconduct or crime by people at Born Free (Stephansen, 2020a):

> Skilled auditors have many good, prominent qualities. Insight into culture and cultural work is not among them. Therefore, it is necessary to defend Shabana Rehman and Born Free. Why do the examiners react so strongly when two artists have gone on a working weekend in a hotel? Do they think they should rent a cabin? Nobody reacts when an auto dealer takes

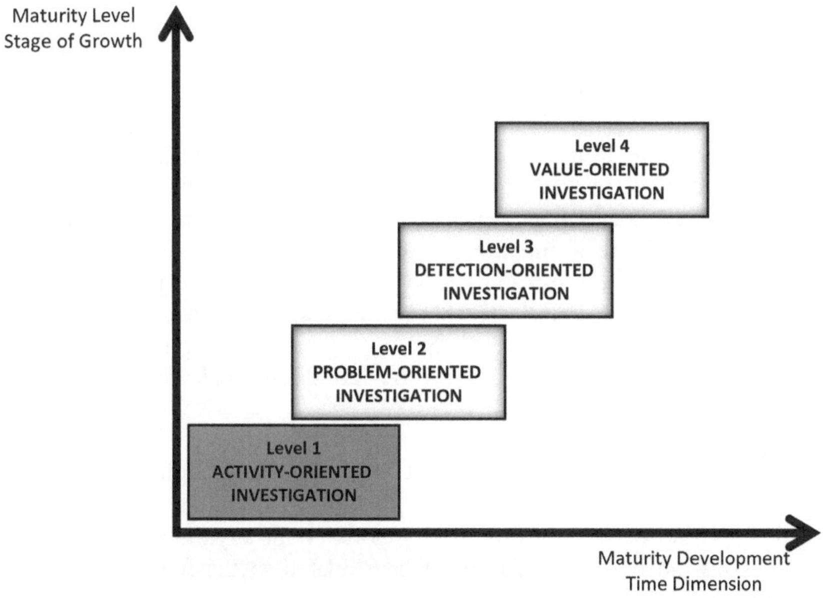

Figure 2.2 Maturity level for the Ernst & Young (2020) investigation at Born Free

> the whole sales department on a team building trip to Monte Carlo – all inclusive, or when local politicians retreat to a mountain resort for their internal seminar.
>
> That it is the Jante Act that emerges becomes clear when the A-ha concert in London is repeatedly highlighted as suspicious – despite the fact that the examiners were told and know that this was completely free, because Zahid Ali knows Magne Furuholmen in A-ha. "EY has not taken a position on the stated explanation from Rehman that there was a need to travel to London to write a script for a school performance", the examiners write. But that they have taken a stand is clear in the next sour sentence: "EY has also not taken a position on whether experienced artists such as Rehman and Ali have a real need to attend several shows and a concert to get 'inspiration' to write school performances, or whether the trip was mainly intended to attend the A-ha concert, as claimed by the whistleblowers", they write.

The previously cited criticism of the attitude of fraud examiners as evidenced in their report is indeed justified. The scornful and skeptical phrasing of many sentences in the report indicates a reluctance to try to understand how creative people work and where they find inspiration.

Reactions from the accused (e.g., Johnsen, 2020a, 2020b; Johnsen et al., 2020) and others (e.g., Stephansen, 2020a, 2020b) support the assessment of a low level of maturity for the report by Ernst & Young (2020), since higher level reports tend to become more acceptable to stakeholders. The negative reactions caused the directorate to invite the accused Born Free and its leader Shabana Rehman to submit a response to the allegations by the fraud examiners. However, the foundation attorney argued that they needed money from withheld funding to be able to provide a substantial response (Bjørdal, 2020)

> Born Free, the foundation led by Shabana Rehman, demands that a suspended grant of three million kroner be paid. Without access to the money, they cannot give a proper answer to the accusations of financial clutter, writes the foundation's lawyer. The three million will be part two of this year's allocation of NOK 6 million over the state budget. In a letter sent to IMDi which the newspaper has been access to, the foundation's lawyer Harald F. Strandenæs writes: "It is required (…) that the grant for the second term 2020 be made available to the foundation immediately".

An issue that examiners overlooked was concerned with contracts that people working for the foundation had to sign. The contract said that hired individuals would be fined if they told anyone about anything in the foundation. This was an obvious violation of laws related to the freedom of speech and expression, as well as the right to blow the whistle when observing wrongdoing (Strand, 2020).

Stephansen (2020e) compared the investigation with the following imagined story about suspected insurance fraud:

> Imagine that your mobile phone is stolen, and you report it to your insurance company. The company replies that they believe you threw it into the sea on purpose, and puts a former police officer to investigate you (there are many of these in the insurance industry). You will be called for an interview, which eventually develops into an interrogation, where you will be pressured and asked leading questions. You firmly refuse, but you are still put off by constantly new allegations from the "investigators". They claim that someone has seen you throw away the phone, but they will not tell who or where it happened. In the report, the company then claims that you are lying, and that you confessed during the "interview". You point out that you have never done it, and discover that large parts of your explanation are not included in the report. You demand that the audio recording be handed over to prove that you are telling the truth. You do not get it, for "privacy reasons".

An interesting piece of information, which confirms the low level of maturity in the investigation by Ernst & Young (2020), is an email received from a daily newspaper in Norway that first blew the story from whistleblowers. Investigative journalists claim that they are in possession of much more documentation regarding Born Free and Shabana Rehman than the fraud examiners were ever able to obtain (Østrem, 2020b):

> We know this case very well. It is not very likely that there is a link here. When the whistleblowers were interviewed, IMDi was actually interested in checking out the case, but what they found in the accounts and appendices indicates that it is reasonably clear that the management of finances has been reprehensible. We have 20 sources independent of each other, and the specific whistleblowers are just a few of them. We have a lot of documentation in addition to the ones EY has provided.

Østrem (2020b) commented earlier that it is not very likely that there is a link. The link she is referring to is a link suggesting the way IMDi's managing director uses fraud examiners and the way her husband as a bank executive used fraud examiners. As DNB chief, Rune Bjerke was responsible for the scandal revealed by the Panama Papers. DNB's associated law firm Hjort was hired by the bank to conduct an investigation, where the conclusion was that Bjerke could not be blamed because he did not know what was going on through DNB Luxembourg in tax havens. In retrospect, it is quite obvious that the Hjort report was a commissioned work. The question then was whether the EY report about Born Free also represents commissioned work. The managing director at IMDi was married to Rune Bjerke. While the order from and preference of DNB seems to have been to acquit Rune Bjerke of any potential blame for the bank scandal, the order from and preference of IMDi seems to have been to shame and blame Shabana Rehman. There was thus a potential need to assess the impartiality of Libe Rieber-Mohn and the entire directorate, since everyone below a biased executive is automatically disqualified to handle the matter. The ministry replied to the request for an impartiality assessment on October 16, 2020, where the ministry letter was signed by Sigrid Bay and Erffan Parandian:

> Incapacity means that the official who is to be involved in deciding the case has such a connection to a case or to the parties to the case that it weakens confidence in his or her impartiality in the individual case. The conditions for incapacity are set out in the Public Administration Act § 6.
>
> According to the Public Administration Act § 8, it is the civil servant himself or herself who assesses own impartiality. If he or she finds reason to do so, he or she may refer the matter to his or her immediate superior for decision. The ministry has not received such an inquiry from the director.
>
> The ministry does not have any information that indicates that IMDi has influenced the report from EY or that they have intended to harm the organization Born Free.

It is important to handle whistleblowing messages carefully and professionally. It is important to protect whistleblowers against retaliation. However, independent examiners should not fall into the trap of trusting whistleblowers and believing what is reported. Examiners have the obligation to question motives of whistleblowers as well, which EY people did not do. For example, when Shabana Rehman and Born Free suddenly got substantial funding from the Norwegian government, others did not get funding, which might cause dissatisfaction and jealousy (Johnsen and Mikalsen, 2020; Johnsen et al., 2020).

Examination Consequences

The investigation report by Ernst & Young (2020) was debated and criticized in the media (e.g., DN, 2020; Gaulin, 2020; Guldberg, 2020; Hussain and Sultan, 2020; Johnsen, 2020a, 2020b; Johnsen et al., 2020; Reymert, 2020a, 2020b; Rolness, 2020; Silvola, 2020; Stephansen, 2020a, 2020b; Strøksnes, 2020; Østrem, 2020a). Born Free with its leader Shabana Rehman hired experts to comment on the investigation and to respond to the directorate. The directorate had so far defined a deadline of October 6 to accept a response from the foundation. The report was dated September 18, so the accused had less than three weeks to respond.

Born Free with its leader Rehman hired attorney Anne Helsingeng to comment on the investigation. She had co-authored the guidelines for private investigations at the association of Norwegian lawyers. Helsingeng was also an active fraud investigator and evaluator of fraud examinations. The foundation hired her to evaluate the work by Ernst & Young (2020). She started her work by requesting more information both from the directorate and from the examiners. In her email to the directorate on September 30, she asked for several documents including minutes from meetings and the original notice from whistleblowers. In her email to Frode Krabbesund at EY, she asked for the contract they had with the directorate as well as minutes from interviews and notes regarding implementation of contradiction statements in the final report.

Born Free with its leader Rehman had already hired attorney Harald Strandenæs to communicate with the directorate IMDi. In its reply to the attorney the directorate wrote on September 30 under the heading "Request for payment of granted state funding – Notice of extension of the basis for withdrawal" (Halse and Selimovic, 2020):

> We refer to the letter of September 24, 2020 on behalf of Born Free, where it is claimed that your letter of September 14, 2020 on behalf of Born Free is in reality still unanswered. IMDi informed in an e-mail to Born Free on September 7, 2020 that IMDi had decided to withhold a second term as a result of findings in connection with the follow-up of the whistleblowing case. In an e-mail to Born Free on September 10, 2020, IMDi informed that the legal basis for the decision on withholding was the grant letter item 3, which states that "if the conditions for receiving a grant are not met, IMDi can withhold the grant". Based on the circumstances that IMDi was aware of at that time, IMDi's assessment was that the conditions for retaining funds were met, and that it would be unjustifiable to pay state aid of NOK 3 million.
>
> In your letter of September 14, 2020, it was stated on behalf of Born Free that IMDi's decision on withholding was to be regarded as an individual decision, and that the public administration act's procedural rules for this had not been followed, including the requirements for prior notice, party access, decision form, content, justification, and right of appeal. At the end of the letter, IMDi's decision of retaining the funds, which Born Free was informed about in an e-mail on September 7, 2020, is also appealed.

The notice of extension of the basis for withdrawal was presented at the end of the letter, where IMDi questioned the practice of Born Free to silence people who have worked for the foundation. The duty of confidentiality had to be signed by anyone who did work for the foundation.

A Norwegian newspaper claimed (in a quote on p. xx of this chapter) that they know the case very well, and that they "have a lot of documentation in addition to the ones EY has provided" (Østrem, 2020b). This newspaper was the first to tell the story according to the version from whistleblowers. The accused did not like it, and they complained to the complaint commission at the Norwegian press association (www.presse.no/pfu/). In the complaint, Shabana Rehman on behalf of Born Free referred specifically to the guidelines for ethical journalism. She claimed that the newspaper had violated several statutes in the guidelines. The newspaper replied that they had to protect their vulnerable sources (Østrem, 2020c).

Attorney Strandenæs (2020c) wrote another letter arguing that the accused was entitled to review documents against her and her foundation. Furthermore, he mentioned in the letter the expected outcome of the review by attorney Helsingeng:

> There will soon be information available about EY's investigation report that will change the media-created image that the foundation Born Free has misused public funds. Regardless, it is of the directorate's self-interest that the case handling is carried out in accordance with the legislation and is thorough and conscientious.

Some of the whistleblowers did disclose their identities in the media: Raime Lima, Laial Janet Ayoub, and Maria Khan. They had all worked for and had left the foundation Born Free. Raime Lima accused Shabana Rehman of spending foundation money on Lima's private services, such as walking Rehman's dogs and buying clothes for her. Laial Janet Ayoub accused Shabana Rehman of spending foundation money on expensive dinner parties with a lot of alcohol. Maria Khan accused Rehman of trying to contact Khan's physician and psychologist. Rehman's response was that Lima had to leave the foundation because of harassment and threats against others at work. Rehman's response was furthermore that both Ayoub and Khan had left Born Free to start their own foundation in competition with Born Free (Strand et al., 2020).

Attorney Helsingeng received more information from the IMDi directorate on October 2. She learned that fraud examiners had been paid NOK 300,000 (USD 30,000). An interesting observation was that the mandate from the directorate differed from the mandate applied by Ernst & Young. While the directorate emphasized financial management documentation, fraud examiners emphasized potential abuse of funds. Involved persons at IMDi included Andreas Halse, Ragnhild Dugstad, Chen Shangquan, Ritika Dhall, Libe Rieber-Mohn, and Tajana Selimovic. In an email of September 22, Selimovic wrote to Shabana Rehman at Born Free: "The Foundation Born Free has the opportunity to express itself in writing in connection with the case. Such an explanation must be in our hands within October 6, 2020."

Over the weekend before this deadline, a number of persons worked intensely to respond to accusations presented in the report and in the media. In addition to Shabana Rehman, Morten Guldberg was the only other person employed by the foundation at this time. Fraud examiner Anne Helsingeng worked on her evaluation of the Ernst & Young report (Helsingeng, 2020), while Harald Strandenæs worked on the legal issues related to termination of public funding. Morten Guldberg made notes about the whistleblowers who had disclosed their identities in the media to present their allegations against Born Free:

- Laial Janet Ayoub had two assignments for Born Free. She reacted to having received the contract for the second assignment too late. She thought it was a violation of the working environment act that she carried out the assignment without a contract. Born Free has acknowledged that due to time pressure, they were late to get this contract in place, but they emphasized that she had a spoken agreement with the foundation that is supposed to be as binding as a written one, and that she was paid according to what was agreed. This was also about a very short-term single assignment associated with her having a conference that launched her own organization, where Born Free financed everything.

- Anna Bostad worked as a volunteer for Born Free for a while. She complained about a number of issues related to her work. For example, she found herself ignored if she did not get a copy of every email in and out of the foundation. She could not get paid by the foundation, since she was on social security funding.
- Thomas Olsen was hired on the basis of projects, while he wanted permanent employment at the foundation. He did not complete his assignments, while he complained about how he was treated at work. When his contract was terminated, he was both upset and angry.
- Michael Holtermann came to the foundation offering his services in web design and graphic work. He said that the current website was very poorly designed and offered to develop a new one. Born Free entered into an agreement with Holtermann to improve the promotional material in connection with conferences and seminars. While the foundation found some of his design work satisfactory, they did not want to pay him more than they had already agreed. Also, they disliked him running his other web design business using their facilities. They suspected he had an alcohol problem where he sometimes stayed overnight in the foundation office. After a while his contract was terminated.
- Raime Lima was a receiver of social benefits because of various illnesses. The social security agency wanted her to get some work training, and Born Free offered her tasks at the foundation. Guldberg noticed that Lima was unable to complete her tasks. One reason was that she did not know how to use Word, Excel, and other computer functions in Microsoft Office. Therefore, she had to be given simpler tasks than originally intended. She complained about the boring tasks. Guldberg gave her feedback, but not in the context and form required in modern organizations where formal and informal rules have to be obeyed when providing negative feedback to people in the organization. She left the foundation before the agreed period for work training was over.

The foundation Born Free was given a deadline of October 6, 2020 to respond to allegations and accusations in the Ernst & Young (2020) report. The foundation submitted its response on the deadline date in a memorandum of 13 pages (Født Fri, 2020). They also held a press conference where all major media were present. Attorney Helsingeng presented her review of the investigation, chair Asker presented his review of facts, account keeper and auditor Magne Tangen presented his review of accounts, attorney Stangenæs presented his review of IMDi, while chief executive Shabana Rehman presented her reactions to accusations. After the press conference, Stephansen (2020b) summarized it by stating that now it was Ernst & Young and IMDi who were left with the shame: "On Tuesday, Born Free and Shabana Rehman had the opportunity to defend themselves against the accusations of money mess and irregularities. Now it is the auditing firm Ernst & Young and IMDi who are left with the shame."

Account keeper and auditor Magne Tangen had been present during the examination interview with Shabana Rehman, which he calls a terrible interrogation where the purpose was to harm her (Mæland, 2020): "I feel that they angled it as negatively as they could. It was about catching Shabana on issues, even though they had received documentation to the contrary earlier, says general manager Magne Tangen at the accounting firm Exacta Services."

Rolness (2020) described what Rehman went through as a Kafka process:

> If you are charged with murder, you have better legal protection than if you are suspected of attending an A-ha concert in London at the state's expense. You have been given a public task to fight social control and a culture of honor. Everyone is happy with the job you do. Until anonymous whistleblowers claim that you exercise social control in the workplace. And before you have the opportunity to cleanse yourself, the state has deprived you of both control and honor – and already granted money.

In addition to the extensive public debate about the work by Ernst & Young (2020) and the coverage by newspaper Vårt Land (Rolness, 2020; Silvola, 2020; Østrem, 2020d), experts suggested various initiatives. For example, legal expert Birthe Eriksen suggested that IMDi should initiate a new fraud investigation with a revised mandate including a review of the first examination by Ernst & Young. Eriksen argued that if IMDi did not do so, then IMDi would be liable for the ruined career of Shabana Rehman with substantial economic loss. There would be a breach of the requirement for proper government case processing if IMDi automatically used the report by Ernst & Young as their sole basis without making a comprehensive assessment of the documented objections and responses from Born Free. Eriksen also argued that Ernst & Young might be held liable for the loss inflicted on Rehman.

Examiners Review Examiners

This book has a number of examination reviews by application of the stage model. An interesting exercise would be to learn how one examiner evaluates the work of another examiner. Examiner Helsingeng was invited by Rehman to evaluate the work of examiner Øglænd. Helsingeng (2020: 2) wrote a report of 14 pages entitled Review of EY's investigation of the foundation Born Free on behalf of IMDi dated October 6, 2020, where she summarized her assessment of the work by Ernst & Young:

> It is my overall assessment of EY's investigation of the foundation Born Free is not sufficiently broad-minded. In my opinion, a too limited mandate has be given by the client IMDi, and not enough time and sufficient funds have been made available so that all aspects could be satisfactory reviewed. For that reason, it may be questioned whether all information relevant to the case has been disclosed. The foundation also does not seem to have had sufficient insight into the notice by whistleblowers and EY's mandate. Correct information at the start of such an investigation can be crucial for the exchange of information and the ability to defend oneself.
>
> EY's report appears in my opinion to be unbalanced, even though the assignment was initially initiated as and accounting audit, and EY believes that they only have commented on financial management, the wording of the report is characterized by EY believing that the foundation does not have sound financial management and that there may be objectionable conditions related to financial dispositions. This permeates in my opinion EY's information presentation and appears as confirmation bias. Overall, the report gives the impression that this is a foundation completely without governance and control.
>
> Furthermore, it appears that the foundation and the foundation's trustees (affected parties) have to a limited extent had the opportunity to safeguard their legal position. Among others, I refer to short deadlines for adversarial proceedings and that there has been a narrow collection of documentation.
>
> It is beyond my remit to assess the individual findings, including whether there are de facto matters worthy of criticism. The same applies if a different methodology would have led to a different outcome.

Born Free arranged a press briefing on Tuesday, October 6, 2020. A number of major media were present. Attorney Strandenæs, attorney Helsingeng, and executive Rehman presented their views. There were expectations that Helsingeng would criticize her fraud examination colleague Øglænd. She did not. Her presentation was even vaguer than the quote from her assessment earlier. In her verbal presentation, she talked about the difficult role of being an examiner, and that the individual examiner Øglænd should not be exposed, but rather only the firm Ernst & Young. Critics afterwards commented that people in the same business of internal investigations avoid being skeptical of each other to avoid reprisal and retaliation.

There is no education in private investigations – sometimes labeled examinations, inquiries, or fact-findings – in Norway. Nevertheless, auditors, lawyers, and other consultants do it, and they are happy to take on all three roles of investigator, prosecutor, and judge. Given that investigation is mainly concerned with reconstructing past events, the tasks are not directly linked to public policing in terms of legitimate force against inhabitants. Nevertheless, the only place investigation is taught is at the police university college in Norway. This is different from the United States, where universities have courses on criminal justice including investigations. Students at US universities can learn approaches to investigations including forensics and then join police forces, including the FBI, after graduation. This is different in Norway, where you have to attend the police university college to be able to sign up for a position as a detective in the Norwegian police force. The only exception in Norway is the Norwegian business school in Oslo, where students can attend an elective course on fraud examinations.

Ernst & Young (2020: 36) formulated their recommendation to IMDi regarding a police report in the following way:

> It is further recommended that IMDi based on the results from the above, consider reporting the circumstances described in this memorandum to the police in order to obtain an assessment of whether the circumstances may have led to a breach of the penalty law or other legislation.

However, IMDi did not follow this advice from the consultants, as director Rieber-Mohn "found it not natural to pursue the case" (Reymert, 2020b). Stephansen (2020e) then argued that Rieber-Mohn probably had noticed that three leading experts by now had criticized the investigation by Ole Jakob Øglænd at Ernst & Young

> She has probably noticed that as many as three leading experts in the field have slaughtered the report from Ernst & Young and pointed at serious procedural errors

- This applies to lawyer Anne Helsingeng, who leads the Bar Association's work on guidelines for investigations.
- This applies to professor Petter Gottschalk, who teaches internal investigations at BI Norwegian Business School.
- And this applies to lawyer Birthe M. Eriksen, who has a doctorate in whistleblowing, was a member of the Governments Notification Committee, and with special expertise in private investigations.

> I have not yet seen any experts who have defended the report.

Stephansen (2020e) claimed that there was a desperate need for a completely new investigation to find out what went wrong in the collaboration between Born Free and the directorate. Strøksnes (2020: 23) reported similarly

> Helsingeng, who spoke very carefully and with many reservations and nuances, said that her impression is that the report is a hybrid, that it has a bias. The report says that no legal assessments should be made, but then the report still does, she said, among other things. Another professor has approached the report in much stronger terms. In an article in Aftenposten

(October 20), business school professor Petter Gottschalk claims that Ernst & Young's investigation would have been given a "failing grade". "The interpretations of facts are speculative and lack both discussion and evidence, where the doubt should have benefitted suspects", writes Gottschalk.

Norwegian Foundation Authority

Born Free was a foundation. When it became publicly known that the foundation might have violated guidelines for use of public funds, the Norwegian foundation authority requested information from Born Free (Stiftelsestilsynet, 2020):

> We refer to that the ministry of education and research has decided to suspend payments to the foundation following inquiries carried out by Ernst & Young on behalf of the directorate for integration and diversity (IMDi). On the basis of the report prepared by Ernst & Young, IMDi has assessed that there are deficiencies in the financial management of the foundation, and that parts of the grants are not considered to have been used in line with the purpose of the grant scheme.
>
> In the authority's assessment, there is a basis for examining whether the board's management of the foundation is in accordance with the foundation act and the foundation's articles of association. The board is the foundation's supreme body, and is responsible for the management of the foundation, cf. the foundation act § 30. The board shall ensure that the foundation's purpose is safeguarded, and that distributions are made in accordance with the statutes of the foundation, and ensure that accounts and asset management are subject to satisfactory control.

Stiftelsestilsynet (2020) then asked in the letter for a number of documents from the foundation. They asked for the board's account of how the board had taken care of its administrative responsibility and supervisory responsibility in the foundation. They also asked the board to explain how the board will handle the situation in the future now that the foundation presumably no longer receives state funds.

Strandenæs (2020d) responded in a letter on behalf of the board at Born Free. He wrote that the foundation certainly has potential for improvements in administrative routines. At the same time, the foundation distances itself from allegations in the Ernst & Young report. The letter explains the combination of relevant expertise among board members and the working procedures followed by the board. Accounting and auditing are also explained in the letter to the authority.

In the response letter to the authority, Strandenæs (2020d: 2) explained:

> The current chairperson of the board, Jan Sverre Asker, took up the position of chairperson of the board at the turn of the year 2017–2018. Asker served as chairperson of the board until April 2019, when he then had to resign due to serious illness. Gerd Fleischer and Solveig Bjørkøy,

respectively, took over as chairperson of the board in the meantime, until Asker was declared healthy and re-elected as chairperson of the board in September 2020. All board members have extensive experience in both business and voluntary organizations. Asker has extensive experience from various positions in the sports sector and has been executive vice president at Gjensidige insurance for over thirty years. Gerd Fleischer has been the leader of self-help for immigrants and refugees (SEIF), and a prominent representative of Norwegian war children. She has long organizational experience.

Regarding the board's work, Gerd Fleischer and Jan Sverre Asker have stated the following: The board has monitored the foundation's two employees very closely, including participating in a number of events and being informed about what should happen in the future. At board meetings after events, the events have been reviewed. This is also reflected in the protocols. A form of project organization has been chosen, where a review of the individual projects, the balance of these and not at least the financial management has been reviewed. A significant focus area for the board has been to ensure the quality of all events. There has been frequent telephone contact between the general manager Shabana Rehman and the board.

The foundation has submitted annual financial statements for 2017, 2018, and 2019 without comments and with a clean report. The foundation is not liable to tax or duty, and does not conduct business for profits. The foundation's accountant Exacta Services has submitted ongoing reports to the foundation's management and has also participated at some of the foundation's board meetings.

This letter by the Born Free attorney was sent to the Norwegian foundation authority in late October 2020. The following review by the foundation authority was not expected to be completed for quite some time. While Ernst & Young completed their review already after one month, the foundation authority tends to spend months and even years before they return to the examined foundation with their conclusion. For example, someone blew the whistle on a foundation for Romani people in 2015, while the foundation review was completed in 2017 (Stiftelsestilsynet, 2017).

Lacking Directorate Response

In the beginning of November 2020, one month had passed since Shabana Rehman and Born Free had responded to the Ernst & Young (2020) allegations and sent the response to IMDi within the short time frame granted to them. Nothing came out of the directorate. Communication director Katarina Heradstveit at the directorate said that "no date has been set for the IMDi's decision, beyond that we have no comment" (Høydal, 2020: 42). Stephansen (2020c) wrote that the Born Free case had risen into a real scandal, and he formulated nine questions addressed to Libe Rieber-Mohn at IMDi:

1 Where are you, Libe Rieber-Mohn? Every time Nettavisen or other media have tried to get answers to questions from you, we were told that you cannot answer because you are in the middle of processing the case. Then I have to ask: What case processing? Did you finish the case already the first weekend after you received the report from Ernst & Young?
2 How many hours did you actually spend depriving Born Free of state funding? You received the heavily criticized report from Ernst & Young on Friday, September 18, in the afternoon. You must have skimmed it fast. Already Monday morning, September 21, the report was published on the government's website, at the same time as the decision to deprive Born Free of state support. The EY report was thus received, processed, and decision made during a weekend.
3 Why was it so urgent? Were you afraid you would be left with the blame, Libe Rieber-Mohn?
4 What did you do to ensure the quality of the report from Ernst & Young? Although much skepticism was caused already at the first reading of the EY report, it was not until the press conference on October 6 that it was really deprived of all honors.
5 Why does Born Free not get access to the audio recordings from the interviews with themselves? The investigation was headed by a former police officer who has previously been criticized for miscarriage of criminal justice.
6 Have you checked the motives of the whistleblowers? The whistleblowers wrote that they were afraid of losing their jobs, but none of them were employed at Born Free.
7 What serious mistakes have you really found? In retrospect, it has turned out that the London trip was paid for by a scholarship, and that the Aha concert was also for free. It has emerged that the so-called spa stay was not a spa stay at all.
8 Do you think this is proper case handling? In my comment a couple of weeks ago, I wrote that; "IMDi director Libe Rieber-Mohn cannot feel good leaving behind an impression where the case handling in an important directorate appears to be lax and impulse or emotion driven".
9 Is this how it should be? Honestly, this is not how it should be. We cannot accept a situation where foundations and organizations become victims of random agency treatment and lose state support, so to speak, overnight, and then they have to sue the state to defend their interests.

Without waiting for a potential response to these questions from director Libe Rieber-Mohn at IMDi, Stephansen (2020d) launched three questions to the next level, which was Guri Melby, minister in the Norwegian government for education and integration:

1 When were the Minister of Education and Integration first informed about the whistleblowing against Born Free? As previously written, the decision to stop the rest of this year's payments to Born Free (6 million) was made

very quickly. It happened in a hectic period before the national meeting of the Liberal Party, where Guri Melby stood for election as leader in competition against Sveinung Rotevatn and Abid Raja. There is nevertheless reason to believe that Melby had time to handle urgent matters in the Ministry. Question two thus follows.

2 Was the Minister of Education and Integration involved in the handling of the case and / or the decision to stop this year's payments to Born Free? This weekend, there has been an influx of information and rumors about personal connections / acquaintances and friendships between various actors in the complex field of immigration and integration. For all involved parties, I think it is best to have such topics clarified immediately, and here it is important to try to be precise in the framing of questions. Question three is therefore divided into two:
3 A. Is the Minister of Education and Integration or others in the political leadership familiar with personal relationships / friendships between the leadership at IMDi and any of the whistleblowers in the Born Free case?
4 B. Is the Minister of Education and Integration or others in the political leadership familiar with personal relationships / friendships between the leadership of IMDi and leaders in other organizations in the area of immigration and integration?

Guri Melby as minister knew about the Born Free case for a long time. The public learned on October 7, 2020 that IMDi had terminated the funding for Born Free and given the money to another foundation (Bjåen, 2020). This was one month before the directorate made its formal decision to terminate the funding (Lindvåg, 2020a). However, the formal decision could be appealed to the ministry (Dhall and Selimovic, 2020), where the next step might be a rivalry among political parties in the Norwegian parliament about the termination of foundation funding to Born Free (Kjørholt, 2020; Lindvåg, 2020b).

The minister, Guri Melby, responded that the ministry learned about the whistleblowing on August 12. She denied that she had been involved in the decision to terminate the funding to Born Free. She denied that she knew of any personal relationships or friendships (Skomakerstuen, 2020).

The director, Libe Rieber-Mohn, responded finally to the questions to her (Rieber-Mohn, 2020):

1 We have been in an internal process where it is not natural to discuss publicly.
2 IMDi has not taken away the support for Born Free. This is up to the parliament to decide.
3 The investigation by Ernst & Young went on for a month.
4 The response from the foundation has been reviewed both by IMDi and experts at audit firm Ernst & Young.
5 The interviews have been transcribed completely and submitted to Born Free.
6 IMDi's assessment is based on the review of finances and accounting at the foundation.

7 Systematic violations of requirements for aid receivers have been identified.
8 We have handled this case in the usual way.
9 What IMDi does is according to common practice.

IMDi continued to pay for services from Ernst & Young in the examination of and responses to Born Free. Attorney Anne Helsingeng learned on October 2 that IMDi had paid NOK 300,000 (USD 30,000) to Born Free. An accumulated invoice dated October 26 shows a total amount of NOK 1,500,000 (USD 150,000). After that date, IMDi continued to use people from Ernst & Young to develop new arguments against Born Free. With these rising costs associated with further investigations and recommendations from Ernst & Young to IMDi, it was relevant to ask the question whether the directorate was in control of its own expenses. The relevance of this question derived from their criticism of Born Free for not having control. The directorate had cut support for Born Free because consultants such as Øglænd believed that the foundation had no proper financial management in place. Øglænd had outlined a financial management scheme that seemed appropriate for organizations with at least two hundred employees. However, the foundation had only two employees.

IMDi paid Ernst & Young NOK 300,000 for the initial report in September. Shabana Rehman at Born Free did not accept the allegations in the report. IMDi then hired the consultants again to respond. An invoice was received from the consulting firm on October 26, which showed an accumulated NOK 1,500,000. Øglænd at Ernst & Young probably continued to work for IMDi also in November. It was therefore not unreasonable to assume that the bill from Ernst & Young would grow from 300,000 to 3 million during the autumn.

One might ask whether IMDi could afford such an expense. According to the state budget, the directorate had operating expenses of 273 million in 2019 and an estimated 293 million in 2020. The budget for 2021 was 305 million. There was thus a 7% growth from 2019 to 2020, and a 4% growth from 2020 to 2021. It was stated in the budget that IMDi "is a strong professional directorate and executive body for integration policy, a premise supplier for the development of the field, and cooperates with sector authorities, municipalities, and county management, among others" (Regjeringen, 2020: 5).

IMDi cannot possibly be a strong directorate in the follow-up of foundations that receive state funding. Normally, IMDi itself should have the competence to investigate Born Free. Instead, the bill from Ernst & Young had grown rapidly during the autumn for work that was heavily criticized by a number of professionals. The fact that IMDi could afford such expenses might imply that IMDi's operating expenses could be cut in the state budget for 2021. Johnsen (2020b) reported early November:

> The auditing company EY has invoiced the Directorate for Integration and Diversity (IMDi) NOK 1.45 million for the investigation of Shabana Rehman's foundation Born Free.

- It is expensive to conduct an audit, but the alternative is that we do not detect violations of the guidelines for government grants. The case processing has now been completed on IMDi's part. The decision can be appealed to the Ministry of Education, and we refer to it for comments on any appeal, writes director of communications and public relations, Katarina Heradstveit, to the newspaper.

Shabana Rehman says the foundation has received support from two lawyers who will work for the organization on a new response, without taking fees.

- We plan to complain the case further to the ministry and to the civil ombudsman, Rehman says.

Petter Gottschalk, professor of business administration at BI, is among those who have criticized the EY report and believes it is based on several misconceptions. In a written comment sent to the newspaper, he expresses surprise that IMDi has spent so much money on an external audit.

- IMDi cannot possibly be a strong professional directorate in the follow-up of foundations that receive state support. Normally, IMDi itself should have had the competence to investigate Born Free. Instead, the bill from EY has grown sharply during the autumn for work that has been slaughtered by a number of professionals, says Gottschalk.

In the middle of November 2020, Shabana Rehman and the board at Born Free were working on the appeal from the directorate to the ministry. She was now frequently contacted by various politicians in the Norwegian parliament. They had read the media coverage of her case and wanted to learn more about it. They were in the middle of the process of approving the government budget for 2021 that was to be passed by the Norwegian parliament before the end of the year. They were mainly listening to Rehman's complaints without indicating whether or not they would interfere in the budget discussions by suggesting in parliament that the state aid to Born Free should be recaptured.

Attorney Harald Strandenæs wrote the formal complaint to the directorate on behalf of Born Free. The letter was 14 pages long and explained the background, processing mistakes, interpretation mistakes, financial management at Born Free, and the invalid decision (Strandenæs, 2020e).

This case study has illustrated the escalating effect of fraud investigations in practice by attorneys. Maybe a dialogue at an early stage between the foundation and the directorate would have reduced the level of conflict.

References

Adler, P.S. and Kwon, S.W. (2002). Social capital: Prospects for a new concept, *Academy of Management Review*, 27 (1), 17–40.

Agnew, R. (2014). Social concern and crime: Moving beyond the assumption of simple self-interest, *Criminology*, 52 (1), 1–32.

Bai, M. (2020). Altså, hvorfor kunne de ikke bare smøre brødskiver, disse innvandrerkvinnene? (So, why could they not just grease slices of bread, these immigrant women?), web-based Norwegian newspaper *Nettavisen*, www.nettavisen.no, published November 3.

Bao, D., Kim, Y., Mian, G.M. and Su, L. (2019). Do managers disclose or withhold bad news? Evidence from short interest, *The Accounting Review*, 94 (3), 1–26.

Bjerknes, O.T. and Fahsing, I.A. (2018). *Etterforskning – Prinsipper, metoder og praksis (Investigation – Principles, Methods, and Practice)*, Bergen, Norway: Fagbokforlaget publishing house.

Bjørdal, S. (2020). Født Fri krever utbetaling for å svare på anklagene (Born Free requires payment to respond to the charges), daily Norwegian newspaper *Vårt Land*, www.vl.no, published September 25.

Bjørkelo, B., Einarsen, S., Nielsen, M.B. and Matthiesen, S.B. (2011). Silence is golden? Characteristics and experiences of self-reported whistleblowers, *European Journal of Work and Organizational Psychology*, 20 (2), 206–238.

Bjåen, B.K. (2020). Tek frå Født Fri – gjev til Bydelsmødre (Take away from Born Free – give it to City Mothers), daily Norwegian newspaper *Vårt Land*, www.vl.no, published October 7.

Bosse, D.A. and Phillips, R.A. (2016). Agency theory and bounded self-interest, *Academy of Management Review*, 41 (2), 276–297.

Brandvold, Å. (2020). Fra frihetskamp til intern strid (From freedom fight to internal conflict), daily Norwegian newspaper *Klassekampen*, published October 30, pages 1, 10 and 13.

Buggeland, S.A., Hassan, A., Johnsen, N. and Kristiansen, T. (2020). Varslet mot Rehman-stiftelse: Mener penger ble brukt feil (Warned against Rehman foundation: Believes money was spent incorrectly), daily Norwegian newspaper *VG*, www.vg.no, published September 25.

Chatterjee, A. and Pollock, T.G. (2017). Master of puppets: How narcissistic CEOs construct their professional worlds, *Academy of Management Review*, 42 (4), 703–725.

Chen, Y. and Moosmayer, D.C. (2020). When guilt is not enough: Interdependent self-construal as moderator of the relationship between guilt and ethical consumption in a Confucian context, *Journal of Business Ethics*, 161, 551–572.

Chrisman, J.J., Chua, J.H., Kellermanns, F.W. and Chang, E.P.C. (2007). Are family managers agents or stewards? An exploratory study in privately held family firms, *Journal of Business Research*, 60 (10), 1030–1038.

Cianci, A.M., Clor-Proell, S.M. and Kaplan, S.E. (2019). How do investors respond to restatements? Reputation and the announcement of corrective actions, *Journal of Business Ethics*, 158, 297–312.

Dhall, R. and Selimovic, T. (2020). *Vedtak om tilbakehold av tilskudd (Decision on withholding of grants)*, letter dated November 2, addressed to chairperson at Born Free, Jan Sverre Asker, from IMDi (integration and diversity directorate).

DN (2020). DN mener: Shabana skuffer, men her er det også mer som skurrer (DN means: Shabana disappoints, but here there is more going on), daily Norwegian business newspaper *Dagens Næringsliv*, September 25, page 2.

Eberly, M.B., Holley, E.C., Johnson, M.D. and Mitchell, T.R. (2011). Beyond internal and external: a dyadic theory of relational attributions, *Academy of Management Review*, 36 (4), 731–753.

Ernst & Young (2020). *Notat vedrørende undersøkelser utført for IMDi (Report concerning investigation conducted for IMDi)*, report of investigation, audit firm Ernst & Young, Oslo, Norway, September 18, 36 pages.

Füss, R. and Hecker, A. (2008). Profiling white-collar crime. Evidence from German-speaking countries, *Corporate Ownership & Control*, 5 (4), 149–161.

Født Fri (2020). *Tilsvar til Integrerings- og mangfoldsdirektoratet (IMDi) fra stiftelsen Født Fri (Response to the directorate for integration and diversity (IMDi))*, Foundation Born Free, Oslo, Norway, 13 pages.

Gaulin, S. (2020). Jeg ble lovet full anonymitet for å si noe negativt om Shabana Rehman (I was promised full anonymity for saying something negative about Shabana Rehman), web-based discussion forum *Subjekt*, www.subjekt.no, published October 13.

Guldberg, M. (2020). Født Fri har brukt pengene rett (Born Free has used the money right), daily Norwegian newspaper *Aftenposten*, published October 7, page 24.

Halse, A. and Selimovic, T. (2020). *Krav om utbetaling av innvilget statsstøtte – Varsel om utvidelse av grunnlag for tilbakehold (Request for payment of granted state funding – Notice of extension of basis for withdrawal)*, letter from IMDi directorate, 2 pages, September 30.

Helsingeng, A. (2020). *Gjennomgang av EYs undersøkelse av stiftelsen Født Fri på oppdrag av IMDi av 18. september 2020 (Review of EY's investigation of the foundation Born Free on behalf of IMDi of September 18, 2020)*, attorney Anne Helsingeng at law firm Bull & Co, Oslo, Norway, 14 pages.

Hussain, M. and Sultan, S. (2020). Shabana Rehman mister statsstøtten: Behandlingen av Født Fri vekker bekymring (Shabana Rehman loses state aid: The treatment of Born Free raises concerns), daily Norwegian newspaper *Dagbladet*, www.dagbladet.no, published October 6.

Høydal, H.F. (2020). Født stri (Born difficult), daily Norwegian newspaper *VG, Helgemagasin* (Weekend magazine), Saturday, October 31, pages 40–50.

Huisman, W. and Erp, J. (2013). Opportunities for environmental crime, *British Journal of Criminology*, 53, 1178–1200.

Johnsen, N. (2020a). Shabana Rehman til VG: -Dette er jo ikke sant (Shabana Rehman to the newspaper: -This is simply not true), daily Norwegian newspaper *VG*, www.vg.no, published September 22.

Johnsen, N. (2020b). Brukte 1,45 millioner på å granske Rehman-stiftelse (Spent 1.45 million to investigate Rehman foundation), daily Norwegian newspaper *VG*, www.vg.no, published November 12.

Johnsen, N. and Mikalsen, H. (2020). Sitter i styret i Født Fri: -Jeg advarte Shabana (Sitting on the board of Born Free: -I warned Shabana), daily Norwegian newspaper *VG*, www.vg.no, published October 5.

Johnsen, N., Hassan, A. and Hansen, F. (2020). Førte regnskap for Rehman-stiftelse: Avviser alle anklager (Kept accounts for Rehman foundation: Denies all charges), daily Norwegian newspaper *VG*, www.vg.no, published October 6.

Jonnergård, K., Stafsudd, A. and Elg, U. (2010). Performance evaluations as gender barriers in professional organizations: A study of auditing firms, *Gender, Work and Organization*, 17 (6), 721–747.

Kakkar, H., Sivanathan, N. and Globel, M.S. (2020). Fall from grace: The role of dominance and prestige in punishment of high-status actors, *Academy of Management Journal*, 63 (2), 530–553.

Kjørholt, D. (2020). Stopper pengestøtten til Født Fri (Stops the money support for Born Free), daily Norwegian newspaper *Klassekampen*, November 3, page 7.

Lange, D. (2008). A multidimensional conceptualization of organizational corruption control, *Academy of Management Journal*, 33 (3), 710–729.

Lehman, D.W., Cooil, B. and Ramanujam, R. (2019). The effects of rule complexity on organizational noncompliance and remediation: Evidence from restaurant health inspections, *Journal of Management*, published online, pages 1–33, doi:10.1177/0149206319842262.

Lindvåg, A.W.H. (2020a). IMDi med endelig konklusjon: Født Fri får ikke statsstøtte (IMDi with final conclusion: Born Free does not get state funding), daily Norwegian newspaper *Vårt Land*, www.vl.no, published November 2.

Lindvåg, A.W.H. (2020b). IMDi stopper støtten til Født Fri (IMDi stops the support for Born Free), daily Norwegian newspaper *Vårt Land*, November 3, page 8.

McClean, E.J., Martin, S.R., Emich, K.J. and Woodruff, T. (2018). The social consequences of voice: An examination of voice type and gender on status and subsequent leader emergence, *Academy of Management Journal*, 61 (5), 1869–1891.

Mesmer-Magnus, J.R. and Viswesvaran, C. (2005). Whistleblowing in an organization: An examination of correlates of whistleblowing intentions, actions, and retaliation, *Journal of Business Ethics*, 62 (3), 266–297.

Mpho, B. (2017). Whistleblowing: What do contemporary ethical theories say? *Studies in Business and Economics*, 12 (1), 19–28.

Mæland, K.B. (2020). Regnskapsfører om granskingsavhør: Det er en drittpakke. De var ute etter å ta Shabana Rehman (The keeper of accounts about investigation interrogation: It is a shit package. They were looking to catch Shabana Rehman), web-based Norwegain newspaper *Nettavisen*, www.nettavisen.no, published October 11.

Østrem, V. (2020a). Født Fri-kritikken: Offenlige midler skal brukes med ydmykhet (The Born Free criticism: Public funds should be used with humility), daily Norwegian newspaper *Vårt Land*, www.vl.no, published September 21.

Østrem, V. (2020b). Vi kjenner denne saken godt (We know this case very well), email from news editor Veslemøy Østrem at daily Norwegian Christian newspaper *Vårt Land*, veslemoy.ostrem@vl.no, dated October 1, 2020.

Østrem, V. (2020c). Saks-id:6863 Shabana Rehman mot Vårt Land – tilsvar fra Vårt Land (Case id. 6863 Shabana Rehman against Vårt Land – response from Vårt Land), Pressens faglige utvalg (The professional committee of the press), www.presse.no/pfu/, Oslo, Norway.

Østrem, V. (2020d). Kafka-kritikk fra Rolness (Kafka criticism from Rolness), daily Norwegian newspaper *Aftenposten*, www.aftenposten.no/meninger, published October 18.

Petrocelli, M., Piquero, A.R. and Smith, M.R. (2003). Conflict theory and racial profiling: An empirical analysis of police traffic stop data, *Journal of Criminal Justice*, 31 (1), 1–11.

Pillay, S. and Kluvers, R. (2014). An institutional theory perspective on corruption: The case of a developing democracy, *Financial Accountability & Management*, 30 (1), 95–119.

Pinto, J., Leana, C.R. and Pil, F.K. (2008). Corrupt organizations or organizations of corrupt individuals? Two types of organization-level corruption, *Academy of Management Review*, 33 (3), 685–709. October 7.

Regjeringen (2020). Tildelingsbrev til Integrerings- og mangfoldsdirektoratet for 2021 (Allocation letter to integration and diversity directorate for 2021), Kunnskapsdepartementet (Ministry of Knowledge), Regjeringen (The Government). www.regjeringen.no, 30 pages.

Rehg, M.T., Miceli, M.P., Near, J.P. and Scotter, J.R.V. (2009). Antecedents and outcomes of retaliation against whistleblowers: Gender differences and power relationships, *Organization Science*, 19 (2), 221–240.

Reymert, P.Å. (2020a). -Født Fri-gransking full av feil (-Born Free investigation full of errors), daily Norwegian newspaper *Vårt Land*, September 24, pages 10–11.

Reymert, P.Å. (2020b). IMDi har valgt å ikke anmelde Født Fri (IMDi has chosen not to report Born Free), daily Norwegian newspaper *Vårt Land*, www.vl.no, published November 2.

Reyns, B.W. (2013). Online routines and identity theft victimization: Further expanding routine activity theory beyond direct-contact offenses, *Journal of Research in Crime and Delinquency*, 50, 216–238.

Rieber-Mohn, L. (2020). Libe Rieber-Mohn svarer Nettavisen og Erik Stephansen (Libe Rieber-Mohn answers Nettavisen and Erik Stephansen), web-based Norwegian newspaper *Nettavisen*, www.nettavisen.no, published November 2.

Rolness, K. (2020). Kafka-prosess mot Shabana Rehman (Kafka process against Shabana Rehman), daily Norwegian newspaper *Aftenposten*, www.aftenposten.no, published October 17.

Ruud, S. (2020). Stiftelse fikk støtte før den var etablert (Foundation received funding before it was established), daily Norwegian newspaper *Aftenposten*, published September 23, page 8.

Sandø, T. (2020). Den såkalte granskingen av Født Fri følger samme mønster som vi opplevde (The so-called investigation of Born Free follows the same pattern as we experienced), web-based Norwegian newspaper *Nettavisen*, www.nettavisen.no, published November 11.

Schnatterly, K., Gangloff, K.A. and Tuschke, A. (2018). CEO wrongdoing: A review of pressure, opportunity, and rationalization, *Journal of Management*, 44 (6), 2405–2432.

Schoultz, I. and Flyghed, J. (2016). Doing business for a 'higher loyalty' How Swedish transnational corporations neutralize allegations of crime, *Crime, Law and Social Change*, 66 (2), 183–198.

Schoultz, I. and Flyghed, J. (2019). From "we didn't do it" to "we've learned our lesson": Development of a typology of neutralizations of corporate crime, *Critical Criminology*, published online doi:10.1007/s10612–10019–09483–09483.

Schoultz, I. and Flyghed, J. (2020a). Denials and confessions: An analysis of the temporalization of neutralizations of corporate crime, *International Journal of Law, Crime and Justice*, published online doi:10.1016/j.ijlcj.2020.100389.

Schoultz, I. and Flyghed, J. (2020b). "We have been thrown under the bus": Corporate versus individual defense mechanisms against transnational corporate bribery charges, *Journal of White Collar and Corporate Crime*, published online doi:10.1177/2631309x20911883.

Silvola, N.M. (2020). Shabana Rehman tar oppgjør med mediene – har klaget Vårt Land til PFU: -Jeg har stått helt sjanseløs (Shabana Rehman attacs the media – has submitted complaint regarding newspaper Vårt Land: -I have been completely without a chance), Norwegian newspaper for journalists *Journalisten*, www.journalisten.no, published October 12.

Skomakerstuen, B. (2020). Melby ikke involvert i Født Fri-avgjørelsen (Melby not involved in the Born Free decision), web-based Norwegian newspaper *Nettavisen*, www.nettavisen.no, published November 3.

Slettholm, A. (2020a). Rehmans pengebruk er Abid Rajas problem (Rehman's money spending is Abid Raja's problem), daily Norwegian newspaper *Aftenposten*, published September 23, page 8.

Slettholm, A. (2020b). Argumentene for å strupe Født Fri-støtten er overbevisende (The arguments for throttling Born Free support are compelling), daily Norwegian newspaper *Aftenposten*, published October 4, page 34.

Stephansen, E. (2020a). Et nødvendig forsvar for Shabana Rehman og Født Fri (A necessary defense for Shabana Rehman and Born Free), web-based Norwegian newspaper *Nettavisen*, www.nettavisen.no, published September 25.

Stephansen, E. (2020b). Nå er det Ernst & Young og IMDi som sitter igjen med skammen (Now it is Ernst & Young and IMDi who are left with the shame), web-based Norwegian newspaper *Nettavisen*, www.nettavisen.no, published October 6.

Stephansen, E. (2020c). Født Fri-saken har vokst til å bli en ekte skandale. Her er ni spørsmål hun må svare på (The Born Free scandal has risen into a real scandal. Here are nine questions she has to answer), web-based Norwegian newspaper *Nettavisen*, www.nettavisen.no, published October 30.

Stephansen, E. (2020d). Rykteflom i helgen: Her er tre spørsmål til statsråden (Flood of rumors this weekend: Here are three questions for the minister), web-based Norwegian newspaper *Nettavisen*, www.nettavisen.no, published November 2.

Stephansen, E. (2020e). Nå gjenstår bare prestisjen i Født Fri-saken (Now only the prestige remains in the Born Free Case), web-based Norwegian newspaper *Nettavisen*, www.nettavisen.no, published November 6.

Stiftelsestilsynet (2017). *Stiftelsestilsynets tilsynsrapport: Stiftelsen romanifolkets / tafernes kulturond (The foundation authority's inspection report: The Romani people's foundation / the cultural fund of the Tatars)*, Lotteri- og stiftelsestilsynet (Lottery and foundation authority), Førde, Norway, February 13, 36 pages.

Stiftelsestilsynet (2020). *Melding om tilsyn: Født Fri (Notification of supervision)*, Lotteri- og stiftelsestilsynet (Lottery and foundation authority), Førde, Norway, September 23, 3 pages.

Strand, T. (2020). Født Fri krevde 25.000 kroner for brudd på taushetsplikt: Ikke lovlig kontrakt, mener ekspert (Born Free demanded 25,000 kroner for breach of confidentiality: Not a legal contract, according to an expert), public Norwegian broadcasting corporation *NRK*, www.nrk.no, published September 25.

Strand, T., Bazaz, R. and Kalajdzic, P. (2020). Født Fri-ansatt: Jeg gikk tur med hundene til Shabana (Born Free employee: I went on walks with the dogs of Shabana), public Norwegian broadcasting corporation *NRK*, www.nrk.no, published September 22.

Strandenæs, H.F. (2020a). *Født Fri-stans i utbetaling for 2. termin og iverksatt gransking (Born Free stop in payments for 2. term and initiated investigation)*, law firm Strandenæs, Oslo, September 14, letter to Libe Rieber-Mohn at IMDi.

Strandenæs, H.F. (2020b). *Tilsvarsfrist – Innhold – Kontradiksjon (Deadline for reply – Contents – Contradiction)*, law firm Strandenæs, Oslo, September 17, letter to EY attention Øglænd, Bøe, and Antzee, 5 pages.

Strandenæs, H.F. (2020c). *Stiftelsen Født Fri. Partsinnsyn og saksbehandling (The Foundation Born Free. Disclosure to Party and Handling of the Case)*, law firm Strandenæs, Oslo, October 2, letter to Libe Rieber-Mohn at IMDi.

Strandenæs, H.F. (2020d). *Brev til Lotteri- og Stiftelsestilsynet (Letter to the Lottery and Foundation Authority)*, law firm Strandenæs, Oslo, October 28, letter to Karsten Karlsen Sunde and May Helen Vik.

Strandenæs, H.F. (2020e). *Klage – Født Fri (Complaint – Born Free)*, letter to the integration and plurality directorate (Integrerings- og mangfoldsdirektoratet, IMDi), November 17, 14 pages.

Strøksnes, M.A. (2020). Når varsellampar blinker raudt (When warning lights flash red), weekly Norwegian newspaper *Dag og Tid* (*Day and Time*), Friday, October 30, pages 18–23.

Sykes, G. and Matza, D. (1957). Techniques of neutralization: A theory of delinquency, *American Sociological Review*, 22 (6), 664–670.

Wheelock, D., Semukhina, O. and Demidov, N.N. (2011). Perceived group threat and punitive attitudes in Russia and the United States, *British Journal of Criminology*, 51, 937–959.

Williams, J.W. (2008). The lessons of 'Enron' – Media accounts, corporate crimes, and financial markets, *Theoretical Criminology*, 12 (4), 471–499.

3 Danske Bank by Plesner

Danske Bank admitted in September 2020 that they had known for years about the bank's practice of collecting outdated and excessive debt from customers. Denmark's financial watchdog Finanstilsynet launched the previous month an inquiry into how Danske Bank had wrongly collected debt from up to 106,000 customers since 2004. The bank blamed IT system errors (Reuters, 2020):

> "There has been knowledge about at least parts of the problem in different parts and levels of the organization, including leaders, during the years", Denmark's largest bank said in a statement. "Despite attempts to manage the problems, the underlying data flaws were never fully addressed, and unfortunately this has caused the issues to continue for several years", it said.

Blaming IT system errors and data flaws is no longer an acceptable excuse for digitized business enterprises such as banks. A computer system is programmed by people according to specifications. If bank managers have provided misleading specifications to computer programmers, then it is a matter of human error. If computer programmers have developed wrongful algorithms and coding, then it is a matter of human error. A computer system never creates errors by itself.

Danske Bank is the largest financial institution in Denmark with a focus on the Nordic region and presence in 16 countries. Danske Bank is listed on the Nasdaq OMX Copenhagen stock exchange. The bank offers financial services, life insurance, pensions, mortgage credit, wealth management, real estate, and leasing services.

The Previous Bank Scandal

The previous scandal at Danske Bank was concerned with money laundering for criminals. Money laundering is the process of removing illegitimate proceeds from attachment to crime such as drug trade and trafficking and introducing the proceeds in the legal economy such as real estate and business enterprises. An important step in the money laundering process is often to achieve detachment

DOI: 10.4324/9781003305071-4

by moving funds through respected banks. Danske Bank was such a bank used by organized criminals and others to delete traces of the origin of large sums of money. Especially in Danske Bank's branch office in Estonia, proceeds were transferred from Russian oligarchs and the Russian mafia, state officials in Azerbaijan, weapon smugglers in Ukraine, criminals in Pakistan, and other suspected places of origins (Hecklen et al., 2020).

The law firm Bruun Hjejle (2018) in Copenhagen, Denmark, was hired by Danske bank to conduct an internal investigation at Danske Bank related to money laundering. The suspicion focused on activities at Danske Bank's branch office in Estonia. Danske Bank paid DKK (Danish kroner) 210 million (about US$ 30 million) for the investigation by the law firm. The investigative knowledge strategy included mainly knowledge workers with legal training at Bruun Hjejle. In addition, forensic experts from PwC and Ernst & Young were assisting the law firm based on accounting and auditing knowledge, and the international data management software company Palantir Technologies deployed its software platform to integrate and enable analysis of the comprehensive magnitude of customer, transaction, and trading data available. CERTA Intelligence and Security was also assisting in these investigative tasks.

The fraud examiners investigated thousands of customers and millions of transactions as well as trading activity. They examined the now terminated non-resident portfolio in the Estonian branch from the time of Danske Bank's acquisition of Sampo Bank completed in 2007 until the termination of the non-resident portfolio in late 2015, with some accounts closing in early 2016. The main focus was on the customers in the non-resident portfolio and their payments and trading activities during this period. The employees and agents of the Estonian branch who handled the non-resident portfolio or could otherwise have been involved were also investigated to uncover potential internal collusion.

The fraud examiners followed the guidelines on investigations issued by the Association of Danish Law Firms as well as the code of conduct issued by the Danish Bar and Law Society. The investigation was assisted by Danske Bank's compliance incident management team as well as the Estonian branch's IT department.

Identified data included 87 million payments for all customers at the Estonian branch, which were transferred into Palantir's software platform to store, structure, and enable data analysis. Relevant external data from other sources than the Estonian branch were also identified, collected, and ingested into the software platform.

The fraud examiners conducted a large number of interviews with relevant persons. For preparation of interviews, they engaged consultants from Promontory. Interviews were conducted with employees, including members of the executive board in the bank as well as members of the board of directors. There were 49 individuals interviewed, and a total of 74 interviews were conducted as part of the investigation. All interviews were conducted in accordance with rules on due process.

The fraud examiners did let suspects and others comment on their findings (Bruun Hjejle, 2018: 20):

> Based on all collected information, the conducted interviews and observations, Bruun & Hjejle assessed the potential institutional and individual accountability. All individuals subject to individual assessment were given the opportunity to review a draft assessment together with relevant material. Also, other individuals with knowledge of the events relevant to the accountability investigation, but not subject to individual assessment, were given the opportunity to review relevant material. Comments and proposed amendments received were subsequently evaluated and reflected where deemed appropriate.

Two years after the fraud examination by Bruun Hjejle (2018), leaked documents from Danske Bank were examined by investigative journalists (Hecklen et al., 2020). Both chief executive officer Thomas Borgen and chairperson at the board Ole Andersen had then resigned from their posts and were subject to criminal investigations by the serious fraud office in Danish police. The former CEO Borgen was sued by 155 investors for USD 270 million in 2020 (Hecklen et al., 2020).

Rather than focusing on real cases of suspected money laundering incidents, fraud examiners only reviewed formal procedures and guidelines in the bank. Rather than focusing on actors handling suspicions, fraud examiners only reviewed activities and transactions. Therefore, the investigation by Bruun Hjejle (2018) belongs at maturity level 2 in Figure 3.1.

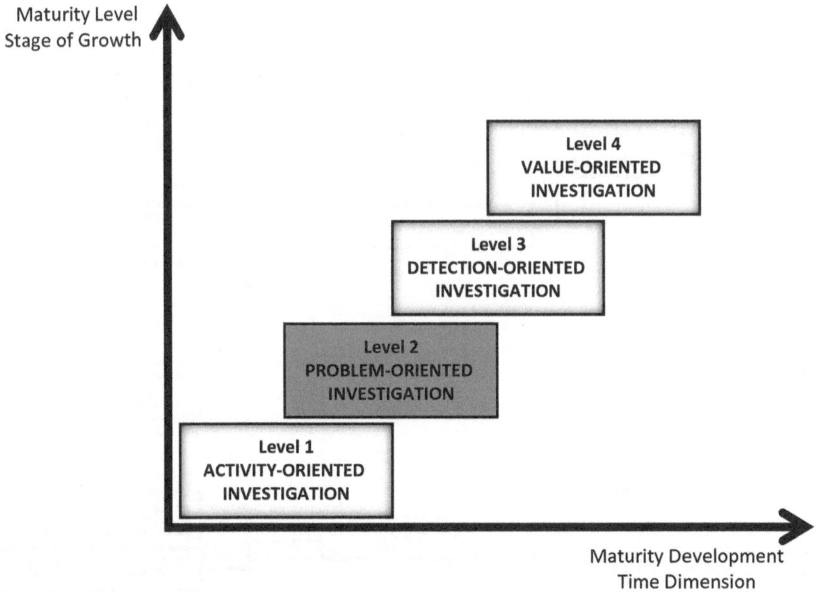

Figure 3.1 Maturity level for the Bruun Hjejle (2018) investigation at Danske Bank

Offender Convenience Themes

The fraudulent debt collection by Danske Bank represents corporate crime to benefit the business and not any specific individual at the bank (Bittle and Hébert, 2020), as illustrated in Figure 3.2.

In many organizations, ends justify means (Campbell and Göritz, 2014). If ends in terms of ambitions and goals are difficult to realize and achieve in legal ways, illegal means represent an alternative in many organizations (Jonnergård et al., 2010). Among most executives, it is an obvious necessity to achieve goals and objectives, while it is an obvious catastrophe failing to achieve goals and objectives. Welsh and Ordonez (2014) found that high performance goals cause unethical behavior. Dodge (2009: 15) argues that it is tough rivalry that makes executives in the organization commit crime to attain goals: "The competitive environment generates pressures on the organization to violate the law in order to attain goals."

Individual executives would like to be successful, and they would like their workplace to be successful. Being associated with a successful business is

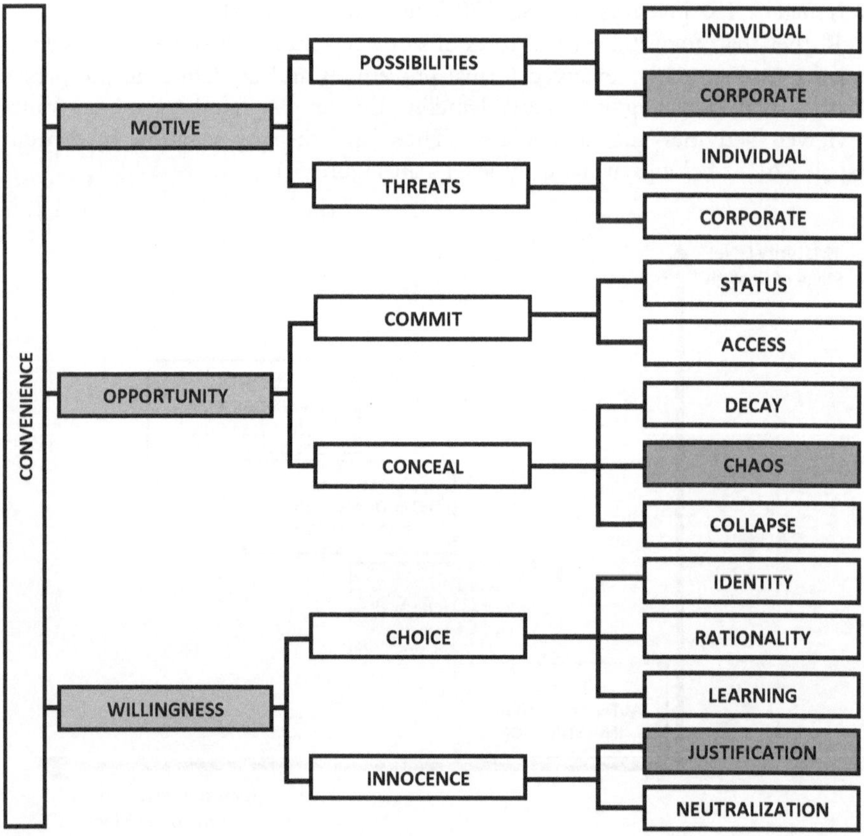

Figure 3.2 Convenience themes in the case of Danske Bank

important to the identity of many executives. They explore and exploit attractive corporate economic possibilities in both legal and illegal ways, so that their organization can emerge just as successful, or as even more successful, than other organizations. Profit orientation becomes stronger in goal-oriented organizations whose aim tends to be an ambitious financial bottom line.

There was a lack of oversight and guardianship that at best can be labeled chaos, as indicated in Figure 3.2. Nobody understood or tried to understand computer code. Bank executives noticed that there were some strange things happening when migrating into a new system, but they continued to study the symptoms rather than the causes. As evidenced by many internal investigation reports by fraud examiners after white-collar crime scandals, internal auditors, external auditors, compliance committees, and other internal and external control units do not function properly (e.g., Bruun Hjejle, 2018). Oversight and control functions tend to be formal units without any insights into the substance of business activities and transactions in computer systems. They tend to review procedures rather than transactions within procedures. Therefore, ineffective control functions are often an important part of the opportunity structure for white-collar crime.

Lack of justification can occur when an offender ignores information related to misconduct and crime. There is simply no need for justification. The upper echelon perspective suggests accordingly that white-collar offenders such as bank executives selectively attend to information when evaluating their own decisions. As argued by Huang et al. (2020) in the upper echelon perspective, elite member's cognitions, values, and perceptions, which are formed by previous experiences, can significantly affect the process of strategic choices. White-collar offenders may receive feedback from a range of actors while selectively ignoring some of the feedback by not paying attention to it (Gamache and McNamara, 2019: 920): "However, corporate executives operate in an environment where they receive feedback from a range of actors, yet we have a limited understanding of whether and to what extent these 'soft performance feedback cues' influence their decision making."

Members of the upper echelon of society where we find white-collar offenders may thus combine neutralization techniques with disregard of negative information related to them personally. They try to choose what information they pay attention to and how they interpret that information.

Fraud Investigation Outcome

The data migration from an old computer system to the Debt Collection System (DCS) in 2004 contained pre-existing incorrect data in relation to outstanding amounts owed by certain customers. Over time an increased level of reliance on and trust in the DCS, a decreased level of institutional knowledge among those involved in the debt collection process, and a declining level of reference to historic paper records have contributed to the persistence of errors in handling the debt of some of the bank's customers.

Employees at different levels in the organization, including managers, at various points in time had known about the problem to varying degrees. The executive management was informed of the systemic flaws affecting the bank's collection systems in May 2019.

A decade earlier, in 2009, Danske Bank launched an initiative known at Lean, which aimed to streamline existing businesses processes in an attempt to become more efficient in case handling. The focus on Lean meant that the employees in the debt collection area were under increasing pressure to rely on the data in DCS when carrying out debt collection and not to spend time looking at files in physical archives. This increased the transitioning into almost complete reliance on the data in DCS, and it implied the elimination of prior manual controls of the flawed data in DCS that had prevented, at least to a certain extent, the data flaws from ultimately impacting the customers wrongfully.

While a correction team was established in 2007 with the purpose of manually correcting the cases in DCS on a continuous basis, the team was closed down again in 2016. The team leader argued then that new cases also included incorrect calculations. Bank management ignored this warning and made a decision not to allocate people to the task of correcting cases. The correction team was re-established in 2019.

Fraud examiners suggest four root causes for the fraudulent debt collection. The first root cause is that accrued interest, fees, and costs on debt was incorrectly aggregated into a single amount and added to the principal amount. The implications of root cause 1 are that the systems do not distinguish between the different types of claims despite the fact that in the context of time-barring principles such claims are subject to different time-barring periods.

The second root cause is incorrect debt origination date. The statutory limitation period starts counting from the date the specific debt is due. When a debt was transferred into DCS, however, the systemic statutory limitation period was effectively set to the date of the transfer – and not the actual due date. The incorrect origination date in DCS made the debt appear younger than it actually is. This meant that it was difficult, using DCS, to identify and control at which point in time the statutory period of limitation should be interrupted to avoid the debt becoming time-barred. The bank may thus have collected debt that at the time of the collection process was time-barred.

The third root cause is the same treatment of guarantors and co-debtors. The bank may have pursued to collect the full debt from each of the debtors, co-debtors, and guarantors. In absence of a manual adjustment in DCS, this meant that if a settlement agreement had been made with a debtor, the system would still attempt to collect the full amount from co-debtors and guarantors.

The fourth and final root cause was separate bank accounts for the principal debtor and related actors such as guarantors. Each account reflects the full debt as being owed. The full debt was consequently recorded on more than one account. Procedures required debtor accounts to be adjusted manually following debtor payments, accrued interest, and other financial items related to the debt. One customer might thus have repaid the debt in full, while the now non-existing debt was still registered as owed by the co-debtor and guarantor.

The total number of potentially impacted customers was 106,000. Under Danish law, if a person or entity has paid an amount due to a mistake, misunderstanding, or as a result of an error, the consequence is that the victim is eligible to a restitution against the offender.

Examiners address the issue of how the bank handled information on identified errors by providing very general answers. The report describes a number of projects and activities, such as the data quality project, group risk management and compliance, and program Athens. It seems that rather than solving problems by correcting programming flaws, groups and projects were organized to discuss the issues. An example is the following sentence where a number of actors are mentioned, but there is no mention of actions (Plesner, 2020: 10): "The bank engaged EY to assist with program Athens and to provide the bank with an analysis and verification of system flaws identified by Plesner."

Examiners thus document a bureaucratic approach to solving technical problems. The manual effort required to review computer code seems ignored. The only manual effort described is concerned with actual transactions in terms of new manual controls regarding calculations for each customer. No new debt collection cases with effect from 2019 were to be initiated without manual calculation being done before. If the manual calculation resulted in different figures compared to the systems figures, then figures in the system were corrected. The bank was thus incapable of solving the underlying systems error; instead, system results were corrected.

The manual correction team was four people, but grew quickly by 21 people to further accelerate the recalculation process. Consultants from Ernst & Young were also engaged to assist with the recalculations. In addition to the new manual control to stop new cases being brought to court before a recalculation, in late 2019 it was also decided to withdraw all current court cases, including debt relief cases, private and business estate, and bankruptcy court cases where the bank was uncertain about the real status for customers. It was decided to compensate all customers for their losses resulting from the identified root causes. To further minimize the risk of over collection of debt, the bank decided to suspend approximately 17,000 customers' debt collection cases until they had been recalculated as part of the ongoing efforts to remediate the identified errors in the bank's debt collection system. These were the cases in which more than 60% of the principal amount had been repaid for which reason there was a higher risk that over collection would take place before the cases had been reviewed. The collection would resume when each case had been reviewed and potential errors corrected. Furthermore, interest would not accrue while collection was suspended.

It was not until 2020 that the real problems in computer systems were addressed. Then an IT implementation plan was set in motion, which included a number of technical safeguards and improvements to the implicated IT system in order to enhance existing and set up additional checks and controls.

Examiners were asked to find out how many customers had been affected by the errors. As a starting point, a total of 402,000 customers with 600,000 accounts were processed.

Examiners found that the total number of possibly impacted customers across systems, and who were at risk of potentially having made overpayments, was 106,000. On the other hand, examiners found that a total of 105,000 customers had not made any payments to the debt when entering the debt collection system. People who were eligible for repayments because of overpayments had so far received on average of DKK 1,000 or 2,000, but they were probably entitled to higher amounts.

While the bank was recalculating accounts for potential overpayments, customers received no information about it. At the time of the investigation in 2020, only 17,000 out of 106,000 customer cases had been recalculated. Therefore, no customers had been contacted so far (Plesner, 2020: 15):

> All customers identified as having been affected by the root causes will be contacted directly by Danske Bank to disclose exactly what has gone wrong, what Danske Bank is doing to ensure that the customer receives proper redress, and what the customer can expect to happen next.

As of September 1, 2020, only 326 customers had received a compensation payment from Danske Bank. The total value of compensation paid to these customers was the equivalent of less than USD 40,000.

Investigation Report Maturity

The investigation report concerning fraudulent debt collection by Danske Bank has 120 pages. The report is addressed to the Danish Financial Supervisory Authority and dated September 10, 2020. The report is a response to the supervisory authority's request for an account of the bank's debt collection system. An account "is a statement made by an actor to explain unanticipated or untoward behavior that is subject to some sort of evaluative inquiry by other actors" (Gottschalk and Benson, 2020: 949). The request for an account from Plesner (2020) was formulated in a three-page letter from the Danish Financial Supervisory Authority dated August 31, 2020. Here we treat the letter as the mandate for the investigation, and the account as the report from the investigation.

The 120-page report has several sections. The first section responds to specific questions raised in the letter from the authority. The second section is written by Danish law firm Plesner concerning the key system and process flaws in Danske Bank's debt collection system and related systems. The third section is a workshop presentation by law firm Plesner regarding key impacts of system and process failures. The fourth section is another memorandum by Plesner on main root causes and Danske Bank's legal obligation to compensate customers. The fifth section is by fraud examiners from audit firm Ernst & Young presenting a data analysis and considerations within debt collection. The

Ernst & Young section seems to be the core of the investigation and builds on previous sections by Plesner. The remaining three sections are a list of potentially derived or correlated issues, a presentation from a conference call, and an overview of the governance structure of the program Athens, which was the label used by Danske Bank to examine its fraudulent debt collection practice.

As a mandate for the investigation, the letter from the Danish Financial Supervisory Authority asks for the following information from Danske Bank (Finanstilsynet, 2020):

1 When did the bank first detect the errors?
2 What exactly do the errors consist of, and how has it affected the customers?
3 How did the bank handle the information about the errors found, including which measures were launched and when and how the bank will avoid new mistakes in the future?
4 How did the bank ensure itself from the time errors were found that similar erroneous recoveries from this time could no longer take place?
5 How many customers are affected by the errors?
6 How has the bank handled the affected customers, including how is the compensation for the individual customer calculated and paid, and what information is given to the customers about errors and calculations?
7 How many customers have per September 1, 2020 received compensation, how many customers does the bank expect to pay compensation to, and when are all customers expected to have been compensated?

Fraud examiners do not provide a real answer to the first question since they obviously have limited knowledge of computer programming and systems design. However, they provide an interesting and relevant answer to the second question in the form of four root causes as previously described. Questions 3 and 4 are linked and open up for very general statements.

Fraud examiners were unable to answer the fifth question, as they only indicated a potential number of victims who had suffered overpayments. In response to question 6, examiners found that no information had been provided to customers while the bank was performing its recalculations. The final question is concerned with compensation paid that examiners were able to answer.

Law firm Plesner was the lead examiner with the tasks of describing key system flaws, assessing key legal and regulatory risks, and assisting Danske Bank to identify possible ways of solving the issues resulting from the system and process flaws (Plesner, 2020: 22):

> In order to deliver on these tasks, we have performed a detailed fact-finding exercise involving a number of interviews of relevant members of staff, participated in meetings held by the group recovery & debt management correction team, and observed how case officers navigate and use the debt collection systems. We have not made an analysis of how the relevant IT systems are coded.

Here examiners admit their reluctance and probable lack of competence in computer programming. They looked at the consequences of wrong computer code, but they did not look at errors in computer code. For trained information technology professionals, computer code is organized as algorithms where certain rules are implemented. For beginners, an if-statement says that a certain condition has to be accepted before execution, while otherwise an else-statement says something else has to happen. It is indeed possible to read computer code, but neither lawyers nor auditors have that kind of training.

The investigation report seems to represent an attempt by Danske Bank management to manipulate contributions from law firm Plesner and audit firm Ernst & Young. Instead of asking Plesner and Ernst & Young to conduct critical and objective reviews and publish their reports independent of Danske Bank, executives at the bank have merged pieces of text from the two firms into their own framework. In their own words, Danske Bank explains their story in the document preceding contributions from the two firms.

As a result of these shortcomings, the maturity of the investigation is at level 2 as illustrated in Figure 3.3. The investigation focused on an issue that needed clarification. Examiners were looking for answers related to debt collection. Once examiners believed they had found answers, the investigation was terminated. No attempt was made to find out who had done what to make the debt collection scandal happen at Danske Bank.

Nobody was held accountable for the customer fraud. Two important types of accountability can be distinguished (Via et al., 2019: 79): "Under outcome

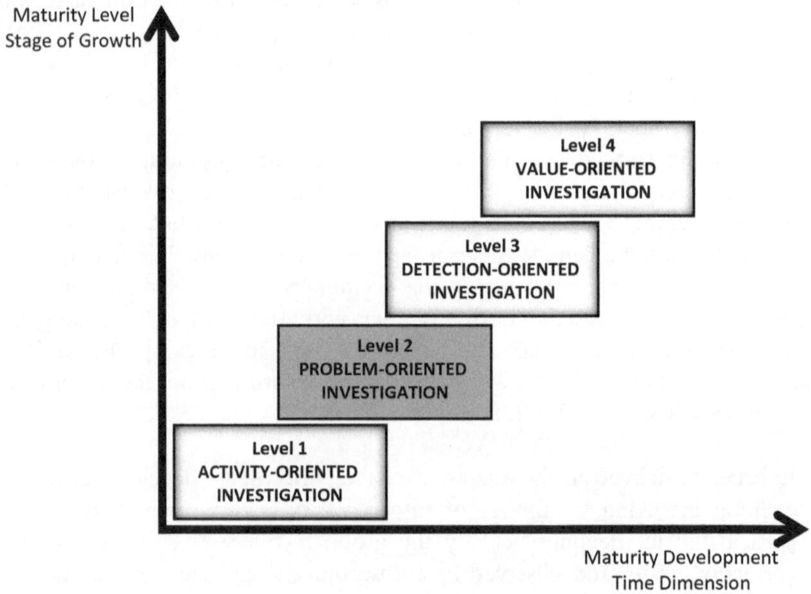

Figure 3.3 Maturity level for combined investigation by Plesner (2020) at Danske Bank

accountability, managers are held responsible for the outcomes or performance effects of their decisions. In contrast, under process accountability, managers are held accountable for the degree to which they can explain and justify their decisions."

Dansk Bank executives do not face either of these two types in the fraud examination report.

References

Bittle, S. and Hébert, J. (2020). Controlling corporate crimes in times of de-regulation and re-regulation, in: Rorie, M.L. (editor), *The Handbook of White-Collar Crime*, Hoboken, NJ: Wiley & Sons, chapter 30, pages 484–501.

Bruun Hjejle (2018). *Report on the Non-Resident Portfolio at Danske Bank's Estonian branch*, report of investigation, 87 pages, law firm Bruun Hjejle, Copenhagen, Denmark.

Campbell, J.L. and Göritz, A.S. (2014). Culture corrupts! A qualitative study of organizational culture in corrupt organizations, *Journal of Business Ethics*, 120 (3), 291–311.

Dodge, M. (2009). *Women and White-Collar Crime*, Saddle River, NJ: Prentice Hall.

Finanstilsynet (2020). *Anmodning om redegørelse om Danske Bank A/S' gældsinddrivelsessystem (Request for account concerning Danske Bank Inc.'s debt collection system)*, Finanstilsynet (The Danish Financial Supervisory Authority), Copenhagen, Denmark, 3 pages.

Gamache, D.L. and McNamara, G. (2019). Responding to bad press: How CEO temporal focus influences the sensitivity to negative media coverage of acquisitions, *Academy of Management Journal*, 62 (3), 918–943.

Gottschalk, P. and Benson, M.L. (2020). The evolution of corporate accounts of scandals from exposure to investigation, *British Journal of Criminology*, 60, 949–969.

Hecklen, A., Ussing, J. and Sommer, M. (2020). 'Beskidte milliarder': Sådan blev hvidvask-sag til Danske Banks største krise. Se tidslinjen over hvidvaskskandalen i Danske Bank ('Dirty billions': This is how money laundering became Danske Bank's biggest crisis), *Danmarks Radio (Danish Public Broadcasting)*, www.dr.dk, published September 21.

Huang, J., Diehl, M.R. and Paterlini, S. (2020). The influence of corporate elites on women on supervisory boards: Female directors' inclusion in Germany, *Journal of Business Ethics*, 165, 347–364.

Jonnergård, K., Stafsudd, A. and Elg, U. (2010). Performance evaluations as gender barriers in professional organizations: A study of auditing firms, *Gender, Work and Organization*, 17 (6), 721–747.

Plesner (2020). *Response to DFSA-letter: Anmodning om redegørelse om Danske Bank A/S' gældsinddrivelsessystem (Response to DFSA letter: Request for account concerning Danske Bank Inc.'s debt collection system)*, investigation report by Danske Bank, law firm Plesner, Copenhagen, Denmark, 120 pages.

Reuters (2020). Danske Bank admits it knew of erroneous debt collection for years, *Financial Post*, www.financialpost.com, published September 11.

Via, N.D., Perego, P. and Rinsum, M. (2019). How accountability type influences information search processes and decision quality, *Accounting, Organizations and Society*, 75, 79–91.

Welsh, D.T. and Ordonez, L.D. (2014). The dark side of consecutive high performance goals: Linking goal setting, depletion, and unethical behavior, *Organizational Behavior and Human Decision Processes*, 123, 79–89.

4 Equinor Energy by PwC

Helge Lund was an ambitious chief executive officer at Norwegian oil company Statoil. He thought Statoil should do more than produce oil in the Norwegian sector of the North Sea. The company had developed a world-leading offshore experience in oil exploration and was ready to expand into other energy sectors and into other parts of the world. One of the corporate fiascos occurred in the United States where Statoil, later named Equinor, recorded a loss of USD 21 billion on its activities between 2007 and 2019 (Hovland and Høgseth, 2020; Lorch-Falch and Tomter, 2021; Mullis, 2020). The victims of the corporate scandal were shareholders at Equinor.

Auditing firm PwC (2020) was hired to investigate the scandal. A corporate scandal is "an unexpected, publicly known, and harmful event that has high levels of initial uncertainty, interferes with the normal operations of an organization, and generates widespread, intuitive, and negative perceptions" externally (Bundy and Pfarrer, 2015: 350). A scandal is a publicized instance of transgression that runs counter to social norms, typically resulting in condemnation and discredit and other consequences such as bad press, disengagement of key constituencies, the severance of network ties, and decrease in key performance indicators (Piazza and Jourdan, 2018). A scandal can be an act of elite deviance that might include financial, physical, and morally harmful behavior committed by privileged members of the organization.

In addition to Helge Lund as the CEO, Statoil's corporate executive committee in 2011 consisted of Torgrim Reitan (CFO), Tove Stuhr Sjøblom (HRM), Øystein Michelsen (Norway), Peter Mellby (International), Bill Maloney (North America), Eldar Sætre (Renewable), Margareth Øvrum (Technology), Tim Dodson (Exploration), and John Knight (Development).

United States Onshore Oil

Investigative journalist at the Norwegian business newspaper *DN* detected and disclosed the substantial losses Equinor had incurred. When the scandal became public, politicians got upset since the Norwegian state previously owned Statoil 100% and now owned 67% of the shares. Politicians asked for a government investigation. When Statoil launched its own investigation by hiring PwC

DOI: 10.4324/9781003305071-5

(2020) and presenting results half a year later, politicians were not satisfied. They still wanted an investigation of the government's role in the scandal.

Norway has a tradition of government investigations into state-owned companies. After the financial crises, the state took over Norway's largest bank DNB as majority shareholder. When the Panama Papers revealed involvement of DNB, fraud examiners were hired to investigate the matter (Hjort, 2016). When the VimpelCom scandal revealed corruption in Uzbekistan, fraud examiners were hired to investigate Telenor where the Norwegian state is a majority shareholder (Deloitte, 2016). An investigation into the government's role in the Equinor scandal would require a mandate focusing on answers to what-, when-, how-, why-, and who-questions.

Since 2007, Equinor has invested around USD 40 billion in the United States, mainly in offshore and onshore oil and gas exploration and production (PwC, 2020: 4):

> Through a series of acquisitions, totaling over 10 billion USD, Equinor built a substantial business in US shale gas and oil, or so called "unconventionals". In 2011, Equinor acquired Brigham Exploration Company (Brigham), a NASDAQ-listed independent oil and gas operator with around 100 employees, for 4.7 billion USD. Equinor grew activity quickly and experienced serious challenges in business support functions such as land management, production revenue accounting, joint venture accounting and procurement. These challenges were wide ranging, and for a period of time resulted in the company losing control over critical business support processes.

The loss of USD 21 billion in the United States was due to impairments of onshore assets (9 billion), expenses due to unsuccessful exploration activities (4 billion), commercial contracts, and internal financing.

Equinor has been present in the US since 1987, when the company established a trading office on Manhattan in New York City. From the mid-1990s, the company involved itself in oil exploration in the deep-water in the Gulf of Mexico where the competitor British Petroleum (BP) caused a serious oil spill in April 2010. After the Deepwater Horizon oil spill, prosecutors brought criminal charges against four BP executives, but none of them ended up in prison (Freeh, 2013; Thompson, 2017). After the oil spill that occurred when the oilrig Deepwater Horizon exploded and sank into the Gulf of Mexico, the environmental protection agency (EPA) in the US became more concerned with activities of oil companies both offshore and onshore. The oilrig explosion killed 11 rig workers and injured many others, and the pipe leaked oil and gas on the ocean floor for 87 days until the Macondo well was capped (Fowler, 2014; Thompson, 2017).

In 2020, Equinor's subsidiaries in the United States had activities in several states with the main offices located in Houston and Stamford. Around 20% of Equinor's production of oil and gas in 2020 came from the US. The company's activities onshore were primarily focused on the Bakken play located in North

Dakota and Montana, and the Marcellus and Utica formations in the Appalachian Basin, which spread across several states in the northeast of the United States. These locations produced 290,000 barrels per day, primarily crude oil in the Bakken and natural gas from the Marcellus and Utica formations. Equinor also held a small position in the Louisiana Austin Chalk.

Offender Convenience Themes

Assuming that the formidable financial losses in the United States were caused by executive ego trips to grow the business, then this case is about executive wrong-doing at Equinor. The motive was corporate possibilities as illustrated in Figure 4.1.

In many organizations, ends justify means (Campbell and Göritz, 2014). If ends in terms of ambitions and goals are difficult to realize and achieve in legal ways, illegal means represent an alternative in many organizations (Jonnergård et al., 2010). Among most executives, it is an obvious necessity to achieve goals

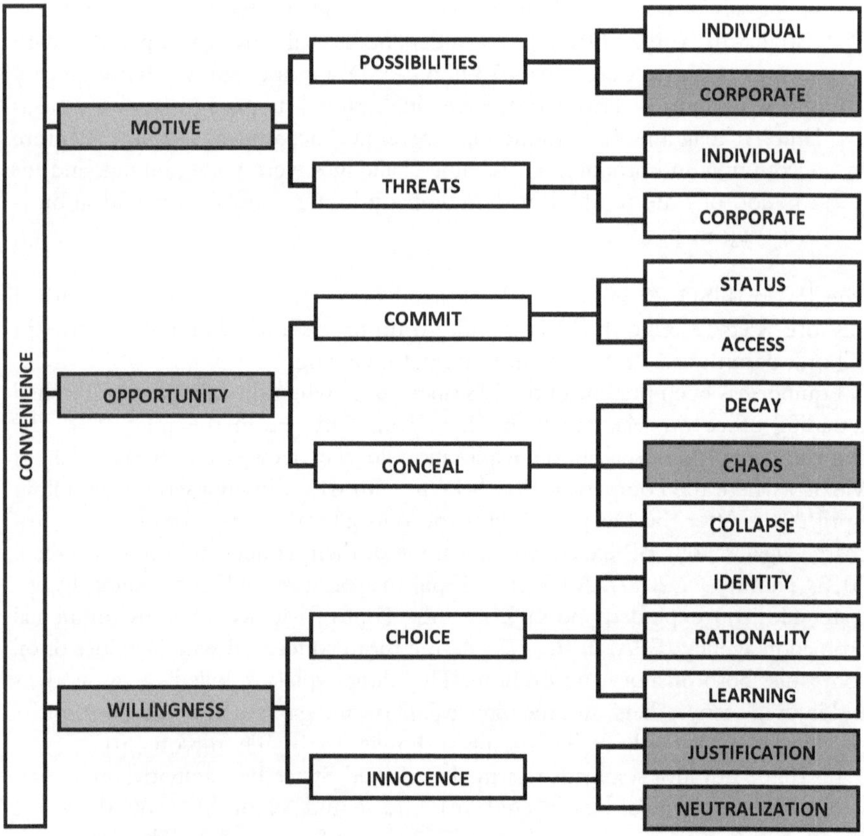

Figure 4.1 Convenience themes in the case of Equinor

and objectives, while it is an obvious catastrophe failing to achieve goals and objectives. Welsh and Ordonez (2014) found that high performance goals cause unethical behavior. Dodge (2009: 15) argues that it is tough rivalry that makes executives in the organization commit crime to attain goals: "The competitive environment generates pressures on the organization to violate the law in order to attain goals."

Individual executives would like to be successful, and they would like their workplace to be successful. Being associated with a successful business is important to the identity of many executives. They explore and exploit attractive corporate economic possibilities in both legal and illegal ways, so that their organization can emerge just as successful, or as even more successful, than other organizations. Growth orientation can become stronger in goal-oriented organizations whose aim tends to be an ambitious financial revenue stream.

When an organization develops and maintains a strong systematic socialization program, employees not only identify with the organization but also its goals. When personal promotion or dismissal, as well as bonuses and benefits, link directly and individually to the achievement of goals, then employees identify even stronger with organizational goals. When the socialization process couples tightly with strong accountability systems, employees perceive individually oriented regulation to achieve organizational goals. The pursuit of goals does not at all imply the absence of crime. The growth focus within an organizational context might increase the frequency of wrongdoing on behalf of the organization for profit or enhancement. A strong emphasis on goal attainment might indeed lead organizational members to engage in ignorance of control mechanisms and illegal acts (Kang and Thosuwanchot, 2017).

Exploitation of attractive corporate economic possibilities can cause environmental pollution.

An example is the oil exploitation in the Gulf of Mexico that caused serious environmental pollution. British Petroleum (BP) operating the Deepwater Horizon platform faced criminal charges amounting to USD 4 billion because of environmental crime. A federal court in New Orleans sentenced BP to pay the record sum (Müller, 2018).

Equinor lacked corporate oversight in the United States as illustrated with chaos in Figure 4.1.

The perspective of principal and agent suggests that when a principal delegates tasks to an agent, the principal is often unable to control what the agent is doing. Agency problems occur when principal and agent have different risk willingness and different preferences, and knowledge asymmetry regarding tasks exists (Bosse and Phillips, 2016).

As evidenced in many internal investigation reports by fraud examiners after white-collar crime scandals, internal auditors, external auditors, compliance committees, and other internal and external control units do not function properly (e.g., Bruun Hjejle, 2018; Deloitte, 2015; Shearman Sterling, 2017). Oversight and control functions tend to be formal units without any insights into the substance of business activities. They tend to review procedures rather than transactions within procedures. Therefore, ineffective control functions are often an important part of the opportunity structure for white-collar crime. For example, at Toshiba Corporation, lack of controls was an important element of the opportunity structure (Deloitte, 2015). Fraud examiners emphasized lack of internal controls by accounting and auditing functions, as well as lack of finance control in each corporate division. At Wells Fargo, corporate control functions were constrained by the decentralized organizational structure (Shearman Sterling, 2017).

In the dimension of personal willingness for deviant behavior in convenience theory, a combination of justification and neutralization occurred, as illustrated in Figure 4.1. The offender denies the act was motivated by self-interest, claiming that it was instead done out of obedience to some moral obligation. The offender appeals to higher loyalties. Those who feel they are in a dilemma employ this technique to indicate that the dilemma must be resolved at the cost of violating a law or policy. In the context of an organization, an employee may appeal to organizational values or hierarchies. For example, an executive could argue that he or she has to violate a policy in order to get things done and achieve strategic objectives for the enterprise (Jordanoska, 2018; Kaptein and Helvoort, 2019; Siponen and Vance, 2010; Sykes and Matza, 1957).

Fraud Investigation Outcome

Examiners found that the underlying causes for the Equinor scandal in the United States were complex. According to the review, the causes include how strategy was developed and implemented, how systems to govern a business were designed, how risk was managed, and how leadership and culture was inefficient. Examiners emphasize the following findings (PwC, 2020: 5):

- Equinor's growth strategy came at the expense of value and control. Rapid growth outpaced and overwhelmed critical business support processes.
- Corporate oversight should have been stronger and did not sufficiently reflect the underlying risks of the business.
- Limited onshore experience in senior leadership teams and lack of continuity in important roles negatively impacted the performance and follow-up of the onshore business.
- From 2014, comprehensive improvement efforts were launched by the administration and reported regularly to the board. Today, the internal control environment in the US is significantly improved.

The decision to operate onshore in the United States was based on overly optimistic predictions of oil and gas prices. When building the US onshore business, Equinor followed a volume growth strategy. Given the relative high oil price at the time, investments in new volumes were also expected to be highly valuable. In 2011, an ambition was set, which was to increase production by 30%, to more than 2.5 million barrels per day in

2020. This proved to be a risky goal that drove behavior at all levels in the company, especially in terms of investments levels without appropriate business cases and reviews. The growth came at the expense of corporate value creation and control in the US onshore business (PwC, 2020: 34):

> Acquisitions and investments were made based on an expectation that the oil price would increase for the foreseeable future. However, in a volatile and cyclical industry, investments should stand the test of both good and bad times. Equinor did not sufficiently test transactions for robustness at a low-price scenario. Key assumptions and risks were not sufficiently understood and challenged by decision makers.

Examiners found that Equinor's experience in the United States was not unique. Many energy companies took positions in the country during the boom years and have since suffered heavy losses. Long periods of rising prices because of growing demand influenced the outlook and executive judgment. Everyone thought in 2011 that an oil price above USD 100 per barrel would be normal. When the PwC report was released in October 2020, the oil price was USD 40 per barrel.

Investigation Report Maturity

The board of directors at Equinor hired PwC (2020) to investigate the corporate scandal. The review team was chaired by Eli Moe-Helgesen, who was a partner at PricewaterhouseCoopers and a state authorized public accountant. The team included Aase Lindahl trained in economics, Hanna D. Opsahl-Ben Ammar trained in risk strategy, Jon Arnt Jacobsen trained in corporate audit, and Ann-Elisabeth Serck-Hanssen trained in asset management. The examination was no independent investigation, since both Jacobsen and Serck-Hansen were employed by Equinor in key positions relevant to the themes of investigation. While Moe-Helgesen, Lindahl, and Ammar were independent of Equinor as employees at PricewaterhouseCoopers, the two other team members were dependent on Equinor as employees at the energy company.

The scope of the investigation was to provide a timeline of events, to extract learning points, and "to provide assurance that adequate actions have been taken" (PwC, 2020: 4). The task of providing assurance is strange in the case that examiners would find lack of adequate actions. This kind of mandate formulation can be damaging to an investigation and should not have been accepted by the examiners. The mandate required answers to three questions: What caused the losses in the US? What caused the control problems in the US onshore business and how have they been followed up? What can Equinor learn to improve?

Rather than focusing on what happened and who did what to make it happen or not happen, the mandate was concerned with learning for Equinor's future business decisions and operations. Examiners only looked back in order to enable Equinor to improve for the future. Examiners avoided any person focus among potentially responsible executives who might deserve blame for the losses (PwC, 2020; 5): "The review team does not point to individual decisions or persons when answering the main questions in this report."

This is an obvious weakness, although examiners claim that no single error or action caused the problems in the United States. Examiners argue that the underlying causes were complex. Examiners suggest that deficiencies in strategy development, governance structure, risk management, leadership, and culture caused the Equinor scandal. While relevant and interesting, this kind of causality is so general that it has little or no value as fraud investigation outcome.

Examiners applied the value chain configuration rather than the value shop configuration in their investigation. A value chain is a sequential approach where examiners identify issues in a linear sequence and order consisting of objective, issues, evaluation criteria, evidence and method, expected findings, and feasibility (PwC, 2020: 9):

1. What do we want to achieve? What do we need to find out?
2. What is the yardstick against which we evaluate?
3. Which information do we need, and how do we obtain it and assure quality of it?
4. What do we expect to find?
5. What are the uncertainties, and are the risks manageable?

A value shop is an iterative approach where examiners identify in an iterative sequence consisting of problems, alternatives, choices, interpretations, and evaluations

1. What is the problem here? What do we want to achieve?
2. How do we do it? What kind of alternative approaches are available to us? What sources of information are available to us?
3. What criteria should we apply to identify the optimal approach to solve the problem?
4. How do we handle pieces of information collected in interviews, from documents and other sources? How do we interpret information in relevant contexts?
5. Did we solve the problem? If not, how do we return to stage 1 of understanding the problem?

As illustrated in Figure 4.2, fraud examiners from PwC (2020) conducted a problem-oriented investigation. The investigation focused on issues that needed clarification. Examiners were looking for answers on things that went wrong and why they went wrong, but they avoided looking at people who made it go wrong. At level 2 in the maturity model, once examiners believe they have found answers, the investigation is terminated. It is important to spend as little resources as possible on the investigation, which should take the shortest possible time. Delamination and management are important for success. The client

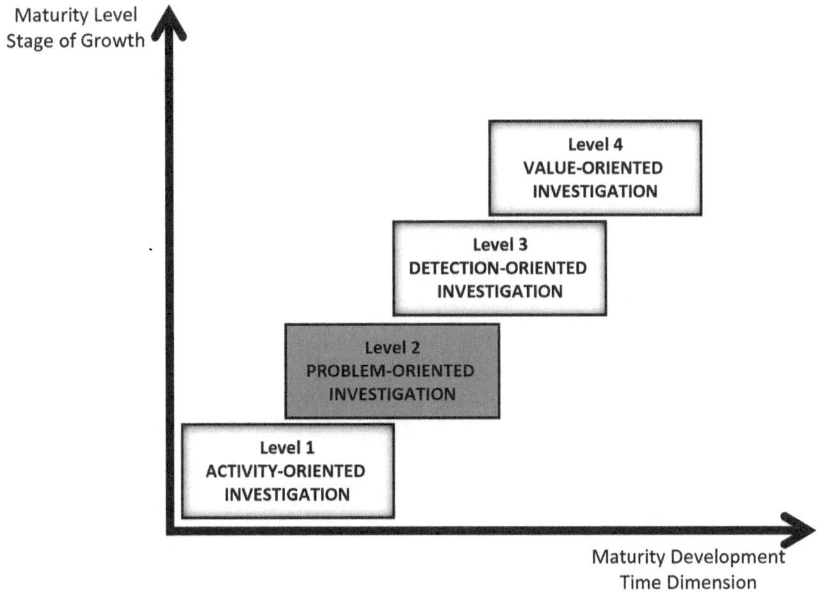

Figure 4.2 Maturity level for the PwC (2020) investigation at Equinor

had an unresolved problem, and the client regulates premises for the investigation. There is no room for investigators to pursue other paths than those that address the predefined problem. They are to map the facts. At this second maturity level, investigators typically attempt to find an answer to the question: How did it happen?

Often, little or nothing comes out of the investigation. The investigation is typically random, amateurish, formalities-focused, somewhat beneficial, but not enough, mainly descriptive, problem-oriented, neutral, unsystematic, inadequate, activity-oriented, shortsighted, fruitless, deviations-oriented, reactive, questions-oriented, and messy. The investigation tends to lack scrutiny, is a collection of information without analysis, and has too many assumptions that make conclusions less valid or invalid. The investigation is superficial and very limited. This stage might deserve the following label: Wishful thinking. At the Equinor investigation, the question of responsibility for the scandal was completely avoided.

References

Bosse, D.A. and Phillips, R.A. (2016). Agency theory and bounded self-interest, *Academy of Management Review*, 41 (2), 276–297.

Bruun Hjejle (2018). *Report on the Non-Resident Portfolio at Danske Bank's Estonian branch*, report of investigation, 87 pages, law firm Bruun Hjejle, Copenhagen, Denmark.

Bundy, J. and Pfarrer, M.D. (2015). A burden of responsibility: The role of social approval at the onset of a crisis, *Academy of Management Review*, 40 (3), 345–369.

Campbell, J.L. and Göritz, A.S. (2014). Culture corrupts! A qualitative study of organizational culture in corrupt organizations, *Journal of Business Ethics*, 120 (3), 291–311.

Deloitte (2015). *Investigation Report, Summary Version, Independent Investigation Committee for Toshiba Corporation*, report of investigation, audit firm Deloitte Tohmatsu, Tokyo, Japan.

Deloitte (2016). *Review – Ownership VimpelCom Telenor*, report of investigation, 54 pages, audit firm Deloitte, Oslo, Norway.

Dodge, M. (2009). *Women and White-Collar Crime*, Saddle River, NJ: Prentice Hall.

Fowler, T. (2014). BP's new tactic in oil spill claims: Go after the 'special master', *The Wall Street Journal*, www.wsj.com, published January 27.

Freeh, L.J. (2013). Independent External Investigation of the Deepwater Horizon Court Supervised Settlement Program, Report of Special Master Louis J. Freeh, www.laed.uscourts.gov, published September 6.

Hjort (2016). *Rapport til styret i DNB (report to the board at DNB)*, bank mentioned in the Panama Papers, report of investigation, 18 pages, law firm Hjort, Oslo, Norway.

Hovland, K.M. and Høgseth, M.H. (2020). Får kritikk i rapport om USA-smell: For lite kontroll (Gets criticism in report on US bang: Too little control), web-based Norwegian newspaper *E24*, www.e24.no, published October 9.

Jonnergård, K., Stafsudd, A. and Elg, U. (2010). Performance evaluations as gender barriers in professional organizations: A study of auditing firms, *Gender, Work and Organization*, 17 (6), 721–747.

Jordanoska, A. (2018). The social ecology of white-collar crime: Applying situational action theory to white-collar offending, *Deviant Behavior*, 39 (11), 1427–1449.

Kang, E. and Thosuwanchot, N. (2017). An application of Durkheim's four categories of suicide to organizational crimes, *Deviant Behavior*, 38 (5), 493–513.

Kaptein, M. and Helvoort, M. (2019). A model of neutralization techniques, *Deviant Behavior*, 40 (10), 1260–1285.

Lorch-Falch, S. and Tomter, L. (2021). Slaget om Obos (The battle of Obos), public Norwegian broadcasting corporation *NRK*, www.nrk.no, published June 22.

Müller, S.M. (2018). Corporate behavior and ecological disaster: Dow Chemical and the Great Lakes mercury crisis, 1970–1972, *Business History*, 60 (3), 399–422.

Mullis, M.E. (2020). Knusende Equinor-rapport: Brukte 180.000 kroner på én kalkun i USA (Crushing Equinor report: Spent 180,000 kroner o none turkey in the USA), web-based Norwegian newspaper *Nettavisen*, published October 9.

Piazza, A. and Jourdan, J. (2018). When the dust settles: The consequences of scandals for organizational competition, *Academy of Management Journal*, 61 (1), 165–190.

PwC (2020). *Equinor in the USA: Review of Equinor's US onshore activities and learnings for the future*, prepared for Equinor ASA's board of directors, October 9, 53 pages, PricewaterhouseCoopers, Oslo, Norway.

Shearman Sterling (2017). *Independent Directors of the Board of Wells Fargo & Company: Sales Practices Investigation Report*, Community Bank, report of investigation, 113 pages, law firm Shearman Sterling, San Francisco, California, USA.

Siponen, M. and Vance, A. (2010). Neutralization: New insights into the problem of employee information security policy violations, *MIS Quarterly*, 34 (3), 487–502.

Sykes, G. and Matza, D. (1957). Techniques of neutralization: A theory of delinquency, *American Sociological Review*, 22 (6), 664–670.

Thompson, R. (2017). With BP settlement claims winding down, Lafayette lawyer Parick Juneau turns attention to Takata air bag recall, *The Advocate*, www.theadvocate.com, published October 29.

Welsh, D.T. and Ordonez, L.D. (2014). The dark side of consecutive high performance goals: Linking goal setting, depletion, and unethical behavior, *Organizational Behavior and Human Decision Processes*, 123, 79–89.

5 Hurtigruten Cruises by Wiersholm

When the Corona virus caused lockdown of most activities, Norway's Hurtigruten cruises used its channels into political decision-makers to convince politicians to open up again for cruise activities. Hurtigruten management was successful, and they could quickly reopen their shipping activities. However, quarantine rules were not followed, suspected cases of the Corona virus were not followed up, and crew members felt their lives were in danger, but were afraid of speaking out (Berglund, 2020a; Valderhaug et al., 2020). When the Corona virus spread on Hurtigruten voyages, senior executives Daniel Skjeldam and Asta Lassesen allegedly attempted to suppress information and prevent disclosure of the scandal (Valderhaug, 2020a, 2020b).

When the Hurtigruten scandal became public, the board at the company hired Norwegian law firm Wiersholm (2020) to investigate the matter. Fraud examiners were to examine the shipping company's handling of passengers infected by the Covid-19 virus during cruise voyages.

After the fraud investigation report was presented in public, Prime Minister Erna Solberg joined many others who were frustrated and angry with the Norwegian cruise and shipping line Hurtigruten, which is supposed to make daily calls at small ports all along the Norwegian coast. Hurtigruten's management had lobbied state officials hard to be allowed to resume cruising, and won their approval, only to violate quarantine rules for its low-paid crew. They were flown in to Norway from the Philippines and put immediately to work on the cruise ship named Roald Amundsen, without going through mandatory ten-day quarantine. Some crew members fell ill during the first of two cruises, and a total of 71 passengers and crew wound up testing positive for the Corona virus (Berglund, 2020b).

Chief examiner Jan Fougner criticized Hurtigruten for being "too eager" to start cruising again when Norwegian authorities reopened for it during the summer. Hurtigruten assumed way too much risk during a pandemic, Fougner said at the press conference, as he pointed to poor communication and, most of all, a culture of fear within the company (Berglund, 2020a).

DOI: 10.4324/9781003305071-6

National Symbol Hurtigruten

Hurtigruten was established in 1893 by government contract to improve travel of persons and transport of goods along the coastline of Norway with its many isolated villages and towns. The Hurtigruten ships connect rural areas on a daily basis that has enabled people to operate and live along the poorly chartered waters, where the voyage is especially difficult during the long and dark winters in the land of the midnight sun during summers. Until the 1940s most ports in the north could not be reached by road, so the sea was the only means of access.

Today, Hurtigruten is just as much a cruise line as a part of the infrastructure for communication in Norway. Ships are sailing along the Norwegian coastline, often deep into fjords with its breathtaking landscapes. In the summer, the midnight sun is a spectacular view to many passengers. The classic voyages offer one- or two-week options. The ultimate journey is from Bergen to Kirkenes and back again. The ports visited by night on the northbound cruise are revealed when visited in daylight on the southbound journey.

During the period July 17–24, 2020, Hurtigruten's vessel Roald Amundsen undertook a cruise from the town of Tromsø, Norway, to Spitsbergen. A person who later tested positive for Covid-19 was a passenger on this voyage. On July 25, the ship once again left Tromsø to undertake another cruise to Spitsbergen. Status regarding the number of infected individuals on August 4, 2020, was 44 passengers and crew members. A total of 544 individuals had been on board the vessel during these two voyages. Any further voyages were suspended until further notice (Wiersholm, 2020: 5): "In a statement made on 3 August 2020, Hurtigruten's Group CEO, Daniel Skjeldam, said "we have failed, we have made a mistake". He communicated that an external investigation would be launched into Hurtigruten's handling of this matter."

The board claimed that it still had confidence in CEO Skjeldam, and that both he and the rest of top management at Hurtigruten needed to learn from all their potentially fatal mistakes (Berglund, 2020a):

> Trygve Hegnar, who leads Hurtigruten's board, has made a career out of criticizing and ridiculing other business executive's mistakes in the various media publications he owns. He nonetheless defended Hurtigruten's CEO here at Thursday's press conference, insisting Skjeldam was still the best person to restore public confidence in the historic shipping line that's run into serious problems with its international cruising.

Hurtigruten is still most known for its operation along Norway's western and northern coast between Bergen and Kirkenes with 34 ports. But as one of the world leaders in exploration travel on sea, the shipping company offers expedition cruises in Antarctica, Greenland, Iceland, Spitsbergen, Alaska, and other destinations. The company operates 11 ships and has more than 2,000 employees.

Hurtigruten was hit by a scandal and a following crisis. A scandal is a publicized instance of transgression that runs counter to social norms, typically resulting in condemnation and discredit and other consequences such as bad press, disengagement of key constituencies, the severance of network ties, and decrease in key performance indicators (Piazza and Jourdan, 2018). A scandal can be an act of elite deviance that might include financial, physical, and morally harmful behavior committed by privileged members of the organization and potentially in cooperation with the state (Rothe, 2020; Rothe and Medley, 2020). A crisis is an unexpected, publicly known, and harmful event that is associated with uncertainty. A crisis is a fundamental threat to a corporation. Ambiguity of cause, effect, and means of resolution often characterize a crisis. Most corporate crises originate from failures within the organization. Scholars denote that organizational crises require timely responses (König et al., 2020).

Prime Minister Solberg and health minister Bent Høie felt betrayed by the national symbol Hurtigruten's management who had pressured them into allowing the cruises. "The health minister and I have said that Hurtigruten deserves all the criticism it's getting", Solberg told NRK (Berglund, 2020b):

> Trade minister Iselin Nybø was also harsh in her assessment of Hurtigruten after its board's and leaders' apologetic press conference on Thursday: "Right now they don't have a very high star, but it's a strong brand, and they have ambitions to rise up again", Nybø said. "Time will tell whether they manage to do so".

Norway's famed but now shamed shipping company announced the suspension of its leader of maritime operations early August while Wiersholm (2020) examiners were conducting their investigation. The virus scandal onboard Roald Amundsen was shaking public confidence in a company long viewed as part of the national heritage. When the fraud examination report was presented in September, it seemed that the top executive, CEO Skjeldam, survived disgrace as chairperson Hegnar expressed strong confidence in Skjeldam at a press conference (Berglund, 2020a).

Offender Convenience Themes

In the following application of convenience theory, it is assumed that the misconduct and wrongdoing was financially motivated. Management wanted the ships back into seas and oceans with passengers to secure revenues. There was a threat of a long-lasting lockdown that might have caused bankruptcy for Hurtigruten as indicated in Figure 5.1. Even though Hurtigruten, like many other companies in Norway, was financially supported by the government during the initial months of the Corona virus pandemic, it was obvious to the board and management that long-term survival would depend on revenues from transport of tourists, inhabitants, goods, and services. As a national symbol, it was important to rescue Hurtigruten. Many researchers have emphasized avoidance

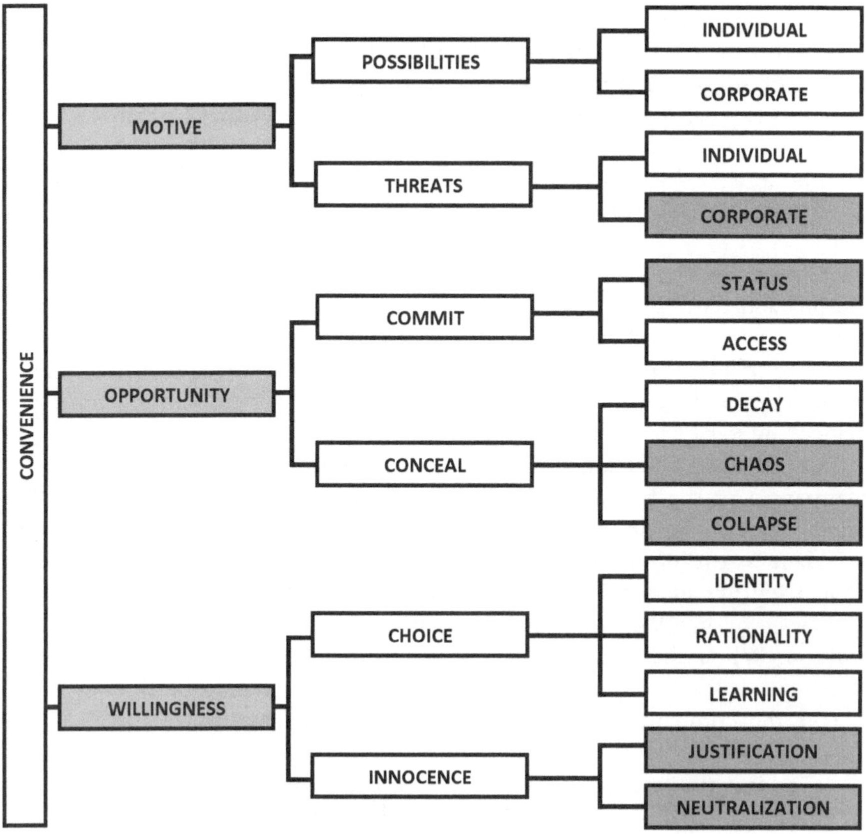

Figure 5.1 Convenience themes in the case of Hurtigruten

of corporate collapse and bankruptcy as an important motive for misconduct and wrongdoing (Blickle et al., 2006; Chattopadhyay et al., 2001; Geest et al., 2017; König et al., 2020; Brightman, 2009; Downing et al., 2019).

The organizational opportunity to sail the ships without relevant protection against the virus for passengers and staff was a matter of status of decision-makers versus staff members who were recruited from low-salary nations. There was power inequality between the elite and others in the company (Patel and Cooper, 2014; Friedrichs, 2010, 2020; Friedrichs et al., 2018; Dearden, 2016; McClean et al., 2018). The costs exceeded benefits for whistleblowers (Keil et al., 2010; Mesmer-Magnus and Viswesvaran, 2005), leading to silence among staff members about what they had noticed. This was in sharp contrast to the Covid-19 outbreak prevention and response regulation aboard Hurtigruten ships (Wiersholm, 2020: 21):

> In the event of suspicion of the discovery of COVID-19 on board, the ship's Doctor must follow reporting directives as stated by the port

> authority where the vessel is destined and inform the Captain who shall inform the Company through the Operation Manager without delay.
>
> For ships operating in Norway, any case of suspicion of discovery of COVID-19, must immediately be reported by the Captain to the Norwegian Coastal Administration via Vardø Sjøtrafikksentral on telephone +47 78 98 98 98 as well as registered electronically in the portal SafeSeaNet Norway.

There was probably an ethical climate conflict (Victor and Cullen, 1988; Murphy and Free, 2015; Murphy and Dacin, 2011), where the business was in a dilemma with safety. Another part of the opportunity structure might be found in rule complexity preventing compliance (Lehman et al., 2019; Huisman, 2020), where rules and guidelines concerning the pandemic were almost constantly changed by local and national officials.

CEO Daniel Skjeldam had a very high status in the company. The chairperson of the board at Hurtigruten, Trygve Hegnar, who was also the largest shareholder in the company for a while, personally head hunted Skjeldam to the position of CEO of the company in the autumn of 2012. That made Skjeldam the youngest leader of a listed Norwegian company as he was born in 1975 and thus 37 years old at the time he took on the position. When the virus scandal emerged, Hegnar quickly expressed complete confidence in Skjeldam, arguing that Skjeldam would be the best man to take the company out of its crisis (Berglund, 2020a):

> Skjeldam thus seems to have survived what's been described as one of the biggest scandals in Norwegian business history. A crushing internal report released Thursday on how Hurtigruten failed to ward off or control a Covid-19 outbreak on board its new ship MS Roald Amundsen points out plenty of mistakes, but none of them seems to have any consequences for the highly paid Skjeldam or others responsible.

High status, as indicated in Figure 5.1, can enable the blame game by misleading attribution to others (Eberly et al., 2011) and scapegoating (Gangloff et al., 2016). Skjeldam's status made him almost too big to fail (Pontell et al., 2014), and to the extent someone was to blame for the scandal and following crisis, it was not him.

The personal willingness dimension of convenience theory focuses on the willingness for deviant behavior among white-collar offenders. Personal willingness for deviant behavior implies a positive attitude towards violating social norms, including formally enacted laws, rules, and regulations (Aguilera et al., 2018). Deviance is a term to describe behavior that contravenes accepted norms, values, and ethical standards (Smith and Raymen, 2018). Deviance is "the failure to obey group rules" (Becker, 1963: 8). Deviance is "a form of behavior that violates organizational norms and that consequently negatively impacts the well-being of the organization and its members" (Michalak and

Ashkanasy, 2013: 20). Deviance is detrimental to organizational performance in several ways, including damaged reputation, exposure to lawsuits, and financial loss (Dilchert et al., 2007).

The willingness derives either from an active choice to commit and conceal offenses, or from the perception of personal innocence when committing and concealing crime. There is little evidence of choice in this case. Rather, innocence is more visible in the case. Justification and neutralization seem visible as convenience themes. The justification by management was to sail ships to create revenues (Schnatterly et al., 2018; Becker, 1963; Chen and Moosmayer, 2020) and to compensate for negative events (Engdahl, 2015; Patel and Cooper, 2014). The justification by staff was to obey orders from peer pressure (Gao and Zhang, 2019; Aguilera and Vadera, 2008) and be loyal to higher authorities (Sykes and Matza, 1957; Schoultz and Flyghed, 2016).

Fraud Investigation Outcome

The investigation report by Wiersholm is 49 pages long. The report spends its first ten pages explaining guidelines for conducting internal investigations. Then it spends ten more pages on rules and regulations in shipping. The foreword is written by chairperson Hegnar, who removes the anonymity for top executives by listing "Leader 2" as CEO Skjeldam, "Leader 1" as operating executive Bent Martini, "Leader 3" as commercial executive Asta Lassesen, and "Leader 7" as chief financial officer Torleif Ernstsen. Other employees mentioned in the report remained anonymous. The mandate for the investigation had the following formulation:

> Law firm Wiersholm, represented by Jan Fougner, Attorney-at-Law, will examine the Subsidiary's handling of the incidence of the Covid-19 virus in connection with the voyages described above. The investigation will include a description of the applicable rules of law, including any internal guidelines applying to the voyages and identify to what extent such guidelines were followed before, during and after voyages. The investigation should provide a basis for understanding what happened and learning from the incident. The investigation will contain recommendations for any further action. The client will ensure that Wiersholm and Wiersholm's aids are granted unlimited access to any records considered by them to be relevant to the execution of the assignment.
>
> Classification company DNV GL is retained to assist Wiersholm in its work. Upon agreement with the Company, Wiersholm may retain other sub-suppliers on behalf of the Company, including technical expertise.

The report by Wiersholm (2020) shows that Hurtigruten management was reluctant to implement effective Corona virus controls. The company had set up a formal control system, but it was never implemented or followed up. Company officials failed to manage a virus control regime, and investigators concluded that management took far too many risks when they resumed cruises in July 2020. Risk is generally a term that relates to negative or undesirable outcomes (Wang, 2020: 1283): "In everyday usage, a risk refers almost exclusively to a threat, hazard, danger or harm which should be avoided if at all possible."

The company was also criticized for poor communications both on board the vessel Roald Amundsen and with health authorities, and for utterly failing to protect both passengers and crew despite repeated claims that they would do so. "The outbreak on the MS Roald Amundsen can't be blamed on any single incident or any one person's actions", concluded Jan Fougner, an attorney from Oslo law firm Wiersholm. The firm, along with classification and consulting firm DNV GL, led Hurtigruten's own investigation of how 71 passengers and crew members ended up testing positive for Covid-19 after the Amundsen's two cruises to Spitsbergen in July (Berglund, 2020a).

Chief investigator Fougner stressed at the press conference that "many have made mistakes", and it would not help to simply blame or fire various individuals (Berglund, 2020a):

> That alone seems to have saved Skjeldam from being dismissed or opting to step down himself, as many expected he would. Skjeldam claimed he and his harshly criticized management team are taking the report seriously, accepting responsibility and promising to do a better job in the future.

The report of investigation is structured around four key phases: preparation, embarkation, measures along the way, and handling of infection outbreaks. In terms of preparation, examiners found that Hurtigruten carried out preparations under demanding circumstances. The preparations meant that a number of new activities were to be carried out in a short time and with fewer employees. Hurtigruten had a risk assessment process that was not sufficient. No overall risk assessment was conducted for risks associated with Covid-19. This shortcoming has influenced the choice and implementation of preventive measures. No training related to the handling of Covid-19 incidents took place before the voyage. The organization of Hurtigruten in a hierarchical and corporate structure made executives reluctant to involve themselves in operational matters. Rather, executive management had simply no review of risks related to the pandemic when sailing ships with many passengers and crew. Examiners emphasize the lack of preparation at all levels of the organization including top management and the board.

At the embarkation phase, Hurtigruten ignored health authority requirements to test foreign crew members and potentially put them in quarantine before working with other crew members and providing service to passengers. There were no single rooms for crew members in case quarantine would become necessary. New crew members arriving from abroad went straight into contact with other crew members and passengers.

In terms of measures along the way, people with illness indications were treated as regular patients by the two doctors onboard. This implied some observation, but relatively fast discharge with improved health. There was suspicion of Corona virus infection, but no testing was conducted by the two ship doctors. They communicated about the issue, but did nothing to follow up on rumors regarding Covid-19 onboard the vessel. Ship management expected that the two doctors would follow up on any indications of infection. This expectation remained even after ship management first received information about crew members put in isolation with Covid-19 symptoms and the need for testing, and then later learned that the information was withdrawn.

When it was discovered during the second voyage that a passenger from the first voyage had been identified with Covid-19, the passengers on the second voyage were not notified. A press release was withheld by agreement with a local doctor pending test results from the infected person's travel companions. The expectation of health authorities in Norway to notify passengers was not met, and warning of passengers was no longer considered after the travel companions of the infected individual tested negative. The communication was characterized by a desire to disprove that the infection might be associated with Roald Amundsen, rather than considering the possibility of infection on board the ship. This is also evidenced by the lack of communication of infection suspicion from the local municipal doctor to public authorities in Norway registering all positive results, which prevented notification to passengers after the positive test result from the passenger sailing on the first voyage. There was no overall understanding of the pandemic. Rather, the relevant perspective was to keep business as usual before the pandemic occurred. At arrival in the city of Tromsø with a confirmed infected person, the person was transported in a taxi with high risk of infecting the taxi driver.

The fourth phase of handling infection outbreaks was very slow. It took time before management reacted to positive test results. All passengers were informed 12 hours later than management. In the meantime, passengers moved freely around, and they were on planes and in other places with many people despite the high risk of infection. Management gathered all crew members for meetings at the same physical location without any restrictions concerning freedom of movement onboard the ship. Crisis management was not implemented according to the crisis management plan, and crisis actions differed and seemed random.

All crises are uncertain events that generate initial negative reactions. An effective response strategy should match external observers' situational attributions of the crisis to prevent cognitive dissonance among observers (Bundy and Pfarrer, 2015: 352):

> A higher situational attributions of responsibility should be matched with a response strategy that accepts more responsibility, and a crisis with lower situational attributions of responsibility should be matched with a response strategy that accepts less responsibility (...) An organization that is under conforming by being defensive in response to a crisis with higher situational attributions risks being perceived as unethical and manipulative.

Hurtigruten management was perceived as unethical and manipulative at the disclosure of the scandal and the following crisis. They seemed not to accept responsibility. However, fraud examiners from Wiersholm (2020) did not blame them.

Investigation Report Maturity

Both Wiersholm and DNV GL have previously worked as paid consultants for Hurtigruten, raising questions about the impartiality of their report (Berglund, 2020a; Brandt, 2020). Many crew members refused to talk to the investigators from Wiersholm (2020), fearing they were not sufficiently independent of Hurtigruten management and board, and that they could thus suffer harassment and reprisals. The fact that examiner Fougner and others at Wiersholm as well as DNV GL had other parallel roles and tasks paid for by Hurtigruten reduces the trust in their objectivity and independence, which in our perspective reduces the maturity level of the investigation report. The maturity level is further reduced by the fact that examiners failed in gaining trust sufficient to access many crew members as interviewees. Both in terms of process and in terms of outcome, the handling of interviewees has to be questioned, and the conclusions based on lacking information sources have to be questioned as well.

Examiners followed the guidelines for private investigations by the Norwegian Bar Association. The guidelines provide some suggestions regarding examination process, but they lack criteria for examination outcome. The guidelines emphasize issues such as the right of contradiction for individuals, whose actions or opinions are subject to investigation.

Examiners avoided the issue of blaming someone for the scandal. While scapegoating is bad, responsibility should be assigned to someone. A scapegoat is a person who is blamed for the wrongdoings, mistakes, or faults of others (Gangloff et al., 2016; Eren, 2020). Scapegoating often occurs after initial denial of wrongdoing or obfuscation of wrongdoing (Gottschalk and Benson, 2020: 949): "Our analysis shows that denial of wrongdoing in several cases is replaced by admission of wrongdoing and scapegoating, while obfuscation of wrongdoing is replaced denial or acceptance of responsibility and scapegoating."

A scapegoat is a person burdened with the wrongdoing of others (Eren, 2020). Medical doctors are close to becoming scapegoats in the Wiersholm (2020) report, while top executives become excused by a bureaucratic structure in the Hurtigruten organization. While the blame game by misleading attribution to others is bad (Eberly et al., 2011; Lee and Robinson, 2000), examiners avoided the task of identifying responsible persons in management.

Ideally, an investigation should answer questions concerned with what happened, how it happened, when it happened, who did what to make it happen or not happen, and why it happened or didn't happen. The latter two questions concerned with responsibility and causality were avoided by fraud examiners from Wiersholm (2020) and DNV GL. Examiners avoided causality in terms of potential motives for the reluctance to consider the pandemic

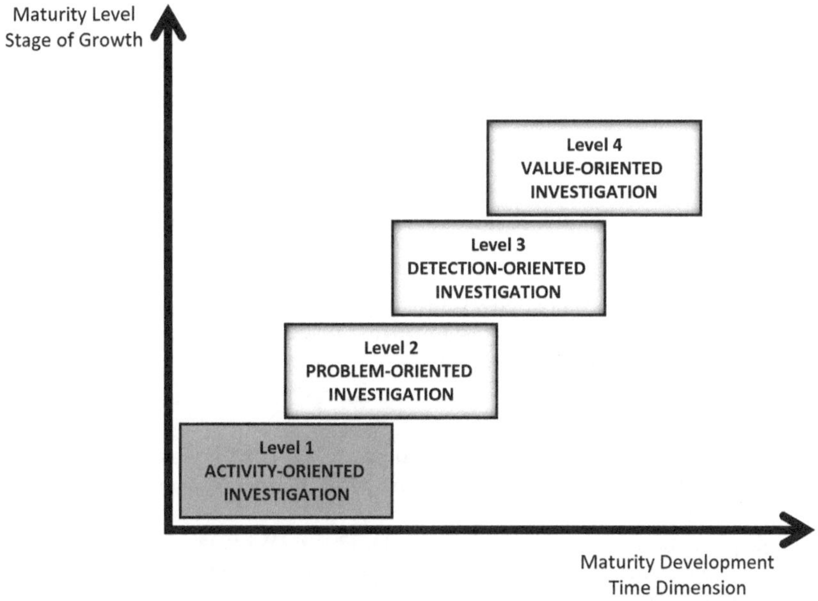

Figure 5.2 Maturity level for the Wiersholm (2020) investigation at Hurtigruten

a serious matter for voyages by Hurtigruten. Here in this chapter, it is suggested that the motive was financial gain to avoid corporate collapse and bankruptcy.

As illustrated in Figure 5.2, Wiersholm (2020) conducted an activity-oriented investigation. The investigation focused on activities that might have been carried out in a reprehensible manner. The examiners looked for activities and prepared descriptions of these. Then examiners made up their minds whether the activities were reprehensible or not.

References

Aguilera, R.V. and Vadera, A.K. (2008). The dark side of authority: Antecedents, mechanisms, and outcomes of organizational corruption, *Journal of Business Ethics*, 77, 431–449.

Aguilera, R.V., Judge, W.Q. and Terjesen, S.A. (2018). Corporate governance deviance, *Academy of Management Review*, 43 (1), 87–109.

Becker, H.S. (1963). *Outsiders: Studies in the Sociology of Deviance*, New York, NY: The Free Press.

Berglund, N. (2020a). Hurtigruten boss survives disgrace, *News in English*, www.newsinenglish,no, published September 17.

Berglund, N. (2020b). Government angry with Hurtigruten, *News in English*, www.newsinenglish.no, published September 18.

Blickle, G., Schlegel, A., Fassbender, P. and Klein, U. (2006). Some personality correlates of business white-collar crime, *Applied Psychology: An International Review*, 55 (2), 220–233.

Brandt, K. (2020). Hvor uavhengig kan og bør en gransking være? (How independent can and should an investigation be?), website *Rett24* for lawyers, www.rett24.no, published October 6.

Brightman, H.J. (2009). *Today's White-Collar Crime: Legal, Investigative, and Theoretical Perspectives*, New York, NY: Routledge.

Bundy, J. and Pfarrer, M.D. (2015). A burden of responsibility: The role of social approval at the onset of a crisis, *Academy of Management Review*, 40 (3), 345–369.

Chattopadhyay, P., Glick, W.H. and Huber, G.P. (2001). Organizational actions in response to threats and opportunities, *Academy of Management Journal*, 44 (5), 937–955.

Chen, Y. and Moosmayer, D.C. (2020). When guilt is not enough: Interdependent self-construal as moderator of the relationship between guilt and ethical consumption in a Confucian context, *Journal of Business Ethics*, 161, 551–572.

Dearden, T.E. (2016). Trust: The unwritten cost of white-collar crime, *Journal of Financial Crime*, 23 (1), 87–101.

Dilchert, S., Ones, D.S., Davis, R.D. and Rostow, C.D. (2007). Cognitive ability predicts objectively measured counterproductive work behaviors, *Journal of Applied Psychology*, 92, 616–627.

Downing, S.T., Kang, J.S., and Markman, G.D. (2019). What you don't see can hurt you: Awareness cues to profile indirect competitors, *Academy of Management Journal*, 62 (6), 1872–1900.

Eberly, M.B., Holley, E.C., Johnson, M.D. and Mitchell, T.R. (2011). Beyond internal and external: A dyadic theory of relational attributions, *Academy of Management Review*, 36 (4), 731–753.

Engdahl, O. (2015). White-collar crime and first-time adult-onset offending: Explorations in the concept of negative life events as turning points, *International Journal of Law, Crime and Justice*, 43 (1), 1–16.

Eren, C.P. (2020). Cops, firefighters, and scapegoats: Anti-money laundering (AML) professionals in an era of regulatory bulimia, *Journal of White Collar and Corporate Crime*, pages 1–12, published online doi:10.1177/2631309X20922153.

Friedrichs, D.O. (2010). Integrated theories of white-collar crime, in: Cullen, F.T. and Wilcox, P. (editors), *Encyclopedia of Criminological Theory*, Volume 1, Los Angeles, CA: Sage Publications, pages 479–486.

Friedrichs, D.O. (2020). White collar crime: Definitional debates and the case for a typological approach, in: Rorie, M. (editor), *The Handbook of White-Collar Crime*, Hoboken, NJ: John Wiley & Sons, chapter 2, pages 16–31.

Friedrichs, D.O., Schoultz, I. and Jordanoska, A. (2018). *Edwin H. Sutherland, Routledge Key Thinkers in Criminology*, London, UK: Routledge.

Gangloff, K.A., Connelly, B.L. and Shook, C.L. (2016). Of scapegoats and signals: Investor reactions to CEO succession in the aftermath of wrongdoing, *Journal of Management*, 42, 1614–1634.

Gao, P. and Zhang, G. (2019). Accounting manipulation, peer pressure, and internal control, *The Accounting Review*, 94 (1), 127–151.

Geest, V.R., Weisburd, D. and Blokland, A.A.J. (2017). Developmental trajectories of offenders convicted of fraud: A follow-up to age 50 in a Dutch conviction cohort, *European Journal of Criminology*, 14 (5), 543–565.

Gottschalk, P. and Benson, M.L. (2020). The evolution of corporate accounts of scandals from exposure to investigation, *British Journal of Criminology*, 60, 949–969.

Huisman, W. (2020). Blurred lines: Collusions between legitimate and illegitimate organizations, in: Rorie, M.L. (editor), *The Handbook of White-Collar Crime*, Hoboken, NJ: Wiley & Sons, chapter 10, pages 139–158.

Keil, M., Tiwana, A., Sainsbury, R. and Sneha, S. (2010). Toward a theory of whistleblowing intentions: A benefit-cost differential perspective, *Decision Sciences*, 41 (4), 787–812.

König, A., Graf-Vlachy, L., Bundy, J. and Little, L.M. (2020). A blessing and a curse: How CEOs' trait empathy affects their management of organizational crisis, *Academy of Management Review*, 45 (1), 130–153.

Lee, F. and Robinson, R.J. (2000). An attributional analysis of social accounts: Implications of playing the blame game, *Journal of Applied Social Psychology*, 30 (9), 1853–1879.

Lehman, D.W., Cooil, B. and Ramanujam, R. (2019). The effects of rule complexity on organizational noncompliance and remediation: Evidence from restaurant health inspections, *Journal of Management*, published online, pages 1–33, doi:10.1177/0149206319842262.

McClean, E.J., Martin, S.R., Emich, K.J. and Woodruff, T. (2018). The social consequences of voice: An examination of voice type and gender on status and subsequent leader emergence, *Academy of Management Journal*, 61 (5), 1869–1891.

Mesmer-Magnus, J.R. and Viswesvaran, C. (2005). Whistleblowing in an organization: An examination of correlates of whistleblowing intentions, actions, and retaliation, *Journal of Business Ethics*, 62 (3), 266–297.

Michalak, R. and Ashkanasy, N.M. (2013). Emotions and Deviances, in: Elias, S.M. (editor), *Deviant and Criminal Behavior in the Workplace*, New York, NY: NYU Press.

Murphy, P.R. and Dacin, M.T (2011). Psychological pathways to fraud: Understanding and preventing fraud in organizations, *Journal of Business Ethics*, 101, 601–618.

Murphy, P.R. and Free, C. (2015). Broadening the fraud triangle: Instrumental climate and fraud, *Behavioral Research in Accounting*, 28 (1), 41–56.

Patel, P.C. and Cooper, D. (2014). Structural power equality between family and nonfamily TMT members and the performance of family firms, *Academy of Management Journal*, 57 (6), 1624–1649.

Piazza, A. and Jourdan, J. (2018). When the dust settles: The consequences of scandals for organizational competition, *Academy of Management Journal*, 61 (1), 165–190.

Pontell, H.N., Black, W.K. and Geis, G. (2014). Too big to fail, too powerful to jail? On the absence of criminal prosecutions after the 2008 financial meltdown, *Crime, Law and Social Change*, 61 (1), 1–13.

Rothe, D.L. (2020). Moving beyond abstract typologies? Overview of state and state-corporate crime, *Journal of White-Collar and Corporate Crime*, 1 (1), 7–15.

Rothe, D.L. and Medley, C. (2020). Beyond state and state-corporate crime typologies: The symbiotic nature, harm, and victimization of crimes of the powerful and their continuation, in: Rorie, M. (editor), *The Handbook of White-Collar Crime*, Hoboken, NJ: John Wiley & Sons, chapter 6, pages 81–94.

Schnatterly, K., Gangloff, K.A. and Tuschke, A. (2018). CEO wrongdoing: A review of pressure, opportunity, and rationalization, *Journal of Management*, 44 (6), 2405–2432.

Schoultz, I. and Flyghed, J. (2016). Doing business for a 'higher loyalty' How Swedish transnational corporations neutralize allegations of crime, *Crime, Law and Social Change*, 66 (2), 183–198.

Smith, O. and Raymen, T. (2018). Deviant leisure: A criminological perspective, *Theoretical Criminology*, 22 (1), 63–82.

Sykes, G. and Matza, D. (1957). Techniques of neutralization: A theory of delinquency, *American Sociological Review*, 22 (6), 664–670.

Valderhaug, R. (2020a). Hurtigruten-topper beskyldes for å ha undertrykket informasjon, daily Norwegian newspaper *Aftenposten*, September 19, page 14.

Valderhaug, R. (2020b). -Vi har hele tiden vært åpne, og det skal vi fortsette med (-We have always been open, and we will continue to do so), daily Norwegian newspaper *Aftenposten*, October 29, page 20.

Valderhaug, R., Jordheim, H. and Christiansen, H. (2020). Rapport: Ikke rart at det gikk galt (Report: No surprise that it went wrong), daily Norwegian newspaper *Aftenposten*, September 18, page 10.

Victor, B. and Cullen, J.B. (1988). The organizational bases of ethical work climates, *Administrative Science Quarterly*, 33, 101–125.

Wang, P. (2020). How to engage in illegal transactions: Resolving risk and uncertainty in corrupt dealings, *British Journal of Criminology*, 60, 1282–1301.

Wiersholm (2020). *Granskningsrapport: Utbrudd av covid-19 på Hurtigruten-skipet MS Roald Amundsen 17.-31. juli 2020 (Investigation Report: Outbreak of Covid-19 on the Hurtigruten ship MS Roald Amundsen July 17 to 31)*, Norwegian law firm Wiersholm, Oslo, Norway, 49 pages.

6 Norfund Foreign Aid by PwC

Norfund is the Norwegian government's investment fund for developing countries. The mission is to create jobs and to improve lives by investing in businesses that drive sustainable development. Norfund is owned and funded by the Norwegian government and is the government's most important vehicle for strengthening the private sector in developing countries and for reducing poverty. Norfund had total commitments of USD 2.5 billion in 2019 in various developing countries.

Norfund reported on May 13, 2020 that the fund had been exposed to a serious case of fraud through a data breach. Two months earlier, on March 16, Norfund transferred USD 9,888,055 to a bank account in Banco Mercantil del Norte, Mexico, which Norfund believed belonged to its client, the Cambodian financial institution LOLC. In fact, the bank account was controlled by a so-called threat actor, who managed to compromise an email account belonging to an employee at Norfund, to register fake domains, and to impersonate Norfund's and LOLC's employees in the conversation (Solgård, 2020; Speed, 2020; Stave, 2020).

In their press release on May 13, 2020, Norfund (2020) claimed to be a victim of "a serious case of fraud through an advanced data breach". The term "advanced" is interesting, as it sometimes indicates and reflects lack of knowledge about the digitalization, applications of information technology, and digital forensics. Norfund hired PwC (2020) to investigate the matter.

Business Email Compromise

The fraud was enabled by business email compromise, where the criminal uses email to impersonate a business executive to request illegitimate payments. The attacker sends an email to someone in the organization who has the ability to execute a financial transaction. Although sent by the criminal, the email looks like it is from the entitled person in the organization. The email typically seems to authorize and request an immediate financial transaction such as an aid payment. The payment is directed to an account owned by the attacker. Immediately when the money arrives in the wrong bank account, the criminal transfers the money to other accounts in other banks and in other jurisdictions

DOI: 10.4324/9781003305071-7

to make it more difficult and impossible for the victim to trace and recover the money. The Norfund fraud was a combination of online identity theft, transnational financial crime, and global money laundering.

The criminal attacker is named Threat Actor in the following. Transnational criminals such as Threat Actor represent a challenge to societies all over the world. Transnational crime encompasses illegal activities that are carried out across national borders, which includes the planning and execution of illegal activities. Globalization has quickly facilitated the spread of these criminal activities. Transnational criminal organizations are organizations that conduct and carry out criminal operations across international borders. A transnational criminal organization may plan a crime in one country, carry it out in another, escape to a third, and keep the proceeds in a fourth country (Gottschalk and Markovic, 2016). Transnational crime has three broad objectives: provision of illicit goods, provision of illicit services, and the infiltration of business and government operations (Albanese, 2012). The Norfund fraud is an example of the latter, where Threat Actor infiltrated Norwegian government operations to steal ten million dollars. Transnational criminal organizations include mafia organizations such as La Cosa Nostra based in Italy, Los Zetas based in Mexico, and Hells Angels Motorcycle Club headquartered in the United States. Such organizations vary in their structure, culture, and fields of activity (Paraschiv, 2013). Some organizations recruit members based on ethnicity, while others recruit criminals based on competence and network. To join Threat Actor, computer skills and finance knowledge are probably required.

Traditional crime generally concerns personal or property offenses that law enforcement has continued to combat for centuries. Cybercrime starting with online identity theft is characterized by being technologically different, it can occur almost instantaneously, and it is difficult to observe and detect by traditional investigative methods. Cybercrime is sometimes easy to track, as digital detectives can follow electronic traces. While the crime scene in terms of computers involved may be easy to track, the criminals as actors are more difficult to find and prosecute. The problem of offender identification occurs because of the relative anonymity afforded by the Internet as well as the transcendence of geographical and physical limitations in cyberspace. Also, decentralized peer-to-peer networks may prevent material from being tracked to a specific location, and sophisticated encryption lets criminals keep online chats private from those policing the web.

Transnational cybercrime encompasses illegal activities carried out across national borders using information technology. Criminals are able to take advantage of a virtually limitless pool of potential victims. This is the case, for example, in online grooming where paedophile offenders find child victims across borders. Similarly, transnational music piracy is committed through a multitude of modus operandi. Also, financial crime in terms of, for example, electronic money laundering is frequently transnational between banking sectors with different legislations and secrecy practices.

Money laundering means securing of the proceeds of the criminal act. The proceeds must be integrated into the legal economy before the perpetrators can use it. The purpose of laundering is to make it appear as if the proceeds were acquired legally as well as disguising its illegal origins. Money laundering takes place within all types of profit-motivated crime, such as embezzlement, fraud, misappropriation, corruption, robbery, distribution of narcotic drugs, and trafficking human beings.

Money laundering has often been characterized as a three-stage process that requires (1) moving the funds from direct association with the crime, (2) disguising the trail to foil pursuit, and (3) making them available to the criminal organization once again with their occupational and geographic origins hidden from view. The first stage is often the riskiest one for the criminals because money from crime is registered with the victim's name in the financial system as the sender of funds. Stage 1 is usually called the placement stage. Stage 2 is often called the layering stage, in which money is moved in order to disguise or remove direct links to the offense committed. The money may be channeled through several transactions, which could involve a number of accounts, financial institutions, companies, and funds as well as the use of professionals such as lawyers, brokers, and consultants as intermediaries. Stage 3 is often called the integration stage, in which a legitimate basis for asset origin has been created. The money is made available to Threat Actor and can be used freely for regular expenditures and investments in legal businesses (Menon and Siew, 2012; Naheem, 2020).

PwC (2020) suggests that banks located in China, Hong Kong, the United Kingdom, and Mexico are often involved in fraudulent transfers. Recent money laundering by criminal organizations in Russia involved Danske Bank in Denmark (Bruun Hjejle, 2018) and Swedbank in Sweden (Clifford Chance, 2020).

According to Joyce (2005), criminal money is frequently removed from the country in which the crime occurred to be cycled through the international payment system to obscure any audit trial. The third stage of money laundering is done in different ways. For example, a credit card might be issued by offshore banks, casino "winnings" can be cashed out, capital gains on option or stock trading might occur, and real estate sale might cause profit. When crime generates significant proceeds, the perpetrators need to find a way to control the assets without attracting attention to themselves or the offense committed. Thus, the money laundering process is decisive in order to enjoy the proceeds without arousing suspicion.

The proceeds of crime find their way into different sectors of the economy. A survey in Canada indicates that deposit institutions are the single largest recipient, having been identified in 114 of the 149 proceeds of crime cases (Schneider, 2006). While the insurance sector was implicated in almost 65% of all cases, in the vast majority, the offender did not explicitly seek out the insurance sector as a laundering device. Instead, because motor vehicles, homes, companies, and marine vessels were purchased with the proceeds of crime, it was often necessary to purchase insurance for the assets.

Executive Email Impersonation

Business email compromise is often associated with CEO fraud. Although it is not known whether the impersonated individual at Norfund was the chief executive, the individual was obviously a high-ranking manager who enjoyed status and trust in the organization. When an email arrived from that Norfund executive, the money transfer of a substantial dollar amount took place without any critical questions or effective controls.

Chief executive officers (CEOs) and other trusted managers typically enjoy substantial individual freedom in their professions with little or no control. The CEO is the only person at that hierarchical level in the organization. Below the CEO, there are a number of executives at the same hierarchical level. Above the CEO, there are a number of board members at the same hierarchical level. But the CEO is alone at his or her level. The CEO is supposed to be controlled by the board, but the board only meets once in a while to discuss business cases. Executives below the CEO are typically appointed by the CEO and tend to be loyal to the CEO. Therefore, power, influence, and freedom are characteristics of CEOs as well as other trusted executives in principal-agent relationships to the CEO.

CEO power and influence can be illustrated by what is labelled CEO fraud in law enforcement. CEO fraud is not fraud by CEOs. Rather, CEO fraud is fraud committed by someone claiming to be the CEO. If someone claims to be the CEO, most people in the organization will do what they are told. As long as they believe that the message stems from the real CEO, they are completely obedient and do as they are told by the fake CEO. The U.S. Federal Bureau of Investigation (FBI) warned in 2016 about a dramatic increase in CEO fraud, email scams in which the attacker spoofs a message from the boss and tricks someone at the organization into wiring funds to the fraudsters. The FBI estimates these scams cost organizations in the United States more than one billion dollars per year. Organizations that are victimized by CEO fraud can be characterized by a combination of CEO power and obedience culture.

Some of the surprises for new CEOs and other executives arise from time and knowledge limitations – there is so much to do in complex new areas, with imperfect information and never enough time. Other surprises stem from unexpected and unfamiliar new roles and altered professional relationships. Still other surprises occur because of the frequent paradox that the more power you have, the harder it is to use it. While several of the challenges may appear familiar, Porter et al. (2004) discovered that nothing in a leader's background, even running a large business within his or her company, fully prepares them to be executives. Given the required struggle for executives to succeed under such circumstances, their subordinates have to cope with initiatives and decisions that may seem random without any clear pattern. After a while with a new CEO, little will surprise those who have to execute CEO decisions. This opens up for CEO fraud, where external criminals can take advantage of an institutional climate where every decision by a CEO is expected to be executed, whether or not the decision makes sense.

CEOs have long been recognized as the principal architects of corporate strategy and major catalysts of organizational change, and the extent to which CEOs can effect change in corporate strategy is thought to be determined largely by the power they possess, and how they decide to apply it (Hambrick and Lovelace, 2018). Thus, CEO fraud is enabled by change initiatives, where CEO behavior itself changes in ways so that there is no suspicion when deviant requests for money transfers occur.

While strategy development as well as organizational change may be at the center of CEO work, many CEOs spend much more time on other – and more minor – matters and issues. Conflicts between individuals in the organization take time to resolve and sudden media attention can steal even more time – and sometimes sleep – from important strategic thinking. Trivial matters tend to occupy much of executives' time. Given an understanding for a stressful situation among employees, CEO fraud is enabled based on the lack of formal rules guiding executive decision-making and implementation.

Many executives discover that they are alone, particularly in difficult times. They have nobody on their side at the same organizational level with whom they can openly discuss how to get out of a crisis situation since they are frequent rivals in the organizational hierarchy. Rather, others in the organization may speculate whether or not an executive will survive in the position and act accordingly to rescue their own future in the business. Therefore, employees who receive strange requests from an alleged executive will be reluctant to contact the real executive to check whether or not they should execute money transfer as requested.

Problem-solving is at the core of executive work, especially with a mindset of solving problems that the executive himself or herself created. Mindsets are conceived as distinct cognitive operations that facilitate problem-solving. The concept dates back to the end of the 19th century and the experimental psychologist Oswald Külpe, who showed that most of human thinking happens without images (imageless thoughts) and that most of it also occurs outside of our awareness. The resulting term, "Bewusstseinslage", literally a "state of mind", was later translated into the concept of mindsets, "Einstellung". Subordinates tend to spend time speculating in the mindset of executives and thus feel distant from communicating with them.

In a leader–follower perspective, followers are supposed to trust their leaders based on their status in the organization (Glasø and Einarsen, 2008; Glasø et al., 2006; Glasø et al., 2010). Status is an individual's social rank within a formal or informal hierarchy, or the person's relative standing along a valued social dimension. Status is the extent to which an individual is respected and admired by others, and status is the outcome of a subjective assessment process (McClean et al., 2018).

Offender Convenience Themes

The assumption in the following is that the so-called threat actor committing so-called advanced data breach is a criminal organization that found it convenient to defraud Norfund based on the criminal business's financial motive, organizational opportunity, and willingness for deviant behavior. A business founded on crime will follow the same business phases and logic in its operation and development as any legal or legitimate business venture. The main difference between a legal and illegal business is one of legislation not one of development (Dean et al., 2010). Both types of business organizations need entrepreneurialism to survive and succeed, where entrepreneurship is the practice of starting new organizations or revitalizing mature organizations, particularly new businesses generally in response to identified opportunities. Entrepreneurial activity is substantially different from operational activity as it is mainly concerned with creativity and innovation. Just like digitalization by application of information technology created new business models and value configurations for legitimate business ventures, so did the communication and technology revolution create new business opportunities for criminal organizations. Criminal organizations – like non-criminal organizations – develop opportunities by entrepreneurship. Criminal organizations – like non-criminal organizations – can organize their businesses in hierarchies, networks, or other forms of structures (Gottschalk and Smith, 2011; McElwee and Smith, 2015; Ramoglou and Tsang, 2016; Smith, 2009; Tonoyan et al., 2010; Welter et al., 2017).

Figure 6.1 illustrates convenience themes for the criminal organization Threat Actor when targeting Norfund. First of all, the financial motive for the criminal organization is the possibility of corporate economic gain. Maybe members of the organization want to climb the hierarchy of needs for status and success (Goldstraw-White, 2012; Maslow, 1943) and suffer from the American dream of prosperity (Cullen, 2010; Schoepfer and Piquero, 2006). The choice of crime might also derive from sensation seeking. Craig and Piquero (2017) suggest that the willingness to commit financial crime by some white-collar offenders has to do with their inclination for adventure and excitement. Offenders are not only seeking new, intense, and complicated experiences and sensations, as well as exciting adventures, they are also accepting the legal, physical, financial, and social risks associated with these adventures. They attempt to avoid boredom by replacing repetitive activities such as regular meetings with thrill and adventures. They search risky and exciting activities and have distaste for monotonous situations.

In the opportunity dimension of convenience theory, most criminals have no status in society (Pontell et al., 2014), but they have access to tools and vehicles to compromise email accounts and register fake domains and impersonate employees involved in financial transactions (Benson and Simpson, 2018; Ramoglou and Tsang, 2016). Concealing crime in the

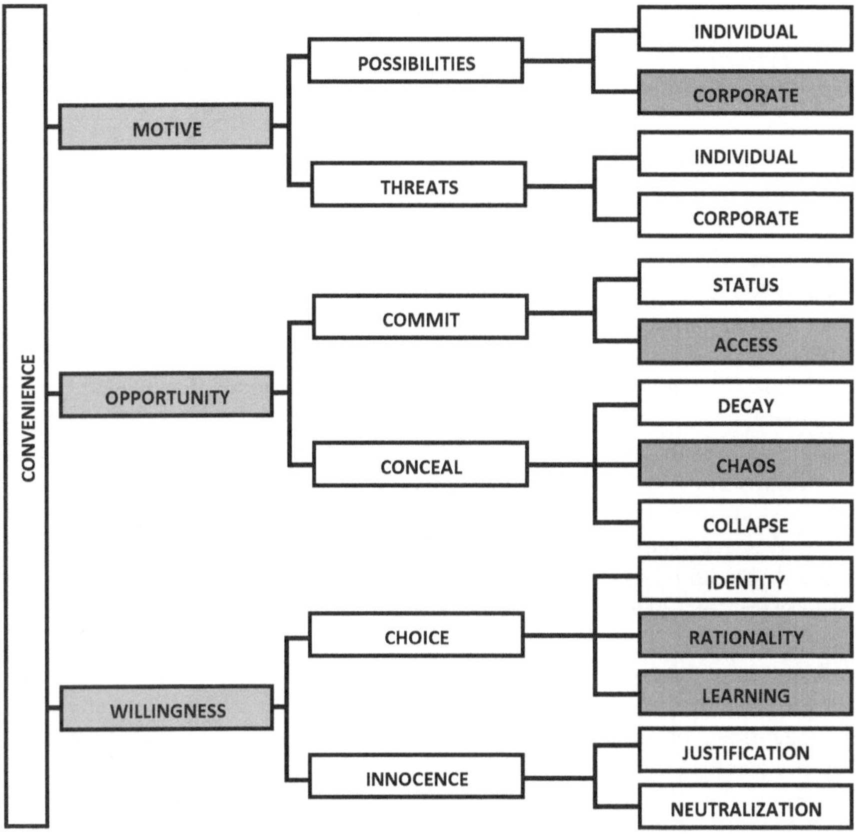

Figure 6.1 Convenience themes for the criminal organization against Norfund

digital financial world is also a matter of access to resources to quickly move money away from the Mexican account while deleting all traces (Adler and Kwon, 2002). An important opportunity theme is also the lack of digital knowledge in the victim organization Norfund and in police forces in Norway and globally that is indicated by chaos in Figure 6.1, where participation in crime networks (Nielsen, 2003) and markets with crime forces (Chang et al., 2005) represents convenient business practice for the criminal organization.

In the willingness dimension of convenience theory, the choice of crime is a rational choice by the criminal organization. The criminals have a perception of benefits exceeding costs (Pratt and Cullen, 2005). If successful, the criminals can experience behavioral reinforcement of deviance over time (Benartzi et al., 2017). The choice of crime is strengthened by learning from other criminals by differential association (Sutherland, 1983) and collectivist value orientations in the criminal organization (Bussmann et al., 2018).

Fraud Investigation Outcome

Norfund (2020) hired fraud examiners from PwC (2020) to assess existing internal controls and routines regarding payments. They were not hired to investigate the fraud case, but they nevertheless provide a description of the sequence of events as follows.

Prior to the fraud on March 16, 2020, the criminal organization Threat Actor comprised an email account belonging to an employee at Norfund on September 27, 2019. The Threat Actor then monitored Norfund's communication for seven months. On March 9, 2020, the criminal actor intercepted email correspondence between Norfund and LOLC about the forthcoming transaction. LOLC is located in Sri Lanka, and the money was destined for Cambodia. Threat Actor managed to change bank account details in the disbursement notice and convinced Norfund that a Mexican bank was used to avoid several bank intermediaries in the transaction. Threat Actor used the Corona virus as a factor to convince LOLC that the bank transfer was delayed. At the same time, the criminals sent emails to Norfund confirming that the funds were received by LOLC to prevent immediate suspicion and potential review by Norfund management.

On April 24, 2020, Threat Actor tried to manipulate a transaction with another Norfund client in Cambodia, First Finance, and asked to change the bank account details to Banco Mercantil del Norte. Norfund's investment manager requested First Finance to confirm the change of banking details. In the meantime, Norfund received an email on April 30 from LOLC stating that the bank account details in the transfer on March 16 were incorrect. Following the discovery of the fraud and fraud attempt, Norfund started reviewing the incident in cooperation with their Norwegian bank DNB, their IT service provider Visolit, as well as reporting the incident to the police.

Police attorney Eivind Kluge at Oslo police district contacted Interpol in France about the case. The Norwegian ministry of foreign affairs contacted Mexican authorities through the Norwegian embassy in Mexico City. However, the police expressed early on that they believed that they would never be able to capture the criminals or retrieve the money stolen (Speed, 2020). Rather than admitting the police force's potential lack of competence and insights into digital fraud locally and globally, the police argued that the criminals were very sophisticated by an "advanced data breach". Key persons at Norfund, such as chairperson Olaug Svarva, chief executive officer Tellef Thorleifsson, and communications executive Per Kristian Sbertoli, communicated a similar message that was supported by PwC's (2020) fraud examiners (Solgård, 2020; Stave, 2020).

However, examiners at PwC (2020: 5) identified the approach used by Threat Actor to defraud Norfund as the well-known technique of Business Email Compromise (BEC):

> In this type of scam, a criminal threat actor uses email to impersonate a business executive or other employees to request fraudulent payments. In Norfund's case, the threat actor leveraged relatively simple techniques in terms of circumventing existing IT security controls. PwC found no signs of malicious software being used.

Norfund had no appropriate IT security controls that could have helped detect the breach, and they had no competent technology expert internally. By intercepting Norfund's email system, Threat Actor had acquired knowledge of Norfund's operations generally and money transfers particularly. Threat Actor was successfully able to manipulate communication between Norfund and its client. The combination of Threat Actor's technical capabilities, digital experience, and understanding of Norfund's communication with clients made the fraud convenient for the criminal organization. Convenience was also caused by Norfund's inability to detect fraud and the Norfund employee's ignorance and naivety, which examiners phrase politely (PwC, 2020: 5): "It's PwC's assessment that the risk management framework could be further developed and improved to ensure Norfund's operational resilience."

The BEC scam that was used against Norfund is quite a common technique (Bakarich and Baranek, 2020: A1):

> Business email compromise (BEC) is a sophisticated email scam targeting companies that frequently work with foreign suppliers or businesses and utilize wire transfers as their regular method of transferring funds. These scams usually involve the compromise of legitimate business email accounts to conduct unauthorized transfers of funds, although other variations include requesting personally identifiable information.

Criminal organizations may use insiders in victim organizations to leak relevant information, bank clerks to open legitimate bank accounts, attorneys to keep secrets because of the attorney–client privilege, police officers to look another way, and various other helpers who the criminals pay off or threaten. When fraud is completed, then money laundering of proceeds from the criminal activity is important.

PwC (2020: 14) identified no singular control failure as the root cause of the incident at Norfund, but rather institutional deterioration that they label "unanticipated interaction of multiple failures in a complex system": "In hindsight, the reasons why such accidents occur may be obvious. However, they are challenging to predict due to the number of actions and pathways that may lead up to them."

Examiners at PwC (2020) conclude that "a chain of unfortunate events, insufficient controls, and human error, all contributed to the incident".

Investigation Report Maturity

Similar to Norfund who used the term "advanced data breach", PwC (2020: 14) claims that "the fraud was carried out by a resourceful and highly motivated threat actor who had an in-depth knowledge of financial transactions, and access to a global payment infrastructure." Such statements seem to be in contrast to PwC's (2020: 5) claim earlier in their report that the technique used is common and "relatively simple":

> In the past few years, the cyber threat landscape has undergone significant changes. Tools, techniques and capabilities that were previously exclusively available to highly resourceful threat actors have not only become easily accessible to less-skilled threat actors, but have also become easier to use. While substantial in terms of the financial losses incurred by Norfund, the LOLC incident was by no means exceptional.

In addition to the seemingly helpless approach to understanding digital fraud, criminal organizations, and identity of potential offenders, the PwC (2020) report seems like a biased work to satisfy the client. The report creates an impression that the main purpose of the review was to confirm that Norfund does what they can to prevent future fraud, for example (PwC, 2020: 27):

> PwC's assessment is that Norfund has a strong commitment to change and sets an appropriate "tone at the top". It is PwC's opinion that following the Alios incident, Norfund conducted a thorough assessment and identified appropriate measures to improve IT security.

In the summer of 2018, one of Norfund's borrowers, Alios, suffered an incident which appears similar to the LOLC incident (PwC, 2020: 26):

> In this incident, a threat actor infiltrated the communication between Alios and Norfund, and manipulated Alios to make a payment to an account under the threat actor's control. Following the incident, Norfund conducted an internal investigation in cooperation with third parties.

PwC (2020) argues that Norfund learned from the episode, while examiners at the same time present excuses for the LOLC incident that happened less than two years later. The client, Norfund, is probably happy with the PwC report that seems less critical and more client friendly than is expected of work by objective and independent examiners. Therefore, the investigation only reaches level 2 in its maturity as illustrated in Figure 6.2.

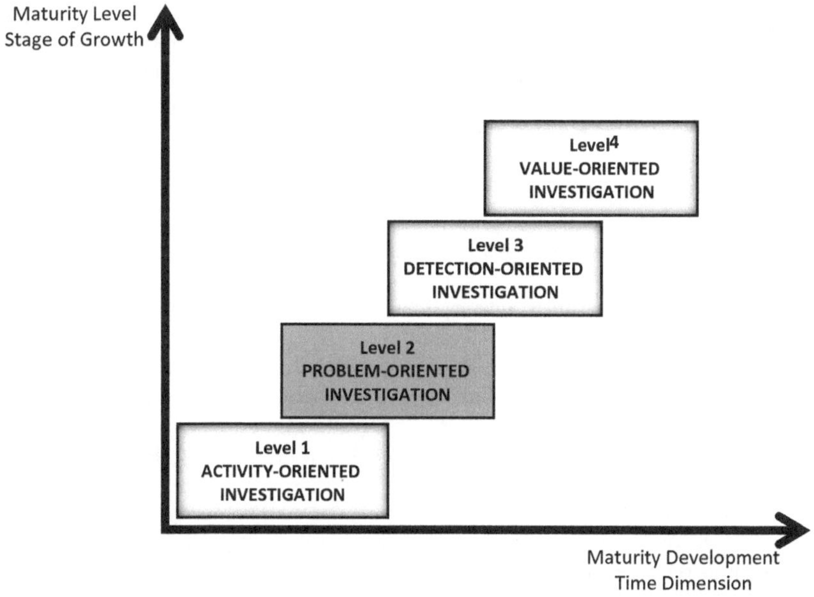

Figure 6.2 Maturity model for internal private investigations applied to PwC (2020)

References

Adler, P.S. and Kwon, S.W. (2002). Social capital: Prospects for a new concept, *Academy of Management Review*, 27 (1), 17–40.

Albanese, J.S. (2012). Deciphering the linkages between organized crime and transnational crime, *Journal of International Affairs*, 66 (1), 1–16.

Bakarich, K.M. and Baranek, D. (2020). Something phish-y is going on here: A teaching case on business email compromise, *Current Issues in Auditing*, 14 (1), A1–A9.

Benartzi, S., Beshears, J., Milkman, K.L., Sunstein, C.R., Thaler, R.H., Shankar, M., Tucker-Ray, W., Congdon, W.J. and Galing, S. (2017). Should governments invest more in nudging? *Psychological Science*, 28 (8), 1041–1055.

Benson, M.L. and Simpson, S.S. (2018). *Understanding White-Collar Crime – An Opportunity Perspective*, 2nd edition, New York, NY: Routledge.

Bruun Hjejle (2018). *Report on the Non-Resident Portfolio at Danske Bank's Estonian branch*, report of investigation, 87 pages, law firm Bruun Hjejle, Copenhagen, Denmark.

Bussmann, K.D., Niemeczek, A. and Vockrodt, M. (2018). Company culture and prevention of corruption in Germany, China and Russia, *European Journal of Criminology*, 15 (3), 255–277.

Chang, J.J., Lu, H.C. and Chen, M. (2005). Organized crime or individual crime? Endogeneous size of a criminal organization and the optimal law enforcement, *Economic Inquiry*, 43 (3), 661–675.

Clifford Chance (2020). *Report of Investigation on Swedbank*, report of investigation, 218 pages, law firm Clifford Chance, Washington, DC, USA.

Craig, J.M. and Piquero, N.L. (2017). Sensational offending: An application of sensation seeking to white-collar and conventional crimes, *Crime & Delinquency*, 63 (11), 1363–1382.

Cullen, F.T. (2010). Cloward, Richard A., and Lloyd E. Ohlin: Delinquency and opportunity, in: Cullen, F.T. and Wilcox, P. (editors), *Encyclopedia of Criminological Theory*, Volume 1, Los Angeles, CA: Sage Publications, pages 170–174.

Dean, G., Fahsing, I., and Gottschalk, P. (2010). *Organized Crime – Policing Illegal Business Entrepreneurialism*, Oxford, UK: Oxford University Press.

Glasø, L. and Einarsen, S. (2008). Emotion regulation in leader-follower relationships, *European Journal of Work and Organizational Psychology*, 17 (4), 482–500.

Glasø, L., Ekerholt, K., Barman, S. and Einarsen, S. (2006). The instrumentality of emotion in leader-subordinate relationships, *International Journal of Work Organisation and Emotion*, 1 (3), 255–276.

Glasø, L., Einarsen, S., Matthiesen, S.B. and Skogstad, A. (2010). The dark side of leaders: A representative study of interpersonal problems among leaders, *Scandinavian Journal of Organizational Psychology*, 2 (2), 3–14.

Goldstraw-White, J. (2012). *White-Collar Crime: Accounts of Offending Behavior*, London, UK: Palgrave Macmillan.

Gottschalk, P. and Markovic, V. (2016). Transnational criminal organizations (TCOs): The case of combating criminal biker gangs, *International Journal of Criminal Justice Sciences*, June–December, 30–44.

Gottschalk, P. and Smith, R. (2011). Criminal entrepreneurship, white-collar criminality, and neutralization theory, *Journal of Enterprising Communities: People and Places in the Global Economy*, 5 (4), 300–308.

Hambrick, D.C. and Lovelace, J.B. (2018). The role of executive symbolism in advancing new strategic themes in organization: A social influence perspective, *Academy of Management Review*, 43 (1), 110–131.

Joyce, E. (2005). Expanding the international regime on money laundering in response to transnational organized crime, terrorism, and corruption, in: Reichel, P. (editor), *Handbook of Transnational Crime and Justice*, London, UK: Sage publications, pages 79–97.

Maslow, A.H. (1943). A theory of human motivation, *Psychological Review*, 50 (4), 370–396.

McClean, E.J., Martin, S.R., Emich, K.J. and Woodruff, T. (2018). The social consequences of voice: An examination of voice type and gender on status and subsequent leader emergence, *Academy of Management Journal*, 61 (5), 1869–1891.

McElwee, G. and Smith, R. (2015). Towards a nuanced typology of illegal entrepreneurship: A theoretical and conceptual overview, in: McElwee, G. and Smith, R. (editors), *Exploring Criminal and Illegal Enterprise: New Perspectives on Research, Policy & Practice: Contemporary Issues in Entrepreneurship Research* Volume 5, Bingley, UK: Emerald Publishing, pages 3–22.

Menon, S. and Siew, T.G. (2012). Key challenges in tackling economic and cyber-crimes – Creating a multilateral platform for international co-operation, *Journal of Money Laundering Control*, 15 (3), 243–256.

Naheem, M.A. (2020). The agency dilemma in anti-money laundering regulation, *Journal of Money Laundering Control*, published online doi:10.1108/JMLC-01-2016-0007.

Nielsen, R.P. (2003). Corruption networks and implications for ethical corruption reform, *Journal of Business Ethics*, 42 (2), 125–149.

Norfund (2020). *Norfund er utsatt for alvorlig svindel (Norfund is exposed to serious fraud)*, Norfund, www.norfund.no, published May 15.

Paraschiv, G. (2013). Conceptualizing transnational organized crime, *Economics, Management, and Financial Markets*, 8 (2), 173–178.

Pontell, H.N., Black, W.K. and Geis, G. (2014). Too big to fail, too powerful to jail? On the absence of criminal prosecutions after the 2008 financial meltdown, *Crime, Law and Social Change*, 61 (1), 1–13.

Porter, M.E., Lorsch, J.W. and Nohria, N. (2004). Seven surprises for new CEOs, *Harvard Business Review*, October, 62.

Pratt, T.C. and Cullen, F.T. (2005). Assessing macro-level predictors and theories of crime: A meta-analysis, *Crime and Justice*, 32, 373–450.

PwC (2020). *Independent assessment of the LOLC incident: Report developed for Norfund, report of investigation*, June 30, 34 pages, PricewaterhouseCoopers, Oslo, Norway.

Ramoglou, S. and Tsang, E.W.K. (2016). A realist perspective of entrepreneurship: Opportunities as propensities, *Academy of Management Review*, 41, 410–434.

Schneider, S. (2006). Privatizing economic crime enforcement: Exploring the role of private sector investigative agencies in combating money laundering, *Policing & Society*, 16 (3), 285–312.

Schoepfer, A. and Piquero, N.L. (2006). Exploring white-collar crime and the American dream: A partial test of institutional anomie theory, *Journal of Criminal Justice*, 34 (3), 227–235.

Smith, R. (2009). Understanding entrepreneurial behavior in organized criminals, *Journal of Enterprising Communities: People and Places in the Global Economy*, 3 (3), 256–268.

Solgård, J. (2020). Norfund ble svindlet for 100 millioner: -Vi har gjort mye, men ikke raskt nok for å styrke våre rutiner og systemer (Norfund was defrauded for 100 million: -We have done a lot, but not fast enough to strengthen our routines and systems), daily Norwegian business newspaper *Dagens Næringsliv*, www.dn.no, published July 9.

Speed, J. (2020). Politiet: Lite trolig at Nordfun får igjen svindelpenger (The police: It is unlikely that Norfund will get back fraud money), foreign aid magazine *BistandsAktuelt*, www.bistandsaktuelt.no, published May 15.

Stave, T.K. (2020). Norfund tar selvkritikk etter gigantsvindel (Norfund takes self-criticism after giant fraud), daily Norwegian newspaper *Aftenposten*, www.e24.no, published July 9.

Sutherland, E.H. (1983). *White Collar Crime – The Uncut Version*, New Haven, CT: Yale University Press.

Tonoyan, V., Strohmeyer, R., Habib, M. and Perlitz, M. (2010). Corruption and entrepreneurship: How formal and informal institutions shape small firm behavior in transition and mature market economies, *Entrepreneurship: Theory & Practice*, 34 (5), 803–831.

Welter, F., Baker, T., Audretsch, D.B. and Gartner, W.B. (2017). Everyday entrepreneurship: A call for entrepreneurship research to embrace entrepreneurial diversity, *Entrepreneurship: Theory and Practice*, 41 (3), 323–347.

7 Obos Housing Facilities by KPMG

Obos is Norway's largest housing developer. Obos' vision is to build the society of the future and, in doing so, fulfill housing dreams. Obos is a member organization where residents and prospects pay an annual membership fee. Obos engages in the development and sale of homes and properties, banking and financial services, property management, real estate brokerage, and other forms of service production in the housing and property sector. The organization is a cooperative owned by its 502,527 members. The cooperative was established in 1929 to provide a solution to housing shortages for low-income families in the capital of Oslo. After World War II, Obos played an important role in building apartment blocks on the eastside of Oslo. The rich people live on the westside of Oslo, while the less fortunate live on the eastside of the city center. Apartments were affordable for poor families as Obos required minimal deposits and favorable loans. To be qualified to buy the most attractive Obos apartments, buyers had to document membership for several decades when moving into the 1950s, 1960s, and 1970s. The suspected fraud was concerned with abuse of position to benefit close acquaintances financially.

According to Holm (2021), Obos is both a member organization and a commercial enterprise:

> The reason lies in the history: The housing construction associations became the mainstay of the social democratic housing policy that really took hold after World War II. The idea was to operate without profit, build rationally, get affordable government loans, and pay a symbolic plot rent. The model worked effectively, and the housing construction associations built more than 200,000 homes during this period. Without Obos and the other housing associations, the Norwegian welfare society would have looked very different.

In the 1980s, a housing market existed where supply of and demand for apartments seemed more in an equilibrium state in Oslo where most people could afford housing on the open market. Then Obos transformed its business into more expensive construction projects with apartments not only with 60 or 70 square meters, but also luxury apartments on the westside of Oslo of more than 100 square meters.

DOI: 10.4324/9781003305071-8

The housing market in Oslo went again out of balance after the year 2000. Obos dwellings in Oslo were 11.5% more expensive in the first quarter of 2016 compared to the same period the previous year (Oesterud, 2016). Social housing was in high demand. However, Obos seemed no longer ready to take on the role of providing affordable housing for low-income families since there was more profit to be made in the higher end of the housing market. Housing development was still the main activity carried out by Obos in the 2020s. The cooperative combined residential construction in Norway, Sweden, and Denmark.

Cooperative Member Revolt

In 2021, former mayor of Oslo, Fabian Stang, claimed that Obos was sabotaging its own social mission (Stang, 2021):

> The housing construction company Obos has had large profits. Bravo! But the profits are kept far away from the owners that are the members. The money is not spent on a careful price reduction on new apartments, which would result in a fall in prices throughout the market. They are used for constantly new activities, further and further away from the basic idea. Many members now see that Obos that they thought was theirs, has turned into a profit seeker. Like when Obos offered an apartment at Majorstuen for NOK 95 million. Obos should first build ordinary homes for ordinary people before the upper part of the luxury market gets its share.
>
> And the sale of an entire block at Ulven. Right in front of the nose of members waiting neatly in line, ready-to-move-in apartments were sold to a rental investor. The board let the sun be shining on themselves in a report they ordered, which said the sale did not violate the law or the statutes of the cooperative.

Holm (2021) phrased the question: Is Obos the solution or the problem?

> There is revolt among Obos' members. They want democracy and a more social profile. For Obos' leadership, the time has come to examine own bowels. 502,000 Obos members who have been passive so far are starting to move themselves. More and more of them have noticed that they have neither power nor influence. Through various schemes, the members are represented at the annual general meeting, but as a member you get minimal information and, for example, membership votes, so-called primaries, are never held, as you have in many other associations. Obos has a board appointed by the general meeting, and in practice it is the board and the administration that have managed the housing association.

Holm (2021) does not answer his own question. However, he suggests that Obos should get to its roots, and he explains how. First, members have to be empowered while management power has to be reduced. Next, a home culture rather than a business culture should dominate the cooperative. Furthermore, architecture and landscaping should go hand in hand with apartment buildings. Finally, management should concentrate on social housing.

Hegtun (2021) phrased a similar question: Has Obos lost its soul?

> Close down Obos! Kick out the leaders! Cut out the investments in Sweden! Reduce prices! In parts of the membership of the housing group Obos, the mood is now very low. In nine days, there may be a riot at the general meeting.

Fraud examiners from law firm KPMG (2021: 1) were hired to conduct a corporate investigation at Obos, based on the following mandate for the examination:

> On April 9, 2021, the board of directors at Obos commissioned KPMG Law to review relevant facts of the Ulven transaction and make associated legal assessments of these. The main purpose of the investigation is to assist the board in assessing whether there have been irregularities or other matters worthy of criticism.
>
> The background for the assignment is that Obos on the occasion of the development at Ulven in Oslo sold two apartment blocks with a total of 182 apartments to the private rental company Quality Living Residential (QLR) for NOK 936 million. In retrospect, criticism has been leveled at Obos from various quarters. The criticism is mainly related to whether the sale fulfills Obos' purpose as a housing association and the members' interests as such. Furthermore, questions have been raised about the relationship between the CEO of Obos and the purchasing representative from QLR, as well as the relationship between the executive director of housing development and his uncle and cousin who invested in QLR.

Obos had sold 182 apartments at Ulven in Oslo to the real estate company Quality Living Residential for NOK 936. The homes were to be rented to the growing corporate market in the area (Jacobsen, 2020):

- Since the apartments we build at Ulven are primarily condominium apartments, we welcome a rental concept with high quality in the area. The sale of Ulven West to one entrepreneur means that the project will be completed quickly, thus shortening the construction activity time for those who already live in the area, says CEO Daniel Kjørberg Siraj in Obos.

The project at Ulven will have park and squares in the immediate vicinity, underground parking, and car-free street gardens. According to the plan, the homes in Ulven West will be ready for occupancy in the spring of 2023. The general contractor is Team Veidekke, which is a construction company (Jacobsen, 2020):

- The plan is to rent out the homes to employees associated with the planned knowledge park Construction City and other knowledge organizations in the area, says Baard Schumann.

Schumann established QLR in 2018. The purpose of the company is to invest in rental projects. The equity in the company was provided by, among others, Oslo Pension Fund, the Baumann family, Wenaas Capital, and Eidissen Consult. Pareto Securities and the Swedish bank SEP assisted in structuring the transaction.

Motive Convenience Themes

Daniel Kjørberg Siraj was appointed chief executive officer at Obos in 2017. His predecessor Martin Mæland held the CEO position for 34 years since 1983. He was a social democrat who had a loyal approach to the vision and mission of Obos as a construction cooperative building ordinary homes for ordinary people. Lars Buer, who held the board chair position, was a trade unionist also committed to the social democracy of Obos as a member organization for ordinary people.

After four years in the position of CEO at Obos, Daniel Kjørberg Siraj became the main target for a membership revolt exemplified by Stang's (2021) article. The revolt included demonstrations in front of Obos headquarters with the demand from members stating on posters that Obos is ours (Sørgjeld, 2021).

In 2021, less than 20% of Obos' revenues came from housing. CEO Siraj did not think that was a problem. He was proud of all the large-scale prestige projects that he had launched. One of them was a giant construction effort to build a completely new city district. Some observers labeled it megalomania (Lundgaard and Sørgjeld, 2021).

CEO Siraj sold an entire block of apartments to an investor who was to make money on rental arrangements. This was in conflict with the basic idea of Obos to provide ownership of ordinary homes to ordinary people. The idea of home ownership is rooted in the Norwegian tradition where very few rent their home. However, CEO Siraj preferred to sell the block to investor Baard Schumann with whom he had a comradely tone (Lorch-Falch and Tomter, 2021).

The main theme for motive convenience was corporate gain to make Obos even more profitable, as illustrated in Figure 7.1. In many organizations, ends justify means (Campbell and Göritz, 2014). If ends in terms of ambitions and goals are difficult to realize and achieve in normal ways, deviant means represent an alternative in many organizations (Jonnergård et al., 2010). Among most executives, it is an obvious necessity to achieve goals and objectives, while it is an obvious catastrophe failing to achieve goals and objectives. Welsh and Ordonez (2014) found that high performance goals cause unethical behavior. Dodge (2009: 15) argues that it is tough rivalry that makes executives in the

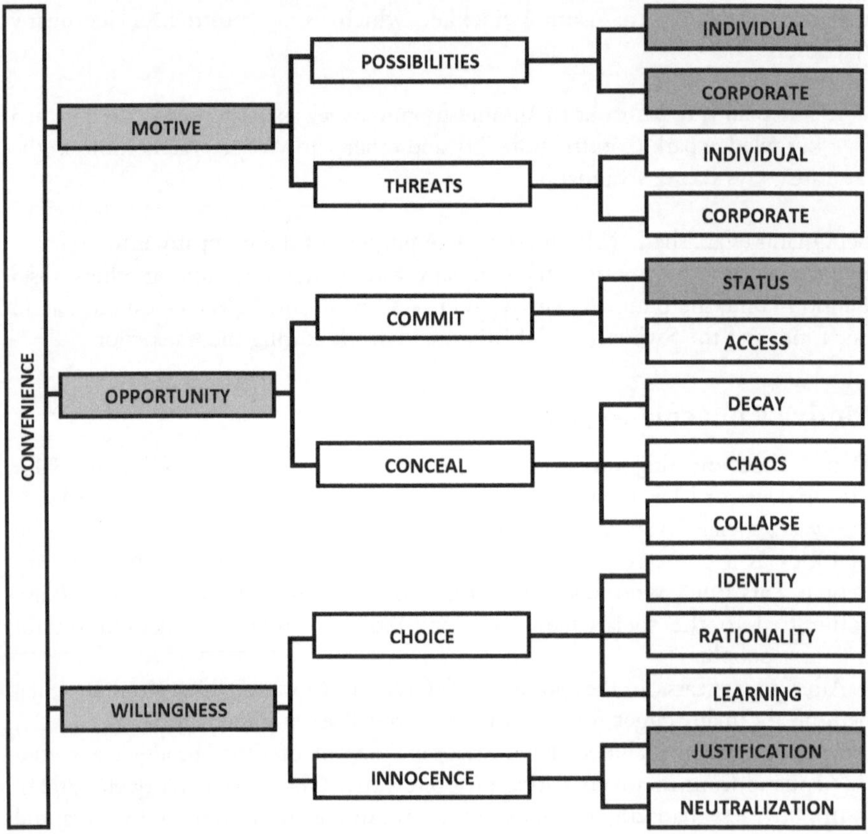

Figure 7.1 Convenience themes in the case of Obos

organization commit wrongdoing to attain goals: "The competitive environment generates pressures on the organization to violate the law in order to attain goals."

Individual executives would like to be successful, and they would like their workplace to be successful. Being associated with a successful business is important to the identity of many executives. They explore and exploit attractive corporate economic possibilities in both legal and illegal ways, so that their organization can emerge just as successful, or even more so, than other organizations. Profit orientation becomes stronger in goal-oriented organizations whose aim tends to be an ambitious financial bottom line.

It seems that Siraj at the individual level wanted to climb in the hierarchy of needs into fame and admiration. Maslow (1943) developed a hierarchy of human needs. Needs start at the bottom with physiological need, need for security, social need, and need for respect and self-realization. When basic needs such as food and shelter are satisfied, then the person moves up the pyramid to satisfy needs for safety and control over their own life situation. Further up in the pyramid, the person strives for status, recognition, and self-respect. While street crime is often concerned with the lower levels, white-collar crime is often concerned with the upper levels in terms of status and success.

Concern for others is sometimes a motive for executive wrongdoing (Agnew, 2014). Helping others can be a self-interested, rational action that claims social concern (Paternoster et al., 2018). In the portrait interview with Siraj, he claims concern for others in his membership in the Pentecostal congregation (Mauno, 2017). He might have satisfied his desire to help others as social concern.

Agnew (2014) suggested that economic wrongdoing can be committed when individuals think more of others than of themselves. An entrepreneur can commit financial crime to ensure that all employees have a job where they can return. A trusted employee can pay bribes to make sure that the company will have new orders to survive in the future. An executive may commit embezzlement to be able to help his adult children to recover after personal bankruptcy. Agnew (2014) argued that social concern consists of four elements, namely that (1) individuals care about the welfare of others, (2) they want close ties with others, (3) they are likely to follow moral guidelines such as innocent people should not suffer harm, and (4) they tend to seek confirmation through other people's actions and norms. That a person puts others before oneself will initially lead to less crime. However, economic crime may be committed where the welfare of others and their success is the motive.

Opportunity Convenience Themes

Several executives objected to the sale of the Ulven block to the investor Schumann who wanted to rent out apartments. One of them was chief housing officer Arne Baumann who looks at himself as a housing provider for members. But the housing director explained that he was loyal to the chief executive (Lorch-Falch and Tomter, 2021):

> Housing director Arne Baumann sees himself as someone who builds homes for the members. According to KPMG, he said that it "tears in the heart of the home builder" to sell a plot in central Oslo to external investors who will rent out. But the director of housing also explained that he was loyal to the CEO.
>
> When the agreement was entered into in May last year, Schumann was given a deadline of October 1, 2020 to put money in place. The money did not appear within the deadline. At the time, both housing director Arne Baumann and director of commercial real estate, Nils Bøhler, thought that Obos should turn around to sell to members. Siraj instead gave an extended deadline to get the agreement realized.

Similarly, the board did not react to the Siraj deviance, and chair Roar Engeland in his account expressed support for the decision, although it led to fewer homes for members (Lorch-Falch and Tomter, 2021):

> Like Siraj, he saw that the sale could provide almost one billion in cash. Money Siraj could spin to get plots for more homes that Schumann bought. However, in the short term, the sale means that there will be fewer homes for the members.

The status of CEO Siraj can explain his ignorance of negative reactions to his business model rather than membership model of the cooperative Obos. Status as convenience theme in the organizational dimension is illustrated in Figure 7.1. Status is an individual's social rank within a formal or informal hierarchy, or the person's relative standing along a valued social dimension. Status is the extent to which an individual is respected and admired by others, and status is the outcome of a subjective assessment process (McClean et al., 2018). High-status individuals enjoy greater respect and deference from, as well as power and influence over, those who are positioned lower in the social hierarchy (Kakkar et al., 2020: 532):

> Status is a property that rests in the eyes of others and is conferred to individuals who are deemed to have a higher rank or social standing in a pecking order based on a mutually valued set of social attributes. Higher social status or rank grants its holder a host of tangible benefits in both professional and personal domains. For instance, high-status actors are sought by groups for advice, are paid higher, receive unsolicited help, and are credited disproportionately in joint tasks. In innumerable ways, our social ecosystem consistently rewards those with high status.

Especially individuals with high status based on prestige rather than dominance tend to be excused for whatever wrongdoing they commit. Individuals who attain and maintain high rank by behaving in ways that are assertive, controlling, and intimidating are characterized as dominant. Individuals who attain and maintain high rank by their set of skills, knowledge, expertise, and their willingness to share these with others are characterized as prestigious (Kakkar et al., 2020).

Willingness Convenience Themes

CEO Siraj does not think that his business model deviates from the social model (Mauno, 2017)

- Do you ever get tired of being confronted with the glossy image of the old, social democratic project Obos – those who built apartments for ordinary people in housing need?
- No, I'm never tired of that story. I think it's a proud story Obos has, and I still like to think that we take social responsibility by building as many homes as possible and start projects that we may not make as much money on, but that help young home buyers, says Siraj.By the way, I was called "an anti-social housing shark" in an editorial in your newspaper. I still remember that. Ha-ha-ha! He laughs.

At the annual general meeting on June 22, 2021, CEO Siraj said he was sorry, as a response to a request that he should step down from the position of chief executive (Lorch-Falch and Tomter, 2021):

> Siraj addressed the congregation and presented the story of Obos. He reminded that the company makes money that goes to housing construction. Last year, the shovel was put in the ground for over 3,000 homes. He apologized if members have perceived the leadership as arrogant. Although the general meeting does not have the power to replace the CEO, Jostein Starrfelt proposed that the board of directors and the supervisory board should start work on replacing the CEO.
>
> - Everyone gets to express their opinions. That's how member democracy works. As a top manager, you have to endure different views on the job you do, Siraj told us before the meeting.
>
> Starrfelt took the floor and asked everyone to think about whether Siraj should continue to steer the ship.
>
> - I do not believe that the CEO has the right expertise, or the deep-seated commitment needed to renew Obos to become a strong, member-driven organization that engages, listens, and delivers, he said.

The willingness to build for the rich and mighty seemed based on a belief that if Obos made money on the rich and mighty, then there would be even better funding for ordinary homes for ordinary people. In the annual report for Obos for 2020, CEO Siraj wrote that he would help young people into their own first homes by sharing space and saving money:

> Obos is more than building homes and making money. One of the biggest innovations is the brand new home purchase model Bostart and Deleie, which open the way into the housing market for many who would otherwise be left out. An absolutely important task for Obos is the major social mission associated with contributing to life between the houses. NOK 567 million have been returned in the five-year period, both to members and living environments in the form of support for sports, culture, local activities, and social meeting places.

CEO Siraj justified his actions as illustrated as the convenience theme along the willingness dimension in Figure 7.1. In a justification, the actor admits responsibility for the act in question but denies its pejorative and negative content. Justifications are different from denials, excuses, or admissions. In a denial, the actor either disavows that anything untoward happened or denies responsibility for whatever it is that happened. In an excuse, the actor admits the act in question is wrong, but denies having full responsibility for it. In an admission, reference is made to the wrongdoer by name as having engaged in the wrongdoing.

Investigation Report Outcome

Fraud examiners from KPMG (2021) found that there was a close relationship between CEO Siraj and QLR executive Schumann. The tone was comradely. They had extensive contact on various business matters. Siraj never considered his impartiality because he thought his relationship with Schumann was exclusively business-like. The board of directors at Obos had no knowledge of the nature and extent of the relationship, but Siraj informed the board at its meeting in November 2018 that Schumann was chairman of the board of a rental fund set up by a financing fund. Siraj and Schumann confirmed to the examiners that they had known each other as industry colleagues for about ten years. They had both been active in the housing policy debate in politics, participated together on municipal committees, and met each other in various industry contexts. On two occasions they participated together in television programs by the Norwegian public broadcaster NRK. Siraj had used the terms good friend and good buddy about Schumann in social media. They had never visited each other privately, participated together in leisure activities, or had social contact of a private nature. They had never done business together privately, exchanged gifts, or covered expenses among themselves or their respective family members. Siraj did not consider the relationship with Schumann to be a private friendship.

Based on these statements of facts as described by KPMG (2021), fraud examiners found that Siraj's impartiality was decent. They found no information that Siraj had acted in disfavor of Obos and in favor of Schumann and Quality Living Residential. They found no evidence of either infidelity or corruption. The relationship did not constitute a conflict of interest according to Obos' ethical guidelines. There were circumstances that could be perceived externally as the relationship also being of a private nature, but according to the ethical guidelines, examiners found that there was no evidence suitable for weakening the confidence in the CEO's impartiality.

This conclusion relates to the second part of the investigation mandate that was concerned with questions about the relationship between the CEO of Obos and the purchasing representative from QLR. The second mandate part also questioned the relationship between the executive director of housing development and his uncle and cousin who invested in QLR (KPMG, 2021: 5):

> Executive vice president housing development heads the housing development division and has been a board member of Ulven Housing in the period from November 22, 2017 to April 29, 2020. He is a board member of Obos New Homes and other Obos companies. During the period as a board member of Ulven Housing, the executive vice president was involved in the case processing of the Ulven transaction. KPMG has evidence

> that the executive vice president of housing development was contacted by telephone by his wealth advisor on September 4, 2020 in connection with the Ulven transaction. The wealth advisor is also an advisor to the family branch that invested in QLR. In the conversation, the executive vice president became aware that the investment company of the uncle and cousin was considering investing in QLR (…) The audio log of this telephone conversation has been reviewed by the external auditor. KPMG is told that the content does not deal with information that was not otherwise publicly known.

As in the case of the CEO, fraud examiners drew the conclusion that they found no evidence to show that the housing executive acted in favor of any other but the employer Obos. The executive did not act in favor of the investor family, nor in favor of himself. There was no basis found for suggesting insider trading, infidelity, or corruption.

The first part of the investigation mandate was concerned with Obos on the occasion of the development at Ulven where Oslo sold two apartment blocks with a total of 182 apartments to the private rental company Quality Living Residential (QLR) for NOK 936 million. In retrospect, criticism was leveled at Obos from various quarters. The criticism was mainly related to whether the sale fulfills Obos' purpose as a housing association and the members' interests as such. KPMG (2021) concluded that the transaction with QLR did not violate rules and regulations at Obos.

Investigation Maturity Assessment

Fraud examiners at KPMG (2021) concluded in their investigation report that neither executives at Obos nor the company Obos did anything wrong. They had been accused of wrongdoing by some cooperative members in the public. But investigators found nothing wrong. One reason for their conclusion was the limited scope of their investigation. It was mainly a legal exercise to find out whether laws, rules, or guidelines were formally violated. They were not, according to the investigation report.

A broader and more relevant perspective would be the vision and mission of Obos as a provider of affordable housing to less fortunate people in the city of Oslo. Since World War II, Obos had received preferential treatment by state and municipal officials to contribute to the social democratic movement of providing all citizens in Oslo with a decent home that they could own themselves. For example, when land areas were regulated for housing, Obos was an important stakeholder in the city of Oslo.

As emphasized by the critics, Siraj and his team had left the basic idea of Obos as a social instrument in society. This was, however, not an issue in the mandate for the investigation. Fraud examiners were lawyers at KPMG (2021) who only looked at formal violations. While fraud examiners might not be blamed for a very limited mandate, it is nevertheless up to them to accept the assignment, reject the assignment, or request a revision of the mandate.

Based on this assessment, the investigation is assigned level 2 in the maturity model in Figure 7.2 as a problem-oriented investigation, where the problem was whether laws and regulations had been violated.

The formalism rather than substance is evidenced not only in the KPMG (2021) report. Ahead of the report, two legal reviews were made public. One legal review was written by Harald Benestad Anderssen, who was a professor of law at BI Norwegian Business School in Oslo. Anderssen (2021: 1) wrote in his note of consideration

> By telephone call and e-mail on April 21, 2021, I have been asked to assess the legality of certain aspects of a real estate transaction Obos has carried out at Ulven in Oslo. This document is a short version of the full report, also submitted today. This document is a short version of the full report, also submitted today. Assessments and statements in this document are short and incomplete. For the full assessments, referral is made to the complete note of consideration. My mandate is to make "a legal assessment of the legality of the transaction in relation to the statutes and the rules of the Housing Construction Act, and with a conclusion as to whether this is contrary to the statutes or not" (…) Based on the discussion above, I conclude as follows: (1) The agreement between Obos and QLR is not in conflict with the Housing Construction Act. (2) The agreement between Obos and QLR is not in conflict with Obos' statutes.

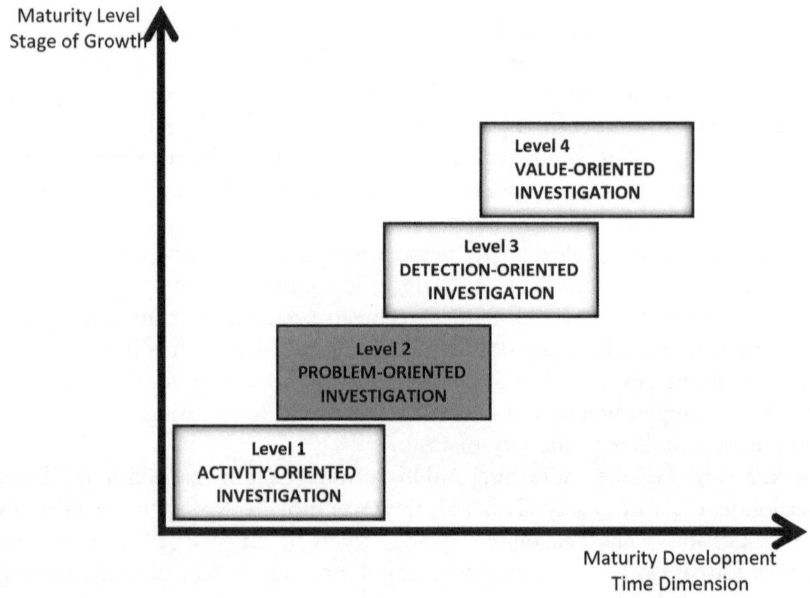

Figure 7.2 Maturity level for the KPMG (2021) investigation at Obos

The complete note of consideration by the law professor was never made publicly available. Nevertheless, it is obvious that the assessment is limited to a narrow perspective of whether or not violations have occurred. There was no assessment of the Ulven transaction being in line with the intentions of Obos statutes. The other legal review by Knudsen and Arvnes (2021: 1) at KPMG was an assessment of the purpose provision of the statutes:

> KPMG Law assists the board of Obos in connection with the investigation of allegations related to Obos' sale of a residential area on Ulven in Oslo to commercial rental business. As part of the mandate, KPMG shall "assess whether the purpose of the sale is in line with Obos' statutes and other relevant rules" (…) The sale of residential area B4 at Ulven in Oslo is in accordance with the statutory purpose of Obos.

While Knudsen and Arvnes (2021) do not find that the Ulven transaction is in line with the main purpose of Obos, they nevertheless conclude that the sale is no violation. The main purpose of Obos is to provide housing to members. The transaction was contrary to the purpose by removing access to 182 apartments for members and transferring those apartments to an outside vendor of rental arrangements.

References

Agnew, R. (2014). Social concern and crime: Moving beyond the assumption of simple self-interest, *Criminology*, 52 (1), 1–32.

Anderssen, H.B. (2021). *Betenkning, kortversjon (Note of Consideration, short version)*, available at www.obos.no, published May 21.

Campbell, J.L. and Göritz, A.S. (2014). Culture corrupts! A qualitative study of organizational culture in corrupt organizations, *Journal of Business Ethics*, 120 (3): 291–311.

Dodge, M. (2009). *Women and White-Collar Crime*, Saddle River, NJ: Prentice Hall.

Hegtun, H. (2021). Granskere har gått inn i PC-en og telefonen hans. «Helt greit», sier presset Obos-sjef (Investigators have entered the PC and his phone. "Quit all right", says the Obos boss), weekly magazine *A-magasinet*, www.aftenposten.no, published June 12.

Holm, E.D. (2021). Er Obos løsningen eller problemet? (Is Obos the solution or the problem?), daily Norwegian newspaper *Aftenposten*, www.aftenposten.no, published June 21.

Jacobsen, S. (2020). Har solgt 182 leiligheter for 936 millioner (Have sold 182 apartments for 936 million), daily Norwegian business newspaper *Finansavisen*, www.finansavisen.no, published December 3.

Jonnergård, K., Stafsudd, A. and Elg, U. (2010). Performance evaluations as gender barriers in professional organizations: A study of auditing firms, *Gender, Work and Organization*, 17 (6), 721–747.

Kakkar, H., Sivanathan, N., and Globel, M.S. (2020). Fall from grace: The role of dominance and prestige in punishment of high-status actors, *Academy of Management Journal*, 63 (2), 530–553.

Knudsen, T.H.R. and Arvnes, E. (2021). *Delrapport til styret i OBOS BBL, Vurdering av vedtektenes formålsbestemmelse, Sammendrag (Sub-report to the board at Obos, Assessment of the statutes' purpose regulation, Summary)*, law firm KPMG, Oslo, Norway, www.obos.no, published June 2.

KPMG (2021). *Ulven-transaksjonen – Granskingsrapport til styret i Obos (The Ulven transaction – Investigation report to the board at Obos)*, law firm KPMG, Oslo, Norway, 34 pages.

Lorch-Falch, S. and Tomter, L. (2021). Slaget om Obos (The battle of Obos), public Norwegian broadcasting corporation *NRK*, www.nrk.no, published June 22.

Lundgaard, H. and Sørgjeld, C. (2021). Milliardene renner inn i Obos-kassen. Men mer enn 80 prosent kommer ikke fra boligbygging (The billions are floating into the Obos cash register. But more than 80 percent do not come from housing construction), daily Norwegian newspaper *Aftenposten*, www.aftenposten.no, published June 21.

Maslow, A.H. (1943). A theory of human motivation, *Psychological Review*, 50 (4), 370–396.

Mauno, H. (2017). Han er pinsevenn og BMW-eier. Men ikke si at han er fra Flekkefjord (He is a Pentecostal friend and BMW owner. But do not say that he is from Flekkefjord), daily Norwegian newspaper *Dagsavisen*, www.dagsavisen.no, published June 25.

McClean, E.J., Martin, S.R., Emich, K.J. and Woodruff, T. (2018). The social consequences of voice: An examination of voice type and gender on status and subsequent leader emergence, *Academy of Management Journal*, 61 (5), 1869–1891.

Oesterud, T.I. (2016). The prices for OBOS housing in Oslo increased by 11.5 percent, *Norway Today*, www.norwaytoday.info, published April 1.

Paternoster, R., Jaynes, C.M. and Wilson, T. (2018). Rational choice theory and interest in the "fortune of others", *Journal of Research in Crime and Delinquency*, 54 (6), 847–868.

Stang, F. (2021). Obos saboterer sitt eget samfunnsoppdrag (Obos sabotages its own social mission), daily Norwegian newspaper *Aftenposten*, www.aftenposten.no, published June 21.

Sørgjeld, C. (2021). På utsiden demonstrerte Obos-opprøret. På innsiden ble de nedstemt (On the outside, the Obos demonstration revolted. On the inside, they were voted down), daily Norwegian newspaper *Aftenposten*, www.aftenposten.no, published June 22.

Welsh, D.T. and Ordonez, L.D. (2014). The dark side of consecutive high performance goals: Linking goal setting, depletion, and unethical behavior, *Organizational Behavior and Human Decision Processes*, 123, 79–89.

8 Samherji Fishing by Wikborg Rein

Samherji is a seafood company in Iceland. The country's largest fishing group was accused of paying bribes to trawl an African country's waters. *Financial Times* reported in November 2019 that two ministers in Namibia had resigned and that Samherji's chief executive had temporarily stepped down over allegations the company paid bribes for fishing quotas in the southern African nation's maritime waters (Cotterill, 2019; Samherji, 2019b). The whistleblower at Samherji was Johannes Stefansson who told WikiLeaks and then Al Jazeera.

Johannes Stefansson came to Namibia in Africa in 2011, where he was assigned the task by the Icelandic seafood company Samherji of looking for business opportunities. To complete the mission, he involved himself in questionable payments to politicians and businesspeople in Namibia and Angola. After a while, he developed a conscience and felt guilty of wrongdoing. He decided to give notice of the situation. The police arrested the former minister of fisheries in Namibia, Bernhard Esau, and indicted him for corruption and money laundering in November 2019. Stefansson provided information to WikiLeaks and then Al Jazeera, where investigative journalist James Kleinfeld interviewed local sources in Namibia. Kleinfeld (2019) then wrote a report on the "Anatomy of a bribe: A deep dive into an underworld of corruption".

Iceland public broadcasting, similar to the BBC in the UK, interviewed the whistleblower and cooperated with Al Jazeera. Al Jazeera's investigative unit secretly filmed officials in Namibia demanding cash in exchange for political favors. It was a story of how foreign companies plunder Africa's natural resources. Using confidential documents provided to Al Jazeera by WikiLeaks, "Anatomy of a Bribe" exposed the government ministers and public officials willing to sell off Namibia's assets in return for millions of dollars in bribes. Al Jazeera journalists spent three months undercover posing as foreign investors looking to exploit the lucrative Namibian fishing industry. The country's minister of fisheries demonstrated a willingness to use a front company to accept a USD 200,000 "donation". Exclusive testimony from a whistleblower, who worked for Iceland's biggest fishing company, revealed that his employer seemingly instructed him to bribe ministers and even the president in return for fishing rights worth hundreds of millions of dollars.

DOI: 10.4324/9781003305071-9

The prosecuting authority in Namibia claimed in December 2019 that the accused officials in the country had received NAD (Namibian dollars) 103 million – equivalent to USD 6 million – in kickbacks to ensure the Icelandic company access to fishing quotas. According to court documents, a large number of false invoices had been made to hide the payments (Kibar, 2020a).

Samherji in Iceland hired fraud examiners at law firm Wikborg Rein in Norway to investigate all of these allegations. The report of investigation was completed in the summer of 2020.

Al Jazeera News Investigation

The broadcasting corporation Al Jazeera investigated allegations and published the report entitled "Anatomy of a bribe: A deep dive into an underworld of corruption", "An Al Jazeera investigation into the corrupt power brokers and global business elites defrauding the Namibian people", and "The storm is brewing – We are preparing ourselves for war" (Kleinfeld, 2019):

> Since Al Jazeera first presented the accused parties with evidence of their alleged wrongdoing, the response has been swift and overwhelming: Minister of Fisheries Bernhard Esau and the minister of justice have both resigned from their cabinet positions; James Hatuikulipi has resigned as the chairman of Fishcor, and has also resigned from his job as the managing director of Investec Asset Management. In the run-up to elections in Namibia, the #Fishrot affair has caused outrage in the country, leading to protests in the capital, Windhoek, with hundreds of people marching to the Anti-Corruption Commission demanding decisive action against corruption in the country. On the day of the elections on November 27, most of the Namibians implicated in the investigation were arrested on charges of corruption, money laundering and fraud.
>
> All the Namibians featured in the Al Jazeera investigation deny all wrongdoing. Sacky Kadhila told The Namibian newspaper that he knew from the start that our undercover reporters were "fake businessmen". "I played along … in order to confirm my suspicions," he wrote. He added that he had reported the matter to the president's lawyer, Sisa Namandje, who in turn claimed he had alerted police.
>
> In Iceland, the scandal has led to the suspension of Samherji's longtime CEO Thorsteinn Mar Baldvinsson, pending an internal investigation. On November 12, Samherji released a statement, saying: "Samherji will co-operate with the relevant authorities that may investigate the fisheries industry in Namibia. If such an investigation will take place, Samherji has nothing to hide." The revelations, reported by Iceland's national broadcasting service RUV (Icelandic National Broadcasting Service – Rikisútvarpiq) and the weekly magazine Stundin, have profoundly shocked this small island nation of 350,000 people. One of the few European countries with no history of colonialism or warmongering, Iceland has long prided itself on its purported

"innocence". Halldora Mogensen, an Icelandic MP with the Pirate Party, put it bluntly: "The myth of Iceland's innocence is dead."

Al Jazeera is an independent news organization funded in part by the Qatari government. In 2006, Al Jazeera Satellite Network was changed to a public utility and private corporation by a public memorandum and articles of association in accordance with the provisions of Qatar Law and was re-named Al Jazeera Media Network. The investigative journalist who wrote the "Anatomy of a bribe" report continued his investigations in Namibia where he detected corruption allegations because of a 5G deal with Huawei. Bribes were offered to politicians to ensure Chinese tech giant Huawei would win an exclusive 5G telecommunication network in Namibia (Kleinfeld, 2020).

Kveikur News Investigation

Johannes Stefansson as whistleblower not only talked to WikiLeaks and Al Jazeera, he also appeared on Icelandic public television. He said that he had approved the payment bribes on behalf of Samherji, and each time with a green light from the company. He claimed that Samherji does whatever it takes to get its hands on the natural resources of other nations. Following the broadcast, Samherji announced that chief executive Baldvinsson had stepped down pending an internal company probe into its Namibian activities. (Cotterill, 2019).

The major newspaper in Namibia, *The Namibian*, followed the corruption scandal closely and reported a number of perspectives on the case. For example, a lawyer suddenly left Namibia after having been interviewed by the Anti-Corruption Commission in connection with the Fishrot fishing quotas corruption scandal (Menges, 2020).

Kveikur is a unit within public broadcasting on Iceland named RUV. Kveikur, the investigative series of RUV, the state broadcaster, has a weekly magazine, *Stundin*. Investigative journalists at Kveikur conduct inquiries that have impacted Iceland. As a result of their work, public officials have been officially censured, the Icelandic parliament has conducted numerous debates, criminal investigations have been instigated, and many stories have led to significant public outcry. Investigative journalists Seljan et al. (2019) published the story "What Samherji wanted hidden":

> This is based on information leaked to Wikileaks which Kveikur has investigated for the past months in collaboration with Al Jazeera Investigation Unit and Stundin. The data leaked to Wikileaks includes thousands of documents and email communication by Samherji's employees. One of them, Johannes Stefansson, also decided to step forward and tell all. Johannes was project manager for Samherji in Namibia until 2016.
>
> "This is criminal activity. It's organized crime. They are benefiting from the country's resources, taking all the money out of the country to invest it elsewhere, in Europe or the US", he says, admitting to having violated the

laws himself. "I violated the law on behalf of Samherji while I was there. I was the man to get the quotas and the connections, on my superiors' orders".

For the past decade Samherji has paid ISK hundreds of millions to high ranking politicians and officials in Namibia with the objective of acquiring the country's coveted fishing quota. For almost a decade, Samherji's Namibian activities have involved three factory fishing trawlers fishing for horse mackerel off the coast. The trawlers have been leased from subsidiaries in Cyprus to two of Samherji's fishing companies in Namibia, Katla, later renamed Mermaria, and Arcticnam, co-owned bySamherji and groups of Namibian quota holders.Samherji has managed to obtain this coveted quota, thus guaranteeing income worth tens of billions ISK. Katla, also known as Mermaria, has been the foremost fishing company and enjoys unusual special terms from the state fishing company, Fishcor, and utilized Namibia and Angola's international agreements.

Investigative journalists at Kveikur included Helgi Seljan Johannsson, Ingolfur Bjarni Sigfussion, Adalsteinn Kjartansson, and Stefan Adalsteinn Drengsson. Three of them published a book in Icelandic entitled "Nothing to hide: On Samherji's trail in Africa" in the spring 2020 (Seljan et al., 2020). In the fall of 2020, Kveikur attempted to get hold of the investigation report by Wikborg Rein submitted to Samherji in the summer. The journalists found that Samherji had not done what they said they would do, which was to give a copy of the report to the prosecutor investigating the case in Iceland. The same applied to Namibian investigators.

Samherji Fishing Press Release

Samherji (2020a) published the following press release on July 29, 2020 using the company website (www.samherji.is/en/moya/news/samherjis-namibia-investigation-finalized):

The Samherji board of directors has received Wikborg Rein's investigation report in relation to the allegations against the company's operations in Namibia. In November 2019, allegations were directed at Samherji and the company's operations in Namibia. The board mandated Norwegian and international law firm Wikborg Rein to assist Samherji in its investigation into the relevant facts. Wikborg Rein is ranked among the leading Nordic law firms within this particular area of law. The firm's lawyers have over decades done vast amounts of similar work for Nordic authorities and international companies.

- Already from the outset we knew that some allegations were outrageous and without basis in reality. One such example related to the German-owned crewing company Cape Cod. The company was dominantly used to pay wages to crews in several countries but portrayed in media as having been a vehicle for a variety of illegal purposes in relation to Namibia. We were further deeply offended by the portrayal of Samherji having exploited a developing nation and walked away with large profits. The total taxes paid in Namibia over the years by entities Samherji was invested in, including income tax, employee tax, export levies, import levies, social security and a number of other payments made to the Namibian state, were about 4 billion Icelandic kroner. That is remarkable in itself considering that Samherji's operations in Namibia were ultimately unprofitable and loss-making, says Mr. Eirikur S. Johannsson, chairman of the Samherji board.

- Other allegations concerned facts about a small part of our global operation in a foreign culture, far from Iceland where we saw a need to have external assistance mapping the relevant facts for us. The alleged facts were simply unknown to us and needed to be scrutinized. So having been faced with serious and fragmented allegations it was very helpful for the Samherji board to receive Wikborg Rein's comprehensive and balanced review of the relevant facts over the years of operation in Namibia, says Mr. Johannsson.

Wikborg Rein has uploaded and analyzed more than a million documents. A large number of relevant personnel have been interviewed. Time has been spent on the ground in several countries, including Namibia. Forensic accounting firm Forensic Risk Alliance (FRA) was also engaged and analyzed payments and other transactions of interest related to the Namibian business. After eight months of work, Wikborg Rein has submitted a comprehensive report substantiating the factual conclusions.

- Having our organization and operations scrutinized is nothing new to Samherji, says Mr. Johannsson.
- In the so-called Central Bank case Samherji was scrutinized for seven years, after which Samherji emerged fully vindicated and victorious. This time we commenced our own investigation and scrutiny in order to get to the bottom of the relevant facts. We have spent vast internal and external resources on this process. Even though the allegations painted a distorted image of our operations, it was important to the company to display to our stakeholders that we take such allegations very seriously, says Mr. Johannsson.

Long before Wikborg Rein's conclusions emerged, Samherji put in place a number of measures to safeguard against further exposure to wrongdoing committed by individuals. All operations in Namibia were stopped already in 2019. On 17 January 2020 Samherji announced that it was in process of launching a modern state-of-the art compliance program which is being implemented throughout our global organization this year: https://www.samherji.is/en/moya/news/samherji-to-implement-corporate-governance-and-compliance-system.

That work is already well underway. Samherji's ambition is to be a pioneer in compliance, governance and internal control within the global fisheries industries.

Samherji will also proactively keep reaching out to relevant authorities that show dedication to mutual cooperation, offering assistance and cooperation during ongoing investigations into the Namibia-related allegations. An agreement is now made for Wikborg Rein to meet with the Icelandic District Prosecutor in the fall. Several meetings have further been held with Namibian authorities in an effort to explore the basis for similar cooperation there.

Once Wikborg Rein have met with relevant authorities, there will be a number of considerations to be taken into account in terms of what findings can be made public and how. We need to assess whether publishing information will jeopardize ongoing investigation in any country. We further need to assess whether publishing certain information will infringe upon laws and regulations concerning protection of individuals mentioned in any findings. Other aspects also need to be taken into consideration.

- We have a need to comment in more detail on the contents of the findings and to rebut allegations that we reacted strongly to when they were made against us last year, says Mr. Johannsson.
- We have respected the integrity of the investigation and left many allegations publicly unanswered despite an urge to comment on them. We equally respect the integrity of still ongoing public investigations. But we will in the coming weeks take a stronger and more vocal stand publicly also in relation to concrete details. Samherji firmly denies that its management ever intended for any subsidiary to engage in wrongful activity, including bribery or money laundering, in order to achieve benefits and will rigorously rebut any further allegation to this effect.

Björgolfur Johannsson was appointed temporarily as chief executive at Samherji while the Wikborg Rein investigated accusations of corruption and money laundering. He expressed already in December 2019 that he did not believe in the allegations that bribes were paid (Schultz and Trumpy, 2019b).

DNB Bank Corrupt Transactions

The alleged corruption payments from Samherji traveled via the Norwegian bank DNB to Esau in Namibia. DNB is Norway's largest lender that faced allegations concerning the Icelandic company that had allegedly transferred money via the bank to bribe Namibian officials. DNB had to investigate the claims. When DNB made the announcement of an internal investigation, Iceland's biggest fishing company, Samherji, said in a statement that it had also hired a law firm to investigate the allegations (Schultz, 2019).

However, at first, Samherji denied any wrongdoing (Samherji, 2019a)

> It has recently been brought to our attention that a former executive of a subsidiary of the company in Namibia, Johannes Stefansson, has spoken to the media and made serious allegations against Samherji's executives, both current and former. We take this very seriously and have engaged the international law firm Wikborg Rein based in Norway to assist us in thorough investigation of our operations in Africa. Until the investigation has been concluded we will not comment on specific allegations
>
> (…)
>
> "All the activities of Samherji and its affiliates were under investigation by authorities for years and no wrongdoings were ever found. All our accounting, e-mails and all other data were thoroughly examined, including that of the companies that have been operating in African waters since 2007. We will not now, like in the past, accept false and misleading allegations of a former employee who once again are prepared by the same parties and media as in the Central Bank-case a few years back," says Thorsteinn Mar Baldvinsson, CEO of Samherji.
>
> At this point in time we believe it is important to disclose that in the beginning of 2016 we came to suspect that something was wrong without operations in Namibia. In order to get better information, we hired a former police officer from the special prosecutor's office to go to Namibia and look into the matter. His investigation led to the dismissal of the aforementioned employee in mid-2016 for unacceptable behavior and conduct. Since then our staff has been trying to take control of our operations in Namibia. During this process the former employee has demanded large sums of money from Samherji.

This statement in a press release from Samherji (2019a) carries the date November 11. It denies any knowledge of wrongdoing and blames the whistleblower Stefansson, who received the blame for misconduct in Namibia. This kind of initial statement is common and similar to initial accounts from companies when they face allegations of misconduct and crime (Gottschalk and Benson, 2020: 949): "Our analysis shows that denial of wrongdoing in several cases is replaced by admission of wrongdoing and scapegoating, while obfuscation of wrongdoing is replaced denial or acceptance of responsibility and scapegoating."

A scapegoat is a person burdened with the wrongdoing of others (Eren, 2020). While CEO Baldvinsson spoke in the previous statement on November 11, he had to step aside three days later, on November 14, when Samherji issued a new press statement (Samherji, 2019b):

> The CEO and board of directors of Samherji have agreed that the CEO Thorsteinn Mar Baldvinsson will step aside for the time being until the

> pending internal investigation into the company's subsidiaries' alleged wrongdoing in Namibia has revealed the key material facts of the matter.

This executive destiny for Baldvinsson is typical as illustrated in the research by Gottschalk and Benson (2020). They found that corporations tend to distance themselves from individuals so that the corporations can survive. Corporations reassign, force to resign, or fire senior leaders. At Samherji, the board hired a new CEO, Bjorgolfur Johannsson, when Baldvinsson had to step down in November 2019. Four months later, Baldvinsson returned to Samherji, now in a position as co-CEO with Johannsson without any real executive power. The company then stated that the fraud examination by Wikborg Rein was to continue (Samherji, 2020a): "Wikborg Rein's reporting lines will remain to the board of directors, and Mr. Johannsson will remain dedicated to providing any assistance needed for Wikborg Rein."

According to Reuters (2019), Samherji transferred more than USD 70 million through a shell company in the tax haven Marshall Islands from 2011 to 2018. Samherji transferred the money through bank accounts in DNB Norway. The bank's largest shareholder is the Norwegian state, which holds 34% stake in the bank (Reuters, 2019):

> The money consisted partly of proceeds from Samherji's questionable and possibly unlawful operations in Namibia where the company bribes officials to get secure access to fishing quotas. The company in the Marshall Islands was used to pay salaries to the crews of Samherji's factory trawlers. These trawlers fished horse mackerel in Mauritania, Morocco, and Namibia.

The Norwegian bank DNB was heavily involved in the Panama Papers scandal, where the bank had helped rich people in their wealth management program to hide large sums of money in tax havens (Brustad and Hustadnes, 2016; Langset et al., 2016; Tanum, 2016). Fraud examiners from law firm Hjort (2016) investigated the case. The bank neglected to monitor its client transactions through the bank and thus risked being a vehicle for money laundering and tax evasion.

The Samherji scandal forced the bank to conduct yet another internal investigation (Reuters, 2019):

> "Like every other bank, we are guided to take action if the clients do not give us the necessary information that we need to have so that the bank can have good control over how the client uses the bank," said DNB's spokesman, Even Westerveld. "This can sometimes mean that the bank freezes the accounts of clients or off boards him. Unfortunately, we do not officially hold count how often this happens within the bank."

Økokrim is the Norwegian national authority for investigation and prosecution of economic and environmental crime, similar to the serious fraud office in the

United Kingdom or the fraud units at the FBI in the United States. They started investigating Samherji and DNB in November 2019 (Ekroll et al., 2019):

> Økokrim is launching an investigation into DNB related to the Icelandic fisheries case. Økokrim has started an investigation at DNB after disclosure of possible corruption and money laundering in an Icelandic fishing company where DNB has been their bank. The Icelandic fishing group Samherji faced accusation of corruption and illegal cooperation with Namibian state officials. Several of them are now in prison, and others are on the run in the country. Samherji faces allegations of having used DNB to transfer money via tax havens, and to an African official who owns a company in Dubai. In total, Samherji allegedly used DNB to transfer NOK 640 million to a tax haven, according to Icelandic media. Økokrim is now investigating Norway's largest financial group.
>
> "The purpose of the investigation is to find out what has happened and whether criminal offenses have been committed. It is natural that we cooperate with the authorities of other countries working on the case complex. We are at an early stage and will not be providing more information about the investigation now," acting Økokrim chief, Hedvig Moe, writes in a press release.

Økokrim is the main source of specialist skills for the police and the prosecuting authorities in their combat against crime of this kind. The board at DNB was headed by Olaug Svarva, and the chief executive at the bank was Kjerstin Braathen. Norwegian business newspaper *Dagens Næringsliv* also reported that Økokrim had started an investigation into DNB's involvement in the Samherji scandal (Solgård and Trumpy, 2019):

> On Wednesday afternoon, Økokrim writes in a press release that they will investigate DNB Bank in connection with the Samherji case, which has been covered by a number of national and international media in recent weeks. "Økokrim has started an investigation against DNB Bank. As reported in several media, the case concerns an Icelandic fisheries group and alleged corruption in Namibia. DNB Bank is referred to as a bank client for the fishing group", the report states.
>
> - The aim of the investigation is to find out what has happened, and whether criminal acts have been committed. It is natural that we cooperate with the authorities in other countries that work on the same case complex. We are in an early phase and will not provide more information about the investigation now, says acting Økokrim executive Hedvig Moe in the press release.
>
> The case concerns the Icelandic fishing giant Samherji on Iceland, which for a number of years is said to have used DNB to squander money

> via tax havens – and to an African official who owns a company in Dubai. It is unknown how much of the funds can be linked to possible money laundering and potential bribery.

Norwegian bank DNB ended the client relationship with Samherji in 2018. This was more than one year after bank executives at DNB learned about the risk and the potential scandal. In 2015, DNB did make a customer update regarding Samherji registered on the Marshall Island, but bank executives failed in establishing an overview of the real owners (Schultz and Trumpy, 2019a; Solgård and Trumpy, 2019).

On the previous and following pages, it is referred to Økokrim, which is the serious fraud office in Norway investigating and prosecuting financial crime. When a new chief executive at Økokrim was appointed, the police agency could no longer investigate the role of the bank DNB in potential money laundering of funds from Iceland to Namibia via Norway. The reason for Økokrim's lack of integrity and impartiality in the case was the background of the newly appointed chief executive. Pål Lønseth, the new executive, was recruited to the agency from the private fraud examination team at audit and accounting firm PricewaterhouseCoopers. In his role as fraud examiner, he had been investigating financial transactions linked to the Samherji scandal. Since the principle is that all subordinates are automatically disqualified if someone higher up is disqualified to handle a matter, Økokrim had to declare that the whole agency might suffer from partiality. Therefore, the investigation of the bank DNB on suspicion of money laundering had to be transferred to one of the police districts in Norway. Each police district has a unit specializing in financial crime. However, those local units are not as qualified at the national agency Økokrim. Therefore, it was reason to expect that DNB would avoid serious scrutiny by a police district unit and thus survive charges even if they were guilty of helping Samherji to launder money for bribes.

Different from Økokrim, local police districts are not part of international law enforcement networks. Therefore, the director of public prosecutions at the higher prosecuting authorities in Norway did not know what to do with the DNB investigation several months after Pål Lønseth had disqualified Økokrim from the investigation. Lønseth was appointed head of Økokrim on Friday, June 12, 2020. Four months later, on October 15, prosecution director Jørn Sigurd Maurud had still not decided what to do with the DNB investigation that was terminated at Økokrim. Police inspector Ole Rasmus Knudsen, who was in charge of white-collar crime investigations in the Oslo police district, had heard nothing about the case being transferred to them. The likely outcome for DNB was again that DNB executives would avoid prosecution in the Samherji scandal, like they avoided prosecution in the Panama Papers scandal four years earlier. However, an investigative journalist became interested in why Maurud seemingly did nothing to allocate the DNB investigation. Maurud then replied on November 2 that the higher prosecuting authorities were in the process of transferring the case to the Oslo police district.

As mentioned earlier, Samherji transferred more than USD 70 million through a shell company in the tax haven Marshall Islands from 2011 to 2018 (Reuters, 2019). Samherji transferred the money allegedly through bank accounts in DNB Norway. In the fall of 2020, Norwegian police seemed reluctant to investigate the matter, almost one year after they first learned about the potential money laundering in the Norwegian bank.

Attorney general Maurud published a press release on September 29, 2020

> The chief at Økokrim has informed the public prosecutor that he considers himself incompetent in four cases that are under investigation by the unit. The attorney general bases the assessment of the question of impartiality on his judgment, and has decided that the case responsibility will be transferred from Økokrim to another regional public prosecutor's office with an associated police district. Until the cases have been moved, no further investigation is currently being carried out. There will be a clarification relatively soon concerning who will take over case responsibility, so that no significant consequences are expected for, among other things, the progress of the investigation. The other public prosecutor's offices and police districts regularly handle cases of financial crime, including extensive and complicated matters, and the attorney general therefore has confidence that the investigation and prosecution are well taken care of in the cases that are transferred. It is in the nature of the cases that Økokrim – as a unit with special responsibility for the case area – in some cases possesses competence that is not as easy to find elsewhere. To the extent that assistance from Økokrim is deemed necessary so that the quality of the investigation does not suffer, the attorney general has, pursuant to section 60 of the criminal procedure act, the opportunity to decide that certain employees at Økokrim may assist in the further investigation, under the direction of the new public prosecutor. Whether this may become relevant will depend on, for example, what kind of criminal act is being investigated, which investigative methods are relevant, and how far the investigation has come already. The attorney general will return to this issue after a closer assessment in the individual case.

Whistleblower Johannes Stefansson

Johannes Stefansson remained active and willing to respond to media requests for interviews. After the press release from Samherji cited earlier, the whistleblower was interviewed by Norwegian business newspaper *Dagens Næringsliv*. The heading of the interview was entitled "The Whistleblower: He announced the biggest corruption case a Norwegian bank has been involved in, but Johannes Stefansson was never contacted by Økokrim" (Kibar, 2020a: 33):

Nobody from Norway has contacted me or my lawyer so far, says Johannes Stefansson, the man who reported the biggest known corruption case a Norwegian bank has been involved in…

It is very strange that I have not heard anything. And there is some concern related to developments in Norway and Iceland. Investigators in Namibia have said that the investigation drags out there and other places, the whistleblower says…

Økokrim has probably known about the case since early 2019, says Stefansson. In a few weeks, he will be ready to return to Namibia for the first time since he blew the whistle – together with a bodyguard with a background from some special forces…

Johannes Stefansson was for many years a very autonomous leader for our business in Namibia. We are in a comprehensive process of implementing systems in our global business so that it can never happen again, writes acting CEO Björgolfur Johannson in an email to us. He characterizes Stefansson's statements about the company as "incorrect, in some respects grossly incorrect"…

Can it affect your credibility that you yourself have been involved in corruption?

That is okay. The documents will speak for themselves. I am just the tour guide.

When a scandal hits a company, then the blame game starts, and scapegoating occurs. Management tries to separate the company from the scandal by identifying an individual to blame (Gottschalk and Benson, 2020). A typical example is given in the previous statement that "Johannes Stefansson was for many years a very autonomous leader for our business in Namibia".

Stefansson worked for 14 months with investigators in Namibia before the case became public knowledge. Namibian investigators sought the assistance of Interpol to conduct investigations in Dubai, the Democratic Republic of Congo, Zimbabwe, Angola, Cyprus, and Spain, in addition to Iceland and Norway. The arrested officials in Namibia were called The Fishrot Six.

Stefansson was originally a fisherman like his father. After being at sea for more than a decade aboard large trawlers in the Atlantic, the Indian Ocean, and eastern Russia, he gradually gained management positions in production facilities at various seafood companies. Soon he got a job in Iceland's largest fishing company with a position that involved a lot of travel. The task for him was to open up new markets for Samherji. He got his first managerial position at Samherji's Moroccan company. As a foreign company, Samherji could not come up with direct bids. However, local actors who won the tenders could resell their rights to parts of an annual quota of tons of horse mackerel. Stefansson quickly had sound agreements signed with three local quota owners.

Bribes in Namibia were seldom in cash. It happened most of the time with invoices. Stefansson had access to the Samherji bank accounts in Namibia. Some minor payments came directly from Norway.

When the scandal became public, Samherji headquarters wanted Stefansson to return immediately to Iceland. He was reluctant to do so in fear of potential reprisals and retaliations. He established contact with an IT expert in South Africa to gather as much information as possible that could document his claims about the company's allegedly corrupt business practice. He saved all the emails from his computer in South Africa. He delayed his return to Iceland with various excuses, at the same time as he shut the rest of the company out of his own dropbox. While Samherji management thought he was on his way home, he secured a total of 40 gigabytes of documentation. He stored everything on several hard drives, which he sent by courier to different parts of the world. It took him two days to empty his personal computer and secure the contents.

Stefansson then received numerous threats, and he observed hacking attempts on his digital equipment. Rumors were spreading about an extravagant lifestyle, affairs with women, alcohol addiction, and drug abuse. At one point in time, he stayed in hiding for five days after receiving a message that they wanted to take him out. He got help from Christian Yema, a Congolese friend he had only known for six months and who was an experienced bodyguard with a background from the military and special force units. Stefansson also got help from the organization Platform to Protect Whistleblowers in Africa, which has provided protection to people in some of the largest corruption cases that have been detected on the African continent – including the latest corruption disclosure related to Angola's president's daughter Isabel dos Santos' business activities.

Stefansson blew the whistle on white-collar crime in the fisheries sector. Witbooi et al. (2020) argue that organized crime in the fisheries sector threatens a sustainable ocean economy

> The threat of criminal activity in the fisheries sector has concerned the international community for a number of years. In more recent times, the presence of organized crime in fisheries has come to the fore (…) Organized criminal groups may share characteristics with conventional businesses, such as their structure and capability, and frequently operate in the white-collar realm. The ability of the network to protect its operations (the protection economy) – through violence, bribery or extortion – is a common, but not necessarily defining, feature of organized crime.

Wikborg Rein Fraud Investigation

Law firm Wikborg Rein headquartered in Oslo, Norway, was hired by Samherji in Iceland to investigate allegations of wrongdoing in Namibia. The law firm was also hired by the Icelandic company to help solve current issues in Namibia. The examiners thus accepted a double role that is problematic. One problem was that the examiners might make mistakes and wrongdoing while solving current issues in Namibia. If they did, then they could not investigate those mistakes or that wrongdoing, simply because you cannot investigate your own action. Another problem was the trustworthiness of the investigation report in terms of independence and objectivity. Critics may easily argue that the report was biased to satisfy the client, who provided the firm with additional legal work.

Unfortunately, the practice of some law firms of taking on additional assignments for clients is not uncommon. While a private investigation by fraud examiners should be independent and objective, where investigators are accountable, it is tempting for a law firm to take on more work for the client. Some law firms are the main legal advisor to the client on a continuous basis. Some audit firms are the main external auditor of the client's accounts on a continuous basis. This is unfortunate, as the reader should be skeptical of investigation reports from such firms.

The following email exchange between the journalist Osman Kibar at daily Norwegian business newspaper *Dagens Næringsliv* and examiners Geir Sviggum and Elisabeth Roscher at Wikborg Rein in August 2020 illustrates the issue

KIBAR: Icelandic media have questioned that Wikborg Rein assisted Samherji in negotiations related to the business even before you were hired for the investigation. Has this been a topic and what is Wikborg Rein's possible comment on this?

SVIGGUM: Wikborg Rein had no ongoing assignments for Samherji when we were instructed by the board to carry out this assignment. We have also never before had any involvement with Samherji's operations in Namibia. So this is incorrect. During the process, it has been desirable for Samherji that we should assist in matters that have had a close and immediate connection to the investigation process and the fact that has been revealed there. This applies, for example, to a controlled closure of the business in Namibia and a legal exit from the country in dialogue with the Namibian authorities. We further assisted in implementing immediate measures to prevent further exposure to the conditions that were the subject of accusations. But all this derives directly from the accusations the company was exposed to in November last year.

It comes as no surprise that the whistleblower, Stefansson, did not want to contribute to Samherji's own investigation of the allegations against the company. Stefansson was repeatedly invited to an interview with Wikborg Rein as part of Samherji's own investigation process. Whistleblowers tend to suffer retaliation (Mesmer-Magnus and Viswesvaran, 2005; Park et al., 2020; Rehg et al., 2009; Shawver and Clements, 2019), misleading presentation of their views, as well as wrongful judgment of their statements in reports of investigations. The preference of cooperating with the criminal justice system, such as public prosecutors, but not with fraud examiners paid by the scandalized company, makes sense.

Given the lack of contribution from the whistleblower Stefansson, the findings in the report of investigation by Wikborg Rein became even less trustworthy. Given the task of reconstructing past events and sequence of events without access to the main source of information, the report became even less complete and objective.

The previously cited email exchange between the journalist Osman Kibar at daily Norwegian business newspaper *Dagens Næringsliv* and examiners Geir

Sviggum and Elisabeth Roscher at Wikborg Rein ended up in a newspaper article in early September 2020 under the heading "Both cleaned up and investigated fishing giant" (Kibar, 2020b: 18):

> Law firm Wikborg Rein assisted the Icelandic fishing giant Samherji in negotiations connected to the business activity after the company hired the firm to investigate Samherji. Norwegian law professors have different views on the roles of Wikborg Rein.
>
> We wrote in the beginning of August that Wikborg Rein has handed over a comprehensive report of investigation of the Icelandic fishing giant Samherji accused of corruption to the client Samherji. The law firm shall, among other things, have reviewed more than one million documents. Icelandic media, led by the state channel RUV, have reported that Wikborg Rein assisted Samherji in negotiations related to business activities in Namibia, after the firm was hired to conduct the investigation – and whether this could affect the independence and impartiality of the law firm.
>
> Professor Petter Gottschalk in the department of leadership and organizational behavior at BI Norwegian Business School says that Wikborg Rein behaves reprehensible.
>
> - Investigators must be independent of everything that has happened, is happening, and can happen. If investigators in other roles perform actions that prove to be unfortunate and harmful, the investigators cannot examine such matters. One cannot examine oneself. Therefore, it is reprehensible that Wikborg Rein has taken on other assignments for Samherji in addition to the investigation, says Gottschalk.
> - That Wikborg Rein has undertaken other assignments for Samherji weakens the credibility of the investigation report. The report can now easily be perceived as commissioned work, he adds.

Samherji remained silent and rejected to disclose the investigation report by Wikborg Rein. Instead, a new press release referred to the report in a manipulative manner to present the white-collar crime case as a matter of a rotten apple. A single, standalone white-collar criminal can be described as a rotten apple, but when several are involved in crime, and corporate culture virtually stimulates offenses, then it is more appropriate to describe the phenomenon as a basket of rotten apples or as a rotten apple orchard, as Punch (2003: 172) defined them: "The metaphor of 'rotten orchards' indicate(s) that it is sometimes not the apple, or even the barrel that is rotten but the *system* (or significant parts of the system)."

Margrét Ólafsdóttir, chief communications officer at Samherji in Iceland, attempted implicitly to blame the whistleblower in her new press release entitled "Fees for quotas were in line with market prices in Namibia" (Samherji, 2020b)

> After Norwegian law firm Wikborg Rein finalized its investigation, into the activities of companies affiliated with Samherji in Namibia on July 28th

and presented its findings to Samherji's board, the company has in various ways corrected and refuted allegations that have been made against it. Samhjeri has now commissioned an analysis of the pricing of the quotas that companies affiliated with Samherji leased while operating in Namibia. The analysis consisted of a comparison of prices in catching agreements between unrelated parties. The comparison confirms that companies affiliated with Samherji paid the market price for quotas. Companies affiliated with Samherji were never allocated any catch quotas in Namibia. Instead, the companies leased the right to quotas that had been allocated to locals.

We have already released information about the losses suffered in Namibia and the taxes paid to local authorities. This statement, however, is related to an audit that Samherji commissioned due to allegations that the price paid for the lease of fishing rights under agreements with Fishcor and Namgomar was far below the market price. While Samherji's companies were operating in Namibia, they leased catching rights from private entities, such as the joint ventures and the company Namgomar, which was granted quotas pursuant to an international fishing agreement between Angola and Namibia. They also leased catching rights from Fishcor, a Namibian-owned fishing company. Samherji firmly denies that quotas were leased from these parties at a price that was lower than the market price. Allegations to that effect are unfounded. In fact, the price paid under the agreements with Fishcor and Namgomar was always equal to or higher than the price paid by Samherji-affiliated companies to other quota holders in Namibia.

The allegations that have been made about the price for quotas form part of a larger narrative according to which companies affiliated with Samherji are accused of having paid bribes to secure catching agreements grossly below market prices. It has also been claimed that companies in the Samherji Group did everything in their power to pay as low tax in Namibia as possible and that these contributing factors, together with the rich profits from operations in Namibia, mean that Samherji was in fact robbing a developing country.

In order to find out what the correct market price was for catch quotas during the years that companies affiliated with Samherji had had operations in Namibia, agreements with six unrelated Namibian companies that held catch quotas were reviewed. Each of these companies was profit-driven and operated in the open market. The price in these agreements was then compared with the price paid by companies affiliated with Samherji under agreements with Fishcor and Nambomar. A total of thirty-nine comparisons were made. In all but one case, the price paid by Samherji for catch quotas under agreements with Fishcor and Namgomar was equal to or higher than the price paid under agreements with other companies. A price comparison was also made in similar agreements made by other commercial fishing companies, domestic and foreign, with quota holders in Namibia. This was done to ensure that the price paid by Samherji's affiliates under agreements with Fishcor and Namgomar was not unreasonably low and also to dispel suspicions that the agreements relied on had been selected explicitly to ensure a favorable outcome. In the vast majority of the contracts examined in this second wave of comparisons, the Fishcor and Namgomar fees were equal to, or higher than, fees in other commercial fishing companies' contracts with Namibian quota holders.

Despite the fact that individual employees did not follow procedures and working methods that Samherji strives for in all its operations, it is clear that the company is responsible for discipline and supervision and must intervene decisively when the required vigilance is not maintained. It seems clear that the leasing of catch quotas in Namibia has in some cases lacked such control and intervention. However, this does not change the main conclusion of this analysis, which is that companies affiliated with Samherji paid market prices for the quota they leased. In the near future, Samherji will continue to correct misrepresentations and at the same time report on procedures and working methods that were deficient.

White-Collar Crime Convenience

Both the briber and the bribed in a corruption relationship have their financial motives, organizational opportunities, and willingness for deviant behaviors. They enter into a relationship with mutual illegal benefits (Huang and Knight, 2017). In Figure 8.1, themes for the briber are with texture, while themes for the bribed are in dark gray. The briber has a motive of obtaining fishing rights in the Namibian ocean zone, which is corporate crime (Bittle and Hébert, 2020), while the bribed can make an extraordinary profit, which is possible because of the individual's decision rights as the minister of fishery. This is occupational crime (Goldstraw-White, 2012; Shepherd and Button, 2019).

Johannes Stefansson had access to resources (Berghoff and Spiekermann, 2018) in terms of corruption payments from Samherji via the Norwegian bank DNB to Esau in Namibia, as suggested by the axis opportunity-commit-access in the figure. It is a rational choice for the briber (Kamerdze et al., 2014) to get involved in corruption to improve corporate profitability in the Icelandic fishing empire of Samherji.

The bribed can neutralize potential feelings of guilt by arguing that he would have triggered the same agreements anyway (Benson, 1985). The briber, Samherji, can neutralize guilt feelings by claiming that they do so much good in Namibia by creating jobs in fisheries and paying taxes to the local government. Samherji can claim that it was necessary to carry out the offense since Namibia is a corrupt country. The offender then claims that the offense belongs in a larger context, where the crime is an illegal element among many legal elements to ensure an important result. The offense was a required and necessary means to achieve an important goal. A bribe represents nothing in dollar value compared to the potential income from a large contract abroad and compared to the local benefit of jobs and business abroad.

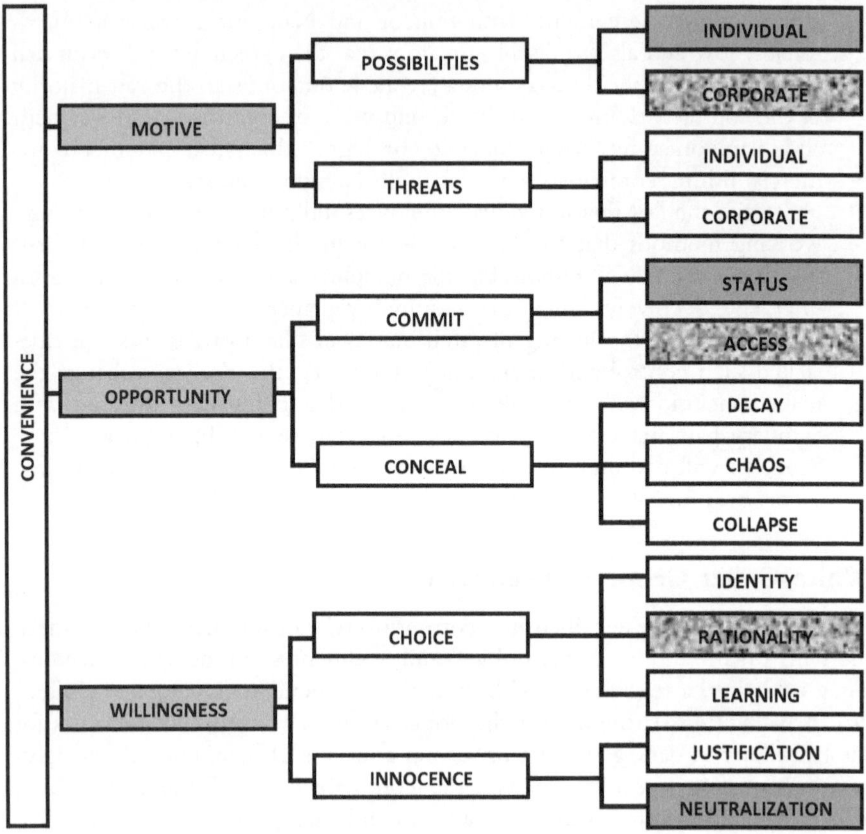

Figure 8.1 Convenience themes in the case of Samherji

Al Jazeera Investigation Evaluation

The investigation report by Kleinfeld (2019) is a documentary television program of 51 minutes accessible at Al Jazeera, YouTube, and other platforms. The documentary was a tremendous success and caused police involvement in Iceland, Norway, and Namibia. It was mature detection-oriented work by investigative journalists at level 3 as indicated in Figure 8.2. The media coverage represented disclosure and clarification of misconduct and crime.

Al Jazeera exposed public figures close to Namibian president Hage Geingob discussing laundering of political contributions. Posing as Chinese investors, Al Jazeera journalists attempted to enter the Namibian fishing industry to acquire highly lucrative fishing quotas for a proposed joint venture with Namibian fishing company Omualu. During the Al Jazeera investigation, Esau requested a donation of USD 200,000 from the Chinese "investors" to the ruling Swapo party, preferably ahead of the nation's general election that was scheduled at

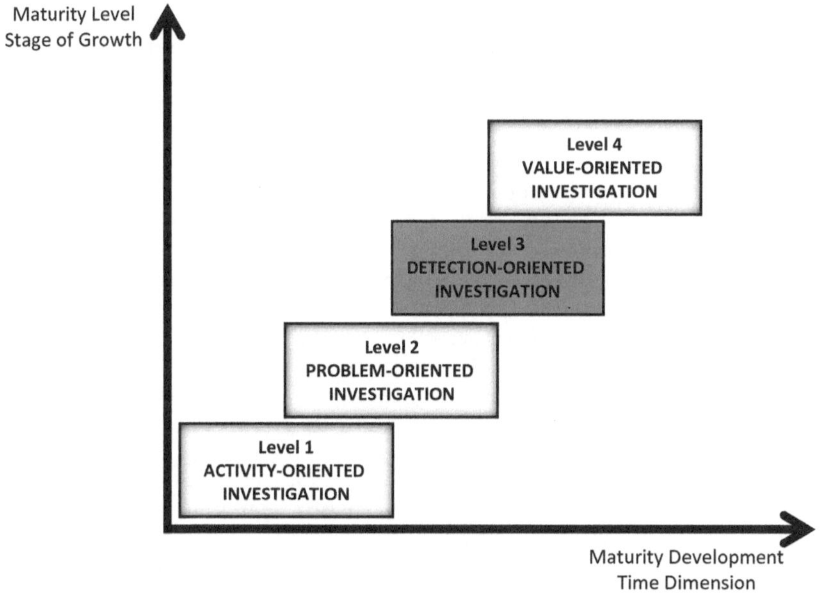

Figure 8.2 Maturity model for investigative journalism by Kleinfeld (2019) at Al Jazeera

that time. Filmed with hidden cameras, Esau is visible when accepting an iPhone from Al Jazeera's reporter.

Under the instructions of Omualu's managing director Sacky Kadhila-Amoomo, the assumed donation should secretly move into the Swapo party, under the disguise of a foreign investment in real estate. Furthermore, the assumed donation should channel through the trust account of Sisa Namandje, who had been the personal lawyer for all Namibian presidents since the nation's independence in 1990.

References

Benson, M.L. (1985). Denying the guilty mind: Accounting for involvement in a white-collar crime, *Criminology*, 23 (4), 583–607.

Berghoff, H. and Spiekermann, U. (2018). Shady business: On the history of white-collar crime, *Business History*, 60 (3), 289–304.

Bittle, S. and Hébert, J. (2020). Controlling corporate crimes in times of de-regulation and re-regulation, in: Rorie, M.L. (editor), *The Handbook of White-Collar Crime*, Hoboken, NJ: Wiley & Sons, chapter 30, pages 484–501.

Brustad, L. and Hustadnes, H. (2016). -Bjerke har forsømt lederansvaret uansett (-Bjerke has neglected the management responsibility regardless), daily Norwegian newspaper *Dagbladet*, www.dagbladet.no, published April 11.

Cotterill, J. (2019). Two Namibian ministers resign in Icelandic fishing scandal, *Financial Times*, www.ft.com, published November 14.

Ekroll, H.C., Breian, Å. and NTB (2019). Økokrim starter etterforskning av DNB i forbindelse med islandsk fiskerisak (Økokrim is launching an investigation into DNB related to the Icelandic fisheries case), daily Norwegian newspaper *Aftenposten*, www.aftenposten, published November 29.

Eren, C.P. (2020). Cops, firefighters, and scapegoats: Anti-money laundering (AML) professionals in an era of regulatory bulimia, *Journal of White Collar and Corporate Crime*, pages 1–12, published online doi:10.1177/2631309X20922153.

Goldstraw-White, J. (2012). *White-Collar Crime: Accounts of Offending Behavior*, London, UK: Palgrave Macmillan.

Gottschalk, P. and Benson, M.L. (2020). The evolution of corporate accounts of scandals from exposure to investigation, *British Journal of Criminology*, 60, 949–969.

Hjort (2016). *Rapport til styret i DNB (report to the board at DNB)*, bank mentioned in the Panama Papers, report of investigation, 18 pages, law firm Hjort, Oslo, Norway.

Huang, L. and Knight, A.P. (2017). Resources and relationships in entrepreneurship: An exchange theory of the development and effects of the entrepreneur-investor relationship, *Academy of Management Review*, 42 (1), 80–102.

Kamerdze, S., Loughran, T., Paternoster, R. and Sohoni, T. (2014). The role of affect in intended rule breaking: Extending the rational choice perspective, *Journal of Research in Crime and Delinquency*, 51 (5), 620–654.

Kibar, O. (2020a). Varsleren (The whistleblower: He announced the biggest corruption case a Norwegian bank has been involved in, but Johannes Stefansson was never contacted by Økokrim), daily Norwegian business newspaper *Dagens Næringsliv*, Saturday, August 8, pages 32–37.

Kibar, O. (2020b). Både ryddet opp for og gransket fiskerikjempe (Both cleaned up and investigated fishing giant), daily Norwegian business newspaper *Dagens Næringsliv*, Tuesday, September 1, pages 18–19.

Kleinfeld, J. (2019). Anatomy of a bribe: A deep dive into an underworld of corruption, news organization *Al Jazeera*, www.aljazeera.com, published December 1.

Kleinfeld, J. (2020). Corruption allegations in Namibian 5G deal with Huawei, news organization *Al Jazeera*, www.aljazeera.com, published July 15.

Langset, M., Ertesvåg, F. and Ensrud, S. (2016). BI-professor: -Det vil bli rettssaker (BI professor: -There will be court cases), daily Norwegian newspaper *VG*, published April 6, page 7.

Menges, W. (2020). Fishrot lawyer fights to stay on as executor, *The Namibian*, www.namibian.com, published August 6.

Mesmer-Magnus, J.R. and Viswesvaran, C. (2005). Whistleblowing in an organization: An examination of correlates of whistleblowing intentions, actions, and retaliation, *Journal of Business Ethics*, 62 (3), 266–297.

Park, H., Bjørkelo, B. and Blenkinsopp, J. (2020). External whistleblowers' experiences of workplace bullying by superiors and colleagues, *Journal of Business Ethics*, 161, 591–601.

Punch, M. (2003). Rotten orchards. "Pestilence", police misconduct and system failure, *Policing and Society*, 13, (2) 171–196.

Rehg, M.T., Miceli, M.P., Near, J.P. and Scotter, J.R.V (2009). Antecedents and outcomes of retaliation against whistleblowers: Gender differences and power relationships, *Organization Science*, 19 (2), 221–240.

Reuters (2019). Norway's DNB investigates allegedly improper Samherji payments to Namibia, *Under Current News*, www.undercurrentnews.com, published November 15.

Samherji (2019a). Statement from Samherji: Press release, www.samherji.is, published November 11 by margret@samherji.is.

Samherji (2019b). Samherji CEO steps aside while investigations are ongoing, www.samherji.is, published November 14 by margret@samherji.is.

Samherji (2020a). Samherji's Namibia investigation finalized, Samherji ice fresh seafood, website, www.samherji.is/en/moya/news/samherjis-namibia-investigation-finalized, Akureyri, Iceland, published by margret@samherji.is.

Samherji (2020b). Fees for quotas were in line with market prices in Namibia, Samherji seafood, www.samherji.is, published September 25 by Margrét Ólafsdóttir, margret@samherji.is.

Schultz, J. (2019). Wikborg Rein-gransker om Samherji: -Planen er å være ute av Namibia innen få måneder (Wikborg Rein investigator about Samherji: -The plan is to be out of Namibia within a few months), daily Norwegian business newspaper *Dagens Næringsliv*, www.dn.no, published December 1.

Schultz, J. and Trumpy, J. (2019a). NRK: DNB brukte mer enn et år på å stenge Samherji-kontoer (NRK: DNB spent more than a year to close Samherji accounts), Norwegian daily business newspaper *Dagens Næringsliv*, www.dn.no, published August 26.

Schultz, J. and Trumpy, J. (2019b). Björgolfur Johannsson ble Samherji-sjef etter hvitvaskingsavsløring: -Jeg tror ikke det har vært noen bestikkelser, Norwegian daily business newspaper *Dagens Næringsliv*, www.dn.no, published December 13.

Seljan, H., Kjartansson, A. and Drengsson, S.A. (2019). What Samherji wanted hidden, Kveikur at *RUV*, public broadcasting on Iceland, www.ruv.is/kveikur/fishrot/fishrot.

Seljan, H., Kjartansson, A. and Drengsson, S.A. (2020). *Ekkert að fela: á slóð Samherja í Afríku (Nothing to hide: On Samherji's trail in Africa)*, VH: Útgefandi.

Shawver, T. and Clements, L.H. (2019). The impact of value preferences on whistleblowing intentions of accounting professionals, *Journal of Forensic and Investigative Accounting*, 11 (2), 232–247.

Shepherd, D. and Button, M. (2019). Organizational inhibitions to addressing occupational fraud: A theory of differential rationalization, *Deviant Behavior*, 40 (8), 971–991.

Solgård, J. and Trumpy, J. (2019). Økokrim har startet etterforsking av DNB (Økokrim has started investiging DNB), Norwegian daily business newspaper *Dagens Næringsliv*, www.dn.no, published November 28.

Tanum, A.C. (2016). DNB Luxembourg – Redegjørelse fra styret (DNB Luxembourg – Statement from the Board), brev til Nærings- og fiskeridepartementet ved statsråd Monica Mæland (letter to the department of industry and fishery attention minister Monica Mæland), April 11, Oslo, Norway.

Witbooi, E., Ali, K.D., Santosa, M.A., Hurley, G., Husein, Y., Maharaj, S., Okafor-Yarwood, I., Quiroz, I.A. and Salas, O. (2020). Organized crime in the fisheries sector threatens a sustainable ocean economy, *Nature*, published online, doi:10.1038/s41586-020-2913-5.

9 Wirecard Banking by KPMG

The background for the investigation of Wirecard by KPMG (2020a, 2020b) was to examine the validity of various accusations that were presented in the press and on the Internet (Chazan and Storbeck, 2020a). Among these allegations, it was suggested that Wirecard has, among other things, recorded higher revenues through fictitious customer relationships, suspicious loan relationships through what is called merchant cash advance, over reporting of profits in the Singapore branch and in the United Arab Emirates, and a suspicious transaction by a company in India (McCrum, 2019). The allegations were concerned with deficiencies in the accounts and mysterious collaborations with third-party companies in countries such as Singapore, the United Arab Emirates, and India (McCrum, 2020; Storbeck, 2020a, 2020b). The suspected fraud was concerned with bankruptcy fraud where trusted executives removed funds to secret destinations before the financial institution collapsed.

The reason why Wirecard wanted to launch an independent investigation was based on these accusations in the media. Especially in the newspaper *Financial Times*, a number of articles were published suggesting that Wirecard used fictitious customers and trading partners to be able to report more income and wealth than was real (Chazan, 2021; Chazan and Storbeck, 2020a, 2020b; Storbeck, 2020a, 2020b, 2021a, 2021b; Storbeck and Morris, 2021; McCrum, 2015, 2019, 2020). The misconduct can be considered a form of fraud where Wirecard tries to deceive potential customers, banks, and investors.

Wirecard was a technology-based financial services company in Germany that began its operation in 2002 as a German payment processor. The company entered the prestigious DAX Index, which lists Germany's top 30 most valuable enterprises (Reuters, 2020). In 2021, Wirecard was bankrupt, and former CEO Markus Brown was in jail (Bloomberg, 2021). Wirecard shareholders had to pay the price for the fraud scandal (Harenbrock and Mergenthaler, 2021):

> German fintech star Wirecard is left in shambles after €1.9 billion were found missing from its books last year. While CEO Braun is in custody and the firm's CFO Marsalek is on the run, shareholders are left in the lurch.

DOI: 10.4324/9781003305071-10

The suspicion started already in 2015 when the *Financial Times* published a series of articles under a title saying, "The House of Wirecard" (McCrum, 2015), which indicated misconduct and collapse inspired by the American political thriller "House of Cards":

> Wirecard is a little known German tech stock worth €5bn, and a puzzle. It offers payment services, owns a Munich bank, and transacts millions of online credit card payments behind the scenes at familiar websites. It grows at breakneck pace but buys obscure payment companies around the world which keep the growth going.
>
> The company says it was founded in 1999, but it went bust after the dotcom crash. The real beginning was 2002, when chief executive Markus Braun took over and injected cash. Three years later Wirecard joined the stock market through the reverse takeover of a defunct call-center business. Allegations of balance sheet inconsistencies were made in 2008. The accuser subsequently landed in jail, and the stock has since been a rocket, rising eightfold. Enthusiastic investors have given Wirecard half a billion euros to spend, and the company used much of it to buy customers, so-called portfolios of relationships, piling almost all the cash its business has produced since 2009 into these customer relationships.

In the *Financial Times* article, McCrum (2015) accused Wirecard, among other things, of a shortfall of €250 million in the balance sheet, which corresponded to three years of company profits. Wirecard denied these allegations, blaming short-selling propaganda. Analysts also agreed with Wirecard that the charges were not true. Furthermore, in 2016, anonymous short sellers of the Wirecard shares made statements in which they accused Wirecard of being involved in money laundering and illegal online gambling. This created greater attention and suspicion among people at the financial supervisory authority in Germany and among private investors. Over the next few years, journalists and short sellers who had spoken badly of Wirecard received so-called fishing emails. There was suspicion that Wirecard was behind these emails in the hope of gaining control of the computers of the critics. In 2019, there was even greater suspicion against Wirecard when the office in Singapore was investigated due to suspicion of fraud. In addition, Wirecard partnered with a third-party company addressed in the Philippines. When investigators went down to this address, they found that the address belonged to a retired fisherman who was unaware that a multinational company was using the same address. On the basis of such findings, there was indeed reason for suspicion of financial crime at Wirecard and great doubt about the company's legitimacy.

Wirecard was first founded in 1999 to handle digital money transactions for pornography and gambling. In 2020, the financial institution went bankrupt (Kagge, 2021). The Wirecard scandal is a series of accounting frauds that resulted in the insolvency of the German payment processor and financial services provider (Storbeck, 2020b). Erikstad (2020) suggests that Wirecard may have been drained of funds before bankruptcy. Wirecard failed in 2019 in its attempt to take over Deutsche Bank, which had not made any profits since 2014 (Håland, 2020). Wirecard's chief executive, Markus Braun, was ambitious both on behalf of the company and on behalf of himself (Solgård, 2020). Wirecard auditor Ernst & Young was in trouble for failing to uncover the fraud (Bugge, 2020).

Motive Convenience Themes

The Wirecard fraud of deceiving potential customers, banks, and investors served the purpose of making them believe that the financial business of Wirecard was more profitable than it actually was. This in turn could potentially lead to financial gains for Wirecard such as greater flow of customer funds, more investors, and improved loan terms for the business. Markus Braun, who was CEO of Wirecard, refused to answer questions after his arrest (Chazan and Storbeck, 2020a):

> Mr Braun refused to answer any questions from MPs, citing his right under German law to remain silent. He declined to answer even basic inquiries, such as what the subject of his PhD thesis was or if he had a daughter.

However, the motive for the fraud can be assessed on the basis of what seems most logical. When Wirecard was established on the German stock exchange (DAX), this put a lot of pressure on the company from the shareholders, who expected a high annual return. The company had seemingly several successful years, and the shareholders received a high annual return. To maintain a good annual return, Wirecard, led by Braun, saw the opportunity to emerge as a larger and stronger company than it really was, to attract new investors. This opportunity arose due to the distinctive organizational structure through the third-party companies it partnered with in Asia and the United Arab Emirates. This was a convenient solution for Wirecard to appear as a large and lucrative company.

The negative gap between performance and public statements increased rapidly. Externally, the company continued as long as possible to appear financially sound and sustainable, while large losses started to occur in 2015. Company management searched for a solution to financial threats. The management of the company, led by CEO Markus Braun, is accused of having falsified the company's accounts to remain attractive to investors and other stakeholders. Braun himself had a large sum invested in stocks at Wirecard, and company decline, and collapse, would thus have personal consequences for him.

In the Wirecard case, the suspicion is that financial crime was committed by manipulating customer relationships as well as creating non-existing partnerships for the purpose of window-dressing to keep everyone happy. Irregularities in the accounting of subsidiaries in Singapore and fake activities in the Philippines are just some of the elements of the fraud scheme to remain in business. The executive's gain increased when the shares of Wirecard rose in value, as not only Braun, but also others in top management had most of their fortune in Wirecard stocks.

At first, the motive was the possibility of creating a market value for Wirecard so high that it exceeded the market value of Deutsche Bank and thereby enabled a possible takeover of Deutsche Bank by Wirecard. It was corporate crime to develop possibilities as illustrated in Figure 9.1. The ambitious business objective probably justified illegal means in the minds of Wirecard executives (Welsh et al., 2019). Both the company and its executives were greedy, where nothing was ever enough (Goldstraw-White, 2012). It was all about making as much profit as possible to improve the market value of the company (Alalehto, 2020).

Storbeck (2020a) wrote about the Wirecard scandal in the UK newspaper *Financial Times* under the heading "Wirecard: The frantic final months of a fraudulent operation":

> A plan to buy Deutsche Bank is now seen as part of a desperate effort to disguise fraud at the German payments group. The codename was "Project

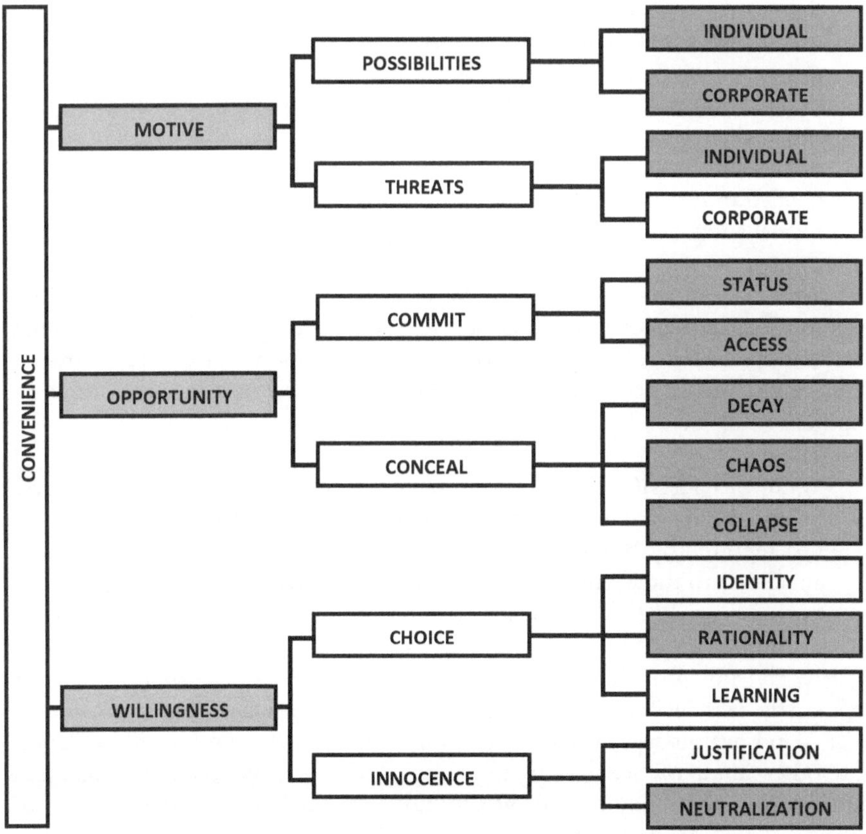

Figure 9.1 Convenience themes in the case of Wirecard

> Panther". Markus Braun, the chief executive of German payments group Wirecard had hired McKinsey & Co to help prepare his most audacious idea yet, a plan to take over Deutsche Bank. In a 40-page presentation last November, the consultants insisted the new entity, to be dubbed "Wirebank", would be "thinking and acting like a fintech, at the scale of a global bank". By 2025, it could generate €6bn in additional profit, McKinsey claimed.
>
> While Germany's largest bank sat on €1.4tn in assets, it was a mere €14bn on the stock market, roughly the same as Wirecard. The McKinsey report promised that the combined stock market valuation would double to close to €50n. A deal to acquire Deutsche Bank would have been the crowning achievement for a company which within a few years had become one of the most valuable in the country, winning the label of "Germany's PayPal". An upstart financial technology company would be running Germany's most illustrious bank. A tie-up with Deutsche Bank had another potential attraction: A deal offered the prospect of a miraculous exit from the massive fraud Wirecard had been operating. Around €1.9bn in cash was missing from its accounts and large parts of its Asian operations were actually an elaborate sham. By blending Wirecard's business into Deutsche's vast balance sheet, it might be possible to somehow hide the missing cash and explain it away later in post-merger impairment charges. There was one catch. To even start preparing such a deal in earnest, the company needed to get a clean bill of health from KPMG, which was conducting a special audit of Wirecard's books.

Wirecard had hired audit firm KPMG (2020a, 2020b) to conduct a fraud examination into an alleged increase in revenue through fictious customer relationships and other forms of accounting manipulation. Wirecard's motive to hire KPMG was to get a clean bill of health from fraud examiners according to Storbeck (2020a):

> With the KPMG investigation in full flow, the Wirecard executives behind the fraud saw Project Panther and a deal with Deutsche, which was first reported by Bloomberg, as one possible way to fend off discover, says an adviser to the payments group who was involved in the discussions. But they also worked on a separate plan: a vast cover-up operation in Asia.

KPMG did not provide a clean bill of health, since fraud examiners in their report criticized Wirecard's internal controls and compliance functions. However, fraud examiners did neither confirm nor reject accounting manipulation and other kinds of financial wrongdoing. Therefore, Wirecard management quickly stated that "no evidence was found for the publicly raised allegations of balance sheet manipulation" (Storbeck, 2020a). Nevertheless, the company collapsed half a year later.

Next, the motive was the possibility of individual enrichment as exemplified by Jan Marsalek who had transferred funds to Asian countries where he later probably was on the run. Marsalek and other executives at Wirecard were young and ambitious, and they wanted to climb the hierarchy of needs for status and success (Maslow, 1943). Maybe they wanted to realize the American dream of prosperity where material wealth is far more important than anything else in life (Cullen, 2010).

Finally, the motive was threats against individual wealth and success as Wirecard moved towards insolvency and bankruptcy. Concealing funds is about avoidance of loss of self-esteem after organizational failure (Crosina and Pratt, 2019). Having personal control over funds can reduce and remove strain, pain, and uncertainty (Thaxton and Agnew, 2018). Having funds can also prevent falling too far from positions in the privileged elite (Benson and Chio, 2020).

Opportunity Convenience Themes

An important part of the opportunity structure for Wirecard was the lack of regulation and oversight by federal authorities in Germany. When the Wirecard scandal was a fact, the German parliament launched an inquiry (Chazan and Storbeck, 2020b):

> Members of parliament set up the parliamentary inquiry last summer as the Wirecard affair began to escalate from a corporate affair into a political scandal. Lawmakers want to know why the authorities seemed so slow to recognize the gravity of the situation at Wirecard, and why Germany's financial regulator BaFin seemed more eager to pursue journalists and short-sellers who had exposed irregularities at the payment processing group than to go after the company itself. The nine members of the investigative committee will also look at why German politicians, including chancellor Angela Merkel, lobbied for Wirecard even after irregularities at the company had come to light. They will also want to know whether Jan Marsalek, the former Wirecard executive who is now on an Interpol wanted list, had any connections to the intelligence services.

The lack of regulation and oversight can be explained by the principal-agent perspective where the principal is both unable and reluctant to monitor the agent (Forti and Visconti, 2020: 65): "The causal loops interconnecting the main features of white-collar crime are strengthened and consolidated within and through corporate organizations, also due to their intersections with institutions of political governance."

Forti and Visconti (2020) conceived all possible dynamic interactions as a system of harms, which – like every system – is more than the sheer sum of single parts. They argue that the elucidation of such a system's dynamics and conditions is much more revealing than any list of single perspectives on white-collar crime. According to principal-agent analysis, exchanges can encourage illegal gain for both principal and agent.

The alleged lobbying for Wirecard by top politicians in Germany opens up the perspective of state-corporate crime. In a state-corporate alignment, the state as well as the corporation can be blamed (Bernat and Whyte, 2020; Rothe, 2020; Rothe and Medley, 2020; Tombs and Whyte, 2003; Zysman-Quirós, 2020). Dynamics of state-corporate crime occur between the national and organizational levels (Bernat and Whyte, 2020: 127): "This growing body of literature on state-corporate crimes takes as its starting points the mutually reinforcing relationships between state institutions and corporations."

The powerful in the upper class of society define their own identity in terms of what is right and what is wrong for them, sometimes in a state-corporate alignment (Tombs and Whyte, 2003; Zysman-Quirós, 2020). If they themselves break their own laws, then there is a need to change the laws rather than punish law violators (Petrocelli et al., 2003).

Another part of the opportunity structure for Wirecard was the lack of whistleblowing and ignorance towards whistleblowers. A single whistleblower tried to talk about the fraud four years before the collapse, but the message was ignored by management at audit firm Ernst & Young (EY), which was responsible for external auditing at Wirecard (Storbeck, 2020b):

> EY was warned in 2016 by one of its own employees that senior managers at Wirecard may have committed fraud and one had attempted to bribe an auditor. The revelation that an EY employee identified suspicious activity at Wirecard four years before the payments group imploded in Germany's largest postwar corporate fraud will increase the pressure on the accounting firm, which audited Wirecard for more than a decade and provided unqualified audits until 2018. EY is already under investigation by Germany's auditor oversight body Apas and is the target of lawsuits from Wirecard investors who lost billions of euros when the company collapsed in June.

Markus Braun reached a very high-status peak at the top of his career before the fraud was revealed. Status is an individual's social rank within a formal or informal hierarchy, or the person's relative standing along a valued social dimension. Status is the extent to which an individual is respected and admired by others, and status is the outcome of a subjective assessment process (McClean et al., 2018). High-status individuals enjoy greater respect and deference from, as well as power and influence over, those who are positioned lower in the social hierarchy (Kakkar et al., 2020: 532):

> Status is a property that rests in the eyes of others and is conferred to individuals who are deemed to have a higher rank or social standing in a pecking order based on a mutually valued set of social attributes. Higher social status or rank grants its holder a host of tangible benefits in both professional and personal domains. For instance, high-status actors are sought by groups for advice, are paid higher, receive unsolicited help, and

> are credited disproportionately in joint tasks. In innumerable ways, our social ecosystem consistently rewards those with high status.

Especially individuals with high status based on prestige rather than dominance tend to be excused for whatever wrongdoing they commit. Individuals who attain and maintain high rank by behaving in ways that are assertive, controlling, and intimidating are characterized as dominant. Individuals who attain and maintain high rank by their set of skills, knowledge, expertise, and willingness to share these with others are characterized as prestigious (Kakkar et al., 2020).

Wirecard was a company that was difficult to understand with numerous daily transactions all over the world. It was a payment processing company that offered infrastructure and services for electronic payments of all sorts of values. Poor and absent control routines combined with lack of transparency made the chances of being detected very small and the possibility of covering up crime convenient.

Misreporting in accounting is often a convenient way of concealing illegal transactions (Qiu and Slezak, 2019). Lack of transparency makes concealment in accounting convenient (Davidson et al., 2019; Goncharov and Peter, 2019). Managers can withhold bad news by accounting misrepresentation (Bao et al., 2019), since financial statements are a substantive component of a firm's communications with its stakeholders. Balakrishnan et al. (2019) found that reduced corporate transparency in accounting is associated with increased corporate tax aggressiveness. Accounting fraud in terms of account manipulation is lacking transparency (Toolami et al., 2019).

Ernst & Young was the external auditor for Wirecard. Concealing illegal transactions may result from the failure of auditors to do their job. Alon et al. (2019) argue that accounting and auditing functions have undergone a legitimacy crisis in recent years. Auditors are supposed to serve as gatekeepers to protect shareholders and other stakeholders, but deviant corporate management tend to hire and control auditors instead of letting auditors report to the board of directors or the supervisory board (Hurley et al., 2019). Skeptical auditors tend to be replaced by less skeptical auditors. Reporting fraud to public authorities will also harm auditors (Mohliver, 2019: 316):

> As organizations, audit firms are often severely penalized for client malfeasance. Yet the individual auditors working for these firms are susceptible to "motivated blindness" stemming from conflicts of interest that bias their moral judgment toward choices that help their clients.

The lack of detection by auditors can also be explained by standardization. Herron and Cornell (2021) found that audit work is standardized which harms auditors' creativity, thereby preventing recognition of and responses to fraud cues. Standardization harms an improvisational style of thinking, tolerance for unpredictability, uncertainty, and open-mindedness that is associated with responses to perceived fraud risk cues.

In the organizational dimension of convenience theory, there are themes related to the convenience of committing crime. Convenience themes address the status of offenders as well as access to resources by offenders as illustrated in Figure 9.1. CEO Markus Braun and other executives at Wirecard were rising stars in German business, where they soon could reach the level of elite members who are too big to fail and too powerful to jail (Kakkar et al., 2020). They used an executive language about their business transactions that auditors from Ernst & Young and examiners from KPMG could not understand (Srivastava and Goldberg, 2017). They applied the blame game by misleading attributions to others in Asia and by scapegoating (Resodihardjo et al., 2015). Executives at Wirecard were entrepreneurial both on the right side and on the wrong side of the law. Entrepreneurs create opportunities where others mainly see problems (McElwee and Smith, 2015). They had legitimate access to premises and systems to be criminal entrepreneurs (Logan et al., 2019). In particular, they had access to strategic resources (Patel and Cooper, 2014).

Scheaf and Wood (2021: 2) found that entrepreneurial fraud has stimulated a wide array of research related to white-collar crime, where they provided the following definition of entrepreneurial fraud: "Enterprising individuals (alone or in groups) deceiving stakeholders by sharing statements about their identity, individual capabilities, elements of new market offerings, and/or new venture activities that they know to be false in order to obtain something of value."

In the organizational dimension of convenience theory, there are also themes related to the convenience of concealing crime. Convenience themes address decay in terms of disorganized institutional deterioration, chaos in terms of lack of oversight and guardianship, and collapse in terms of criminal market structures as illustrated in Figure 9.1. Institutional deterioration was based on legitimacy (Crosina and Pratt, 2019). Interference and noise in crime signals (Szalma and Hancock, 2013) helped conceal misrepresentation in accounting (Qiu and Slezak, 2019) and prevented effective auditing (Balakrishnan et al., 2019).

There were signs of chaos, such as lack of control in principal-agent relationships (Wall-Parker, 2020), where the board did not know what top management was doing, and top management did not know what local branch managers were doing. Sense making of actions was difficult for outsiders (Weick et al., 2005). While there was an instance of whistleblowing related to misconduct in Singapore, costs did exceed benefits for whistleblowers (Tankebe, 2019). In addition to lack of control in principal-agent relationships, problems in sense making of actions for outsiders, and costs exceeding benefits for whistleblowers, an ethical climate conflict also contributed to chaos (Potipiroon and Wongpreedee, 2020). While some ignored violations of laws in achieving goals, others wanted to watch compliance, which created an ethical climate conflict. Collapse is also evident as some Wirecard executives involved themselves in markets with crime forces (Freiberg, 2020) and in crime networks (Geest et al., 2017).

Willingness Convenience Themes

In police interrogation, Braun denied allegations and said he had not committed any illegalities. The specific suspicions indicate that the background for Wirecard actions lies in keeping the company attractive and profitable, and this may indicate that there is a reason for neutralization of guilt. It might either be considered a necessary rescue of the company or a way of thinking that the actions should not be considered criminal. Braun was very reticent in his answers, which makes it difficult to concretize the background for the actions. There is a large degree of disclaimer on the part of Braun, also through claims that it is Wirecard that is the victim here. It seems that Braun and Wirecard justify actions in the form of condemning those who criticize. They ordered the report from KPMG on the basis of accusations in the media and in particular the *Financial Times*.

In the willingness dimension of convenience theory, there are thus themes related to the convenience of deviant behavior. Convenience themes address the choice of crime and the feeling of innocence as illustrated in Figure 9.1. The rational choice of accounting manipulation had benefits exceeding costs if Wirecard was successful in taking over Deutsche Bank. The rational choice perspective suggests that crime is a rational choice if benefits exceed costs (Müller, 2018). Wirecard executives were sliding on the slippery slope over on the wrong side of the law (Gamache and McNamara, 2019). Some Wirecard executives lacked self-control (Craig and Piquero, 2016).

Investigation Report Outcome

KPMG (2020a, 2020b) conducted the investigation on the premises of Wirecard AG, as well as at KPMG's branch offices between October 31, 2019, and April 24, 2020. In addition, KPMG inspected documents on the premises of the auditor and conducted interviews with Wirecard business partners on their premises in Dubai, the Philippines, and, in one case, via video conferencing. KPMG determined the scope and nature of the relevant investigation activities independently and at their discretion in accordance with the examination mandate.

KPMG (2020a: 12) examined the amount and existence of revenues from the TPA business relationships between Cardsystems Middle East, Wirecard UK & Ireland, as well as Wirecard Technologies and the respective relevant TPA partners:

> KPMG can, as a result of the forensic investigation conducted in relation to the investigation period 2016 to 2018, neither make a statement that the revenues exist and are correct in terms of their amount, nor make a statement that the revenues do not exist and are incorrect in terms of their amount. To this extent, there is an obstacle to the investigation.

In our perspective of evaluating the KPMG investigation, the examiners failed in establishing facts concerning the existence or non-existence of revenues. A different approach in terms of knowledge strategy and information strategy might have been successful.

Within a few days of investigation, KPMG realized that Wirecard's core payments processing operations in Europe were not making any money – a fact that Wirecard had never disclosed to investors (Storbeck, 2020a): "All of the profit was generated by the operations overseen by Mr Marsalek, Wirecard's Asia business, where the processing of transactions was outsourced to third-party business partners."

Jan Marsalek claimed that €1.9 billion in cash was transferred from Singapore to the Philippines and into a bank account in the name of Manila-based lawyer Mark Tolentino. KPMG discovered that two months after the money supposedly was paid into Tolentino's account, Wirecard still did not have a contractual relationship with the new trustee, nor had it conducted background checks on him (Storbeck, 2020a).

In their final report, KPMG examiners detailed shortcomings in Wirecard's internal controls and compliance functions and outlined severe doubts about the company's accounting practices (Storbeck, 2020a), but they did not draw any definitive conclusions. KPMG neither verify the existence of the outsourced business nor the cash in escrow accounts, and they describe "the dogged obstruction by Wirecard and its business partners" (Storbeck, 2020a).

The examiners' report presents results of the investigation activities into third-party acquiring in regard to (1) existence and revenues from third-party acquirers (TPA) business, (2) customer relationships in the TPA business, and (3) descriptions of the TPA business in Wirecard's annual statements:

1 Questionable amount and existence of revenues, in particular with reference to allegedly questionable customer relationships. KPMG (2020a: 13) examiners could not make a statement regarding existence and correctness of numbers: "This is due to deficiencies in the internal organization and, in particular, to the unwillingness of the Third-Party Acquirers to participate in this special investigation in a comprehensive and transparent manner".
2 Questionable customer relationships. KPMG (2020a: 28) examiners could not verify the existence and correctness of customer names: "According to the information available, the names given in the press were 'account name' designations or aliases under which the revenues of customers referred to a TPA partner were recorded at the time. As we could not be provided with the actual names of the 43 alleged customers (aliases) quoted in the press, KPMG was unable to verify the existence of these customer relationships for the investigation period 2016 to 2018".
3 Questionable descriptions of third-party business in annual statements. KPMG (2020a: 30) provides no clear answer: "The presentation of debtor risk and existing customer risk in the report casts doubt on whether the scope of these risks in relation to the TPA business is sufficiently apparent to addressees of the financial statements. With regard to the debtor risk, the presentation made in the management report could give the

impression that the risk from chargebacks is exclusively related to the receivables from the acquiring area. However, according to the information obtained, the chargeback risk in Wirecard's TPA business actually affects a considerable portion of the escrow accounts reported as cash and cash equivalents."

The examiners' report presents results of the investigation activities into digital lending business in regard to (1) amount and composition of the merchant cash advance business, (2) legal permissibility of business activities in Turkey and Brazil, (3) business background of certain lending activities, (4) acts at subsidiaries in Singapore, and (5) payment to a middleman in India:

1 Questionable amount and composition of the merchant cash advance business in the context of the company's disclosures. KPMG (2020a: 37) provides no clear answer: "According to an internal memorandum submitted to KPMG, the published information on the volume of merchant cash advance should be used to explain business models. It is said not to be a defined product, but a value-added service, which is in part an integral component of Wirecard's services. This volume is therefore a management estimate based on various assumptions and calculations". Examiners neither questioned the management estimate nor inquired into assumptions and calculations.
2 Questionable legal permissibility of Wirecard's business activities in Turkey and Brazil in connection with the merchant cash advance product. KPMG (2020a: 39) conducted no independent investigation in Turkey but trusted instead a law firm paid for by Wirecard: "In the course of the investigation of the permissibility of the merchant cash advance business in Turkey, KPMG reviewed results summarized in the memorandum of a law firm commissioned by Wirecard. With regard to the appropriateness of the structure of the merchant cash advance business with international customers ('international merchants'), including Wirecard Bank, KPMG concluded that the transactions with international customers in Turkey were legally permissible". A similar conclusion was drawn for Brazil based on "the information we received" (KPMG, 2020a: 40). The passivity of examiners in obtaining information is striking.
3 Questionable business background of possible unsecured loans granted to a specific company. Again, KPMG (2020a: 42) was unable to reconstruct past events: "In 2018, Wirecard Asia Holding Pte. Ltd, Singapore, granted company 4 several unsecured loans with a total volume of EUR 115 million with a one-year term for the purpose of 'merchant cash advance business'. Since KPMG did not receive any information on the customers of company 4 in the course of the investigation – in particular, not on the customers forwarded by Wirecard to company 4 – KPMG could not determine which companies or persons participated economically and to what extent in the loans granted to company 4 for 'merchant advance purposes'". The passivity of examiners in obtaining information is again striking.

4 Whistleblower alleging that there are indications of fraudulent acts at Wirecard subsidiaries in Singapore. KPMG (2020a: 45) base again their assessment on secondary sources: "In response to the whistleblower's accusations in spring 2018, Wirecard AG engaged Law Firm 1 to conduct a compliance audit and, at a later date, engaged Law Firm 2 to conduct an internal investigation. The background was that the compliance audit of Law Firm 1 has weaknesses. For example, the data basis, in particular consisting of accounting data and e-mail traffic, was not completely saved. The incompleteness of the data basis could not be fully remedied in the course of the investigation by Law Firm 2. EY Audit has supplemented individual results of the compliance audit and the internal investigation of the Law Firms 1 and 2 respectively, with its own auditing activities – including the use of EY FIS. As a result, the investigation activities of Law Firm 2 and the auditing activities of EY Audit under the extended audit procedures were not carried out on a complete data and information basis. Therefore, it cannot be ruled out that the investigation activities of Law Firms 1 and 2 and the auditing activities of EY Audit within the framework of the extended audit procedures would have come to a different conclusion if a complete database had been available. EY Audit has carried out auditing activities on the basis of the available data in relation to the accusations made". While fraud examiners here express that deviance is possible, they made no attempt to interview the whistleblower or others who could tell where to find evidence.

5 Questionable payment of excessive purchase price to middleman in India. Fraud examiners at KPMG (2020a: 50) admit another failure despite attempted background research: "The auditors were unable to identify the beneficial owner of Fund 1. The background research by KPMG also failed to identify the beneficial owner of Fund 1. Consequently, the accusation that Fund 1 is an intermediary cannot be conclusively clarified. Since knowledge of the beneficial owner is of essential importance for the question of who benefited from the purchase price, further investigations are not useful at this time as long as the identity has not been clarified. According to the information provided to KPMG, Wirecard AG does not know the beneficial owner of Fund 1".

KPMG (2020a: 59) presents the following text under the heading "Conclusion": "KPMG issues this report to the best of its knowledge and belief on the basis of the documents submitted to KPMG, information provided and its own investigation activities, and with reference to the Code of Professional Conduct."

This is certainly no conclusion regarding findings. However, as there were no findings and no fraud investigation outcome, the chosen conclusion text illustrates the complete failure of Sven-Olaf Leitz and Alexander Geschonneck at KPMG.

Investigation Maturity Assessment

Maybe it was no coincidence that Wirecard hired KPMG (2020a, 2020b) to investigate allegations in the media, since Markus Braun had been a former KPMG consultant and because KPMG had other assignments for Wirecard as well (McCrum, 2020). These kinds of relationships reduce the trust in investigation objectivity and investigator integrity.

Storbeck (2020a) suggests that Wirecard "needed to get a clean bill of health from KPMG" to prepare for a deal "blending Wirecard's business into Deutsche's vast balance sheet". If examiners had delivered a report of investigation according to such client expectations, it would be a commissioned work lacking independence and objectivity. However, the investigative journalist Storbeck (2020a) concludes that "the approval from KPMG never came". While there was no approval in the investigation report, there was also no conclusion. Lack of conclusion is surprising, as Wirecard only six months later collapsed into insolvency after it was exposed as one of Germany's biggest postwar accounting frauds. There are thus certainly grounds to suggest that while KPMG examiners did not provide approval, they avoided condemnation of Wirecard board and management by claiming that they were unable to reconstruct critical events.

Wirecard's motive for a clean bill of health from KPMG was also evidenced by the statement of board members to chairman Wulf Matthias that "we told him that he needed the audit to protect himself and his money" (Storbeck, 2020a). KPMG was thus far from an ideal initiation situation for the investigation. The ideal situation is a client who has a genuine interest in finding out what happened, how it happened, when it happened, and who did what to make it happen or not happen. The initiation stage for the investigation was dominated by client expectation that fraud examiners would refute with clear evidence what Wirecard was accused of in the media and elsewhere. While influenced by this expectation, KPMG did not meet such an expectation.

Another relevant issue to consider at the initiation stage is the extent to which KPMG's competitor Ernst & Young (EY) might implicitly be criticized if KPMG would find solid evidence of wrongdoing. The global audit business is characterized by shifting roles in fraud examinations, where they investigate each other. Chairman Matthias argued that EY was "evaluating the matters sufficiently". Maybe next time EY will investigate failing audit by KPMG, which might influence KPMG's extent of criticism of EY. The blame game among global audit firms seems restricted by industry loyalty.

According to Storbeck (2020a), "40 forensic accountants from KPMG started to dig through Wirecard's books". While the number of examiners might seem impressive, the knowledge strategy is interesting. Probably, not all examiners were forensic accountants. Almost always lawyers are the dominating professionals participating in internal investigations. The relevant knowledge strategy for the challenge of reconstructing activities at Wirecard includes investigative interviewing since key people normally are willing to tell if they trust the interviewers. Since the examination team was dominated by forensic accountants who searched data and transactions, it is not at all obvious that they successfully accessed individuals who had insights into what was going on inside Wirecard globally.

This seeming lack of relevant information sources is further evidenced by the lack of whistleblowing (KPMG, 2020a: 9): "At the end of the investigation, we received confirmation that no information had been received through the whistleblower system."

All existing information and information submitted during the examination period to Wirecard's internal whistleblowing system regarding the subject of investigation was to be forwarded to KPMG. It is thus interesting to note that nothing was received through the whistleblowing system. While it is obvious in the aftermath that employees had relevant information to contribute through the whistleblowing system, the reasons for not contributing information might vary among employees. One typical reason is the fear of retaliation and reprisals that have harmed so many whistleblowers in the past. Another typical reason is the lack of trust in those who handled the messages (Mesmer-Magnus and Viswesvaran, 2005; Park et al., 2020; Rehg et al., 2009; Shawver and Clements, 2019).

According to Storbeck (2020a), Sven-Olaf Leitz and Alexander Geschonneck, the two veterans KPMG partners running the fraud examination, told CEO Markus Braun that the documents on the escrow accounts were not good enough. They insisted on seeing original documents, ideally directly obtained from OCBC. Escrow is a legal concept describing a financial instrument whereby an asset or escrow money is held by a third party on behalf of two other parties that are in the process of completing a transaction. OCBC bank is located in Singapore.

Jan Marsalek attempted to manipulate KPMG examiners by arranging a series of meetings in Manila introducing KPMG to the alleged Wirecard trustee for escrow accounts (Storbeck, 2020a). KPMG was unconvinced, but did not conduct interviews independent of Marsalek, which fraud examiners should have done. Fraud examiners failed in having separate meetings with important information sources in the Philippines, Dubai, and Singapore. One of the meetings monitored by Marsalek was with Christopher Bauer who ran PayEasy, which processed high-risk transactions for Wirecard – mostly payments for pornography, gambling, and gaming. A few months after the meeting, Bauer was reported dead.

According to Storbeck (2020a), KPMG told Wirecard that fraud examiners where thinking of terminating their work because of obstacles to the investigation. But they did not. To preserve fraud examiner integrity, they might have done so. Instead, KPMG extended the deadline for submission of their report.

The first draft of the KPMG report was not accepted by the client. KPMG revised the report of investigation before it was published (Storbeck, 2020a). Whether or not the revision represented commissioned work that harmed KPMG's integrity is not obvious.

The investigation was hit by the Corona virus pandemic on March 12, 2020, when examiners were no longer able to travel. They had to conduct video conferencing with interviewees for the remaining investigation period until submission of their report on April 27. Generally, digital media reduced the quality of information compared to face-to-face interaction.

Fraud examiners admit that they failed in verifying information (KPMG, 2020a: 6):

> The basis of our investigation and evaluation were the documents received and information provided, but it was not possible for us to verify the completeness and authenticity of the documents and documentations provided to us. Consequently, we cannot make any conclusive statement as to whether these documents and information are complete, accurate, and free of contradictions. Nor can we conclusively assess whether all information and evidence relevant to the assessment has been made available to us. In this respect, we also cannot rule out the possibility that we would have come to a different conclusion if we had been aware of additional information or documents.

Investigative interviewing and digital forensics might have helped solve this problem (Goodman-Delahunty and Martschuk, 2020). Collins and Carthy (2018) studied the relationship between rapport and communication during investigative interviews. Attention, positivity, and coordination are important rapport components. Rapport is a close and harmonious relationship in which individuals understand each other and are sympathetic to each other. The purpose of investigative interviewing is to gain information, and persons providing information may not always be motivated to do so, especially if the persons perceive being subject to suspicion or blame for misconduct. The aim is for the examination interviewer and the information source to have a productive relationship that builds on cooperation and respect. An interview takes place because the interviewer assumes that the subject of an interview has information of value to the interviewer.

Digital forensics is the recovery and investigation of material found in digital devices. For example, email accounts and mobile phones tend to have personal and sensitive information that could lead examiners towards conclusions. Search engines might have been applied by fraud examiners on all digital devices available to executives at Wirecard.

A further action to verify information is triangulation where several sources confirm or disconfirm the same piece of information. By combining multiple observers, documents, and theories, examiners can overcome the weakness of single source investigations.

Fraud examiners admit that they did not even try to verify information (KPMG, 2020a: 7): "KPMG points out that KPMG has not carried out an authenticity check, in particular for documents delivered on or after April 17, 2020."

Anonymous providers of information are an unreliable, yet often important, source in fraud investigations. Examiners have to assess the reliability of the information as well as the source, but KPMG (2020a: 9) seemingly ignored that important task in assessing anonymous reports:

> During our special investigation, KPMG was provided with information and documents by third parties, in part anonymously. KPMG examined these pieces of information and documents with regard to their relevance to the areas under investigation and took them into account to the extent they were related to one of the areas under investigation. KPMG included these pieces of information and documents in its investigation to the extent that KPMG in its discretion considered this to be necessary for the purposes of the investigation.

KPMG (2020a: 10) blame Wirecard for their lack of cooperation and thus avoid self-blame for failing:

> Wirecard AG did not supply some of the documents requested by KPMG in the course the investigation (…) Wirecard repeatedly postponed individual agreed interview appointments (…) The transfer of transaction data at least for the years 2016 and 2017 required the support of the TPA partners, which has so far been lacking.

Self-blame is rare and often non-existent. Nobody will blame oneself for a negative event. Self-blame is attributing a negative event to one's behavior or disposition (Lee and Robinson, 2000).

The failing investigation is confirmed by KPMG (2020a: 12), who label it an obstacle rather than a failure as presented earlier in this chapter:

> KPMG can, as a result of the forensic investigation conducted in relation to the investigation period 2016 to 2018, neither make a statement that the revenues exist and are correct in terms of their amount, nor make a statement that the revenues do not exist and are incorrect in terms of their amount. To this extent, there is an obstacle to the investigation.

Based on this review, the assessment of the KPMG investigation results in the lowest possible maturity level as illustrated in Figure 9.2.

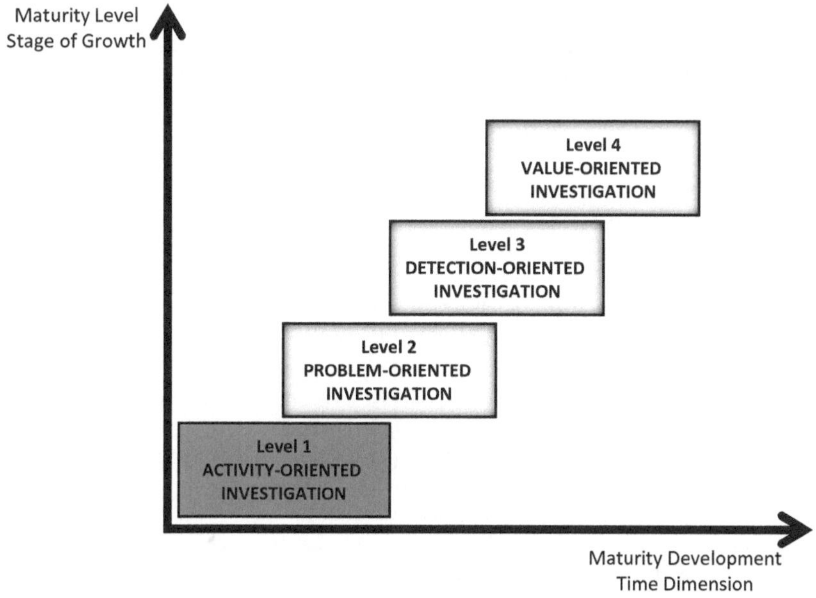

Figure 9.2 Maturity level for the KPMG (2020a, 2020b) investigation at Wirecard

References

Alalehto, T. (2020). Corporate crime: A logical misconception, but with one analytical point, *Journal of Financial Crime*, published online doi:10.1108/JFC-04-2020-0063.

Alon, A., Mennicken, A. and Samsonova-Taddei, A. (2019). Dynamics and limits of regulatory privatization: Reorganizing audit oversight in Russia, *Organization Studies*, 40 (8), 1217–1240.

Balakrishnan, K., Blouin, J.L. and Guay, W.R. (2019). Tax aggressiveness and corporate transparency, *The Accounting Review*, 94 (1), 45–69.

Bao, D., Kim, Y., Mian, G.M. and Su, L. (2019). Do managers disclose or withhold bad news? Evidence from short interest, *The Accounting Review*, 94 (3), 1–26.

Benson, M.L. and Chio, H.L. (2020). Who commits occupational crimes, in: Rorie, M. (editor), *The Handbook of White-Collar Crime*, Hoboken, NJ: John Wiley & Sons, chapter 7, pages 97–112.

Bernat, I. and Whyte, D. (2020). State-corporate crimes, in: Rorie, M.L. (editor), *The Handbook of White-Collar Crime*, Hoboken, NJ: Wiley & Sons, chapter 9, pages 191–208.

Bloomberg (2021). Jailed ex-Wirecard CEO sues chubb to pick up his legal bills, *Bloomberg*, www.bloomberg.com, published May 10.

Bugge, W. (2020). Wirecard-revisor i trøbbel for å ikke ha avdekket milliardsvindelen (Wirecard auditor in trouble for failing to uncover billionaire fraud), daily Norwegian business newspaper *Dagens Næringsliv*, www.dn.no, published June 26.

Chazan, G. (2021). Wirecard given no 'privileged treatment' says German finance deputy, *Financial Times*, www.ft.com, published April 21.

Chazan, G. and Storbeck, O. (2020a). Wirecard: The scandal spreads to German politics, *Financial Times*, www.ft.com, published September 29.

Chazan, G. and Storbeck, O. (2020b). Wirecard's Markus Brown says regulators not to blame in scandal, *Financial Times*, www.ft.com, published November 20.

Collins, K. and Carthy, N. (2018). No rapport, no comment: The relationship between rapport and communication during investigative interviews with suspects, *Journal of Investigative Psychology and Offender Profiling*, published online doi:10.1002/jip.1517.

Craig, J.M. and Piquero, N.L. (2016). The effects of low self-control and desire-for-control on white-collar offending: A replication, *Deviant Behavior*, 37 (11), 1308–1324.

Crosina, E. and Pratt, M.G. (2019). Toward a model of organizational mourning: The case of former Lehman Brothers bankers, *Academy of Management Journal*, 62 (1), 66–98.

Cullen, F.T. (2010). Cloward, Richard A., and Lloyd E. Ohlin: Delinquency and opportunity, in: Cullen, F.T. and Wilcox, P. (editors), *Encyclopedia of Criminological Theory*, Volume 1, Los Angeles, CA: Sage Publications, pages 170–174.

Davidson, R.H., Dey, A. and Smith, A.J. (2019). CEO materialism and corporate social responsibility, *The Accounting Review*, 94 (1), 101–126.

Erikstad, T. (2020). Wirecard kan ha blitt tappet for midler før konkurs (Wirecard may have been drained of funds before bankruptcy), daily Norwegian business newspaper *Dagens Næringsliv*, www.dn.no, published August 11.

Forti, G. and Visconti, A. (2020). From economic crime to corporate violence: The multifaceted harms of corporate crime, in: Rorie, M.L. (editor), *The Handbook of White-Collar Crime*, Hoboken, NJ: John Wiley & Sons, chapter 5, pages 64–80.

Freiberg, A. (2020). Researching white-collar crime: An Australian perspective, in: Rorie, M.L. (editor), *The Handbook of White-Collar Crime*, Hoboken, NJ: John Wiley & Sons, chapter 26, pages 418–436.

Gamache, D.L. and McNamara, G. (2019). Responding to bad press: How CEO temporal focus influences the sensitivity to negative media coverage of acquisitions, *Academy of Management Journal*, 62 (3), 918–943.

Geest, V.R., Weisburd, D. and Blokland, A.A.J. (2017). Developmental trajectories of offenders convicted of fraud: A follow-up to age 50 in a Dutch conviction cohort, *European Journal of Criminology*, 14 (5), 543–565.

Goldstraw-White, J. (2012). *White-Collar Crime: Accounts of Offending Behavior*, London, UK: Palgrave Macmillan.

Goncharov, I. and Peter, C.D. (2019). Does reporting transparency affect industry coordination? Evidence from the duration of international cartels, *The Accounting Review*, 94 (3), 149–175.

Goodman-Delahunty, J. and Martschuk, N. (2020). Securing reliable information in investigative interviews: Coercive and noncoercive strategies preceding turning points, *Police Practice and Research*, 21 (2), 152–171.

Håland, S. (2020). De elendige: Hva feiler det tyske banker? (The miserable: What is wrong with German banks?), daily Norwegian business newspaper *Dagens Næringsliv*, www.dn.no, published July 27.

Harenbrock, K. and Mergenthaler, T. (2021). Wirecard shareholders pay the price for fraud scandal, *Deutsche Welle*, www.dw.com, published March 19.

Herron, E.T. and Cornell, R.M. (2021). Creativity amidst standardization: Is creativity related to auditors' recognition of and responses to fraud risk cues? *Journal of Business Research*, 132, 314–326.

Hurley, P.J., Mayhew, B.W. and Obermire, K.M. (2019). Realigning auditors' accountability: Experimental evidence, *The Accounting Review*, 94 (3), 233–250.

Kagge, G. (2021). Merkel må forklare seg om hjelp til selskap anklaget for milliardsvindel (Merkel must explain herself about help to companies accused of billion fraud), daily Norwegian newspaper *Aftenposten*, Thursday, April 22, page 24.

Kakkar, H., Sivanathan, N. and Globel, M.S. (2020). Fall from grace: The role of dominance and prestige in punishment of high-status actors, *Academy of Management Journal*, 63 (2), 530–553.

KPMG (2020a). *Report Concerning the Independent Special Investigation at Wirecard AG*, April 27, audit firm KPMG, Munich, Germany, 74 pages.

KPMG (2020b). *Bericht über die unabhängige Sonderuntersuchung, Wirecard AG, München*, 27. April, audit firm KPMG, Munich, Germany, 74 pages.

Lee, F. and Robinson, R.J. (2000). An attributional analysis of social accounts: Implications of playing the blame game, *Journal of Applied Social Psychology*, 30 (9), 1853–1879.

Logan, M.W., Morgan, M.A., Benson, M.L. and Cullen, F.T. (2019). Coping with imprisonment: Testing the special sensitivity hypothesis for white-collar offenders, *Justice Quarterly*, 36 (2), 225–254.

Maslow, A.H. (1943). A theory of human motivation, *Psychological Review*, 50 (4), 370–396.

McClean, E.J., Martin, S.R., Emich, K.J. and Woodruff, T. (2018). The social consequences of voice: An examination of voice type and gender on status and subsequent leader emergence, *Academy of Management Journal*, 61 (5), 1869–1891.

McCrum, D. (2015). The House of Wirecard, *Financial Times*, www.ft.com, published April 27.

McCrum, D. (2019). Wirecard's suspect accounting practices revealed, *Financial Times*, www.ft.com, published October 15.

McCrum, D. (2020). Wirecard: The timeline, *Financial Times*, www.ft.com, published June 25.

McElwee, G. and Smith, R. (2015). Towards a nuanced typology of illegal entrepreneurship: A theoretical and conceptual overview, in: McElwee, G. and Smith, R. (editors), *Exploring Criminal and Illegal Enterprise: New Perspectives on Research, Policy & Practice: Contemporary Issues in Entrepreneurship Research*, Volume 5, Bingley, UK: Emerald Publishing.

Mesmer-Magnus, J.R. and Viswesvaran, C. (2005). Whistleblowing in an organization: An examination of correlates of whistleblowing intentions, actions, and retaliation, *Journal of Business Ethics*, 62 (3), 266–297.

Mohliver, A. (2019). How misconduct spreads: Auditors' role in the diffusion of stock-option backdating, *Administrative Science Quarterly*, 64 (2), 310–336.

Müller, S.M. (2018). Corporate behavior and ecological disaster: Dow Chemical and the Great Lakes mercury crisis, 1970–1972, *Business History*, 60 (3), 399–422.

Park, H., Bjørkelo, B. and Blenkinsopp, J. (2020). External whistleblowers' experiences of workplace bullying by superiors and colleagues, *Journal of Business Ethics*, 161, 591–601.

Patel, P.C. and Cooper, D. (2014). Structural power equality between family and nonfamily TMT members and the performance of family firms, *Academy of Management Journal*, 57 (6), 1624–1649.

Petrocelli, M., Piquero, A.R. and Smith, M.R. (2003). Conflict theory and racial profiling: An empirical analysis of police traffic stop data, *Journal of Criminal Justice*, 31 (1), 1–11.

Potipiroon, W. and Wongpreedee, A. (2020). Ethical climate and whistleblowing intentions: Testing the mediating roles of public service motivation and psychological safety among local government employees, *Public Personnel Management*, published online doi:10.1177/0091026020944547.

Qiu, B. and Slezak, S.L. (2019). The equilibrium relationships between performance-based pay, performance, and the commission and detection of fraudulent misreporting, *The Accounting Review*, 94 (2), 325–356.

Rehg, M.T., Miceli, M.P., Near, J.P. and Scotter, J.R.V (2009). Antecedents and outcomes of retaliation against whistleblowers: Gender differences and power relationships, *Organization Science*, 19 (2), 221–240.

Resodihardjo, S.L., Carroll, B.J., Eijk, C.J.A. and Maris, S. (2015). Why traditional responses to blame games fail: The importance of context, rituals, and sub-blame games in the face of raves gone wrong, *Public Administration*, 94 (2), 350–363.

Reuters (2020). Germany's DAX index gets shake-up in wake of Wirecard scandal, *Reuters*, www.reuters.com, published November 24.

Rothe, D.L. (2020). Moving beyond abstract typologies? Overview of state and state-corporate crime, *Journal of White-Collar and Corporate Crime*, 1 (1), 7–15.

Rothe, D.L. and Medley, C. (2020). Beyond state and state-corporate crime typologies: The symbiotic nature, harm, and victimization of crimes of the powerful and their continuation, in: Rorie, M. (editor), *The Handbook of White-Collar Crime*, Hoboken, NJ: John Wiley & Sons, chapter 6, pages 81–94.

Scheaf, D.J. and Wood, M.S. (2021). Entrepreneurial fraud: A multidisciplinary review and synthesized framework, *Entrepreneurship: Theory and Practice*, published online doi:10.1177/0422587211001818, pages 1–36.

Shawver, T. and Clements, L.H. (2019). The impact of value preferences on whistle-blowing intentions of accounting professionals, *Journal of Forensic and Investigative Accounting*, 11 (2), 232–247.

Solgård, J. (2020). "Bestemors favorittbank" ga milliardlån til tidligere Wirecard-sjef ("Grandma's favorite bank" gave billions in loans to former Wirecard boss), daily Norwegian business newspaper *Dagens Næringsliv*, www.dn.no, published July 9.

Srivastava, S.B. and Goldberg, A. (2017). Language as a window into culture, *California Management Review*, 60 (1), 56–69.

Storbeck, O. (2020a). Wirecard: The frantic final months of a fraudulent operation, *Financial Times*, www.ft.com, published August 25.

Storbeck, O. (2020b). Whistleblower warned EY of Wirecard fraud four years before collapse, *Financial Times*, www.ft.com, published September 30.

Storbeck, O. (2021a). Prosecutors delayed arrest warrant for Wirecard's Jan Marsalek, *Financial Times*, www.ft.com, published January 29.

Storbeck, O. (2021b). German parliament expands probe into EY's audits of Wirecard, *Financial Times*, www.ft.com, published April 22.

Storbeck, O. and Morris, S. (2021). BaFin files insider trading complaint against Deutsche Bank board member, *Financial Times*, www.ft.com, published April 19.

Szalma, J.L. and Hancock, P.A. (2013). A signal improvement to signal detection analysis: fuzzy SDT on the ROCs, *Journal of Experimental Psychology: Human Perception and Performance*, 39 (6), 1741–1762.

Tankebe, J. (2019). Cooperation with the police against corruption: Exploring the roles of legitimacy, deterrence and collective action theories, *British Journal of Criminology*, 59, 1390–1410.

Thaxton, S. and Agnew, R. (2018). When criminal coping is likely: An examination of conditioning effects in general strain theory, *Journal of Quantitative Criminology*, 34, 887–920.

Tombs, S. and Whyte, D. (2003). Scrutinizing the powerful: Crime, contemporary political economy, and critical social research, in: Tombs, S. and Whyte, D. (editors), *Unmasking the Crimes of the Powerful*, New York, NY: Lang, pages 3–48.

Toolami, B.N., Roodposhti, F.R., Nikoomaram, H., Banimahd, B. and Vakilifard, H. (2019). The survey of whistleblowing intentions for accounting frauds based on demographic individual differences among accounting staff, *International Journal of Finance and Managerial Accounting*, 4 (14), 1–13.

Wall-Parker, A. (2020). Measuring white collar crime, in: Rorie, M.L. (editor), *The Handbook of White-Collar Crime*, Hoboken, NJ: John Wiley & Sons, chapter 3, pages 32–44.

Weick, K.E., Sutcliffe, K.M. and Obstfeld, D. (2005). Organizing and the process of sensemaking, *Organization Science*, 16 (4), 409–421.

Welsh, D.T., Bush, J., Thiel, C. and Bonner, J. (2019). Reconceptualizing goal setting's dark side: The ethical consequences of learning versus outcome goals, *Organizational Behavior and Human Decision Processes*, 150, 14–27.

Zysman-Quirós, D. (2020). White-collar crime in South and Central America: Corporate-state crime, governance, and the high impact of the Odebrecht corruption case, in: Rorie, M.L. (editor), *The Handbook of White-Collar Crime*, Hoboken, NJ: John Wiley & Sons, chapter 23, pages 363–380.

10 Stanland Autobiography

Craig Stanland in the United States is a white-collar convict who recently wrote his autobiography. The title of his autobiography is "Blank Canvas – How I reinvented my life after prison" (Stanland, 2021). The book focuses on the terrible consequences that he suffered from his detected wrongdoing. He had exploited the warranty policy of his employer to privately make money on spare parts that were not requested by his employer's customers. He was arrested by the FBI and sentenced to two years in federal prison, followed by three years of supervised release, and was ordered to pay USD 834,307 in restitution. He lost his wife, his homes, his cars, his career, and his identity – according to the autobiography.

Autobiographies by convicted white-collar offenders are an interesting and relevant source of information to review the convenience in financial motives, organizational opportunities, and personal willingness for deviant behavior. Examples include Benulic (2018) in Sweden, Middelhoff (2017) in Germany, Belfort (2008) in the United States, Olav (2014, 2015) in Norway, and Kerik (2015) in the United States. They all wrote their autobiographies while in jail for financial crime committed in a professional setting. They were all members of the elite in society as privileged individuals in private business or public administration.

White-Collar Support Member

One of the members of Jeff Grant's white-collar support group at website www.prisonist.org was Craig Stanland. In 2021, he published his book; "Blank Canvas: How I reinvented my life after prison" (Stanland, 2021). He started his book with a voicemail message that he received on October 1, 2013:

> "Mr. Stanland, this is Special Agent McTiernan with the FBI. We are at your residence and have a warrant for your arrest. You will need to call us and come home immediately, or we will issue an APB with the federal marshals for your arrest."

The following text can be found on the back cover of his book:

DOI: 10.4324/9781003305071-11

In 2021, Craig Stanland made a choice that would cost him everything. After he had exploited the warranty policy of one of the largest tech companies in the world for almost a year, the FBI finally knocked on his door. He was arrested and sentenced to two years in federal prison, followed by three years of supervised release, and was ordered to pay $834,307 in restitution. He lost his wife, his homes, his cars, his career, and even his identity. He wanted nothing more than to die.

The FBI posted on their website (www.fbi.gov) on June 10, 2014, a notice that a Stamford man was sentenced to federal prison for running a USD 800,000 fraudulent computer networking parts scheme:

> Deirdre M. Daly, United States Attorney for the District of Connecticut, announced that CRAIG A. STANLAND, 40, of Stamford, was sentenced today by U.S. District Judge Janet Bond Arterton in New Haven to 24 months of imprisonment, followed by three years of supervised release, for fraudulently obtaining hundreds of computer networking parts from Cisco Systems Inc. According to court documents and statements made in court, from October 2012 until he was arrested October 1, 2013, STANLAND operated a service contract fraud scheme in which he purchased or controlled approximately 18 service contracts for Cisco networking parts.

Stanland used aliases such as "Alan Johnston of Opex Solutions" and "Kyle Booker of KLB Networks" to make hundreds of false service requests to Cisco to replace purportedly defective computer networking parts. Cisco then shipped replacement parts to various addresses, where Stanland sold the new parts to third parties to enrich himself. The total loss to Cisco was USD 834,307.

In May 2021, Craig Stanland posted the following blog on the white-collar support group website at www.prisonist.org:

> On September 30th, 2013, I had what many would call,
>
> "It all."
>
> A successful career, multiple homes, nice cars, nice watches, I ate at the finest restaurants in Greenwich and Manhattan. I was married to an amazing and beautiful woman.
>
> On October 1st, 2013, I lost it all.
>
> Even though I had "it all," I never thought I did, and what I did have, I didn't feel worthy of.
>
> I didn't feel worthy of my success; I didn't feel worthy of my beautiful wife.
>
> I was chasing anything and everything outside of myself to feel whole. To feel complete. To be someone people would respect, like, and love.
>
> I was desperately trying to become someone I would respect, like, and love.
>
> Chasing, chasing, chasing.
>
> I was on a treadmill, trying to catch the horizon.

The next purchase, the next high, the next extravagant dinner – all of them would make me feel worthy and complete. I would be someone.

Until the rush would inevitably fade, and I'd be off to the races, chasing the next thing. It was exhausting.

My self-worth and my identity were inextricably tied to the things I owned, the things I purchased, and my ability to purchase those things.

I was my BMW's, my Panerai watches, my $300 bottle of Rioja, my Platinum Amex Card.

I had no idea what I was doing at the time. I had no idea of the absurdity of the task I was taking on. I was trying to fill a broken glass with my things and utterly blind to the fact that I never could.

The equipment I was selling was becoming more commoditized, the profit margins were shrinking, and so were my paychecks.

My job performance was also dwindling; I was too consumed with chasing.

My dwindling checks and performance were a direct threat to my very identity and sense of worth. I had to do something.

I could have been honest with myself and my wife. I could have told the truth that I couldn't maintain our lifestyle.

I didn't. I was too afraid; I was too scared to be seen as "less than." I couldn't find the courage to shed the facade I created.

I had to do something else to maintain this house of cards.

I discovered an opportunity to exploit our partner companies warranty policy for my financial gain. This would solve the problem; this would make everything ok.

For just under a year, I committed fraud against one of the largest technology companies in the world.

I committed this fraud in the face of my heart telling begging me not to.

With each click of the mouse, each time hit the enter button to perpetuate the fraud, my heart spoke,

"Don't do this."

"This is not the way."

"You know this isn't right."

And I ignored it every time.

It came to a screeching halt on October 1st, 2013, when the FBI caught up with me.

I was arrested and charged with one count of mail fraud.

This was the first day on my long descent to rock bottom.

I pleaded guilty and was sentenced to two years of federal prison.

I was consumed with shame. I destroyed for my life; I ruined my wife's life.

I hated the man I had become; I hated the choices I made. I hated the crystal clear clarity that I did this.

That I was wrong.

That I was responsible.

That I could have avoided all this suffering if only I had been honest.

I had to make the pain stop; I begged the hand of death to kill me in my sleep, suicide became a viable option.

This was my rock bottom.

I was lucky; my best friend of over thirty years visited me in prison. It was from here that my life turned around.

This was the day I started to rebuild.

If you had told me that eight years later, I would experience one of the most emotional, transformational, joyful, transcendent experiences of my life resulting from that pain, I would have thought you were insane.

But that's precisely what happened.

On May 13th, 2021, I carried three heavy cardboard boxes up four flights of stairs into my apartment in Brooklyn.

I carefully opened the boxes with a razor knife, removed the packing paper and saw, and held, for the first time, my experience in its physical manifestation.

I took all of that pain, all of the shame, all of the embarrassment, all of the guilt, all of the fear, and I alchemized it into a book.

"Blank Canvas, How I Reinvented My Life After Prison"

I wrote it because I had to.

I know that sharing my experience at rock bottom will help someone with theirs. They will see that they are not alone.

This book took over six years to write, spread across eight drafts and approximately one million words. I had to write those one million words to get to the fifty-two thousand in the book that capture the truth of my experience.

It's the truth that will help someone who feels right now how I once felt.

Writing is a solitary practice. It's me and the words.

But the emotions and the experiences I capture, that's not only me.

That's my family, friends, and the Progressive Prison Ministries. They guided me and supported me on my rapid descent to rock bottom and the slow journey out.

To know that you're not alone when you feel most alone is one of the most powerful realizations we can have.

This is what our family and friends do; this is what a community does- they inform us that we are not alone.

Sometimes that's all we need.

The Progressive Prison Ministries is that community.

Jeff Grant wrote about Craig Stanland that he is a powerful example of how to come back from the depths of professional and personal destruction and despair, survive and evolve in prison, and become a better, more fulfilled person living the life God intended for him. However, the most interesting aspect of the autobiography is not necessarily how Craig Stanland claimed he reinvented his life after prison, but rather his reason for regret of white-collar crime. His regret is not caused by the victimization of his employer or his violation of the law, but rather by the consequences of his detected wrongdoing. If his wrongdoing had not been detected, or if the detection would not have such serious consequences for him, then it seems that Stanland thinks he has committed no serious wrongdoing.

Offender Convenience Themes

Craig Stanland experienced that his paycheck at work was shrinking. Much of his salary was based on a bonus arrangement that resulted in less money. At the same time, he had recently bought an expensive home, and he enjoyed meals at fashionable restaurants with his wife that he had recently married. These were elements of his individual possible motives as indicated in Figure 10.1.

Stanland (2021: 28) described his desire and excitement regarding a house that was too expensive for him:

> We went to more open houses than I can count searching for this home. We knew we found it the moment we walked through the front door. It

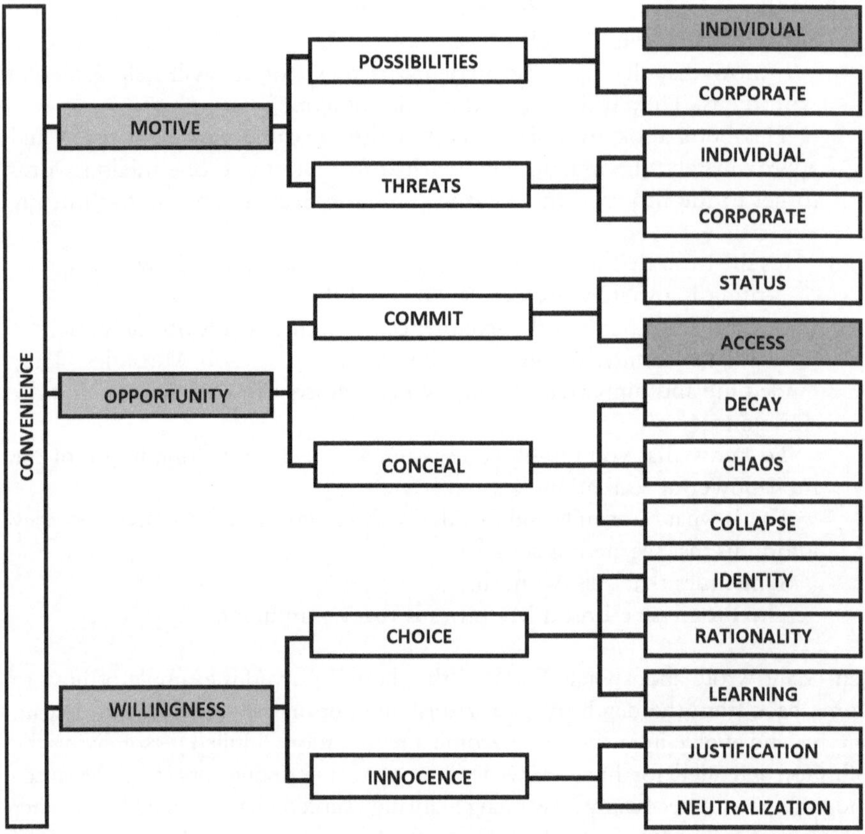

Figure 10.1 Convenience themes in the case of Craig Stanland

> was new construction, and we would be the first to live in it. The kitchen opens to the living room, the Wolf range with its red knobs begging to be used. The master bath a sea of white Carrara marble. A guest bedroom for family and friends. Moving from our small one-bedroom, we would have more room for Kyla's growing vintage furniture business. This was the next chapter in our lives.

The court exemplified his restaurant spending in the following text (Stanland, 2021: 70):

> On April 20, 2013, Mr. Stanland went to Polpo restaurant, located in Greenwich, Connecticut, where he ordered the octopus appetizer, the spaghetti Bolognese, tiramisu for desert, and a bottle of Purple Angel wine. The total cost of the meal: $236.54.

He was living paycheck to paycheck. The paychecks were still big, but the bills were even bigger. He was spending more than he was making. Each month, he stressed how he would pay the American Express bill. He was worried how to maintain a lifestyle he was growing tired of. It was the crushing weight of maintaining an illusion, the lies, deception, and energy required to keep it alive. He found it exhausting. He was constantly living in the future, spending money he did not have.

The main convenience theme in the opportunity structure was access to resources in his position as presented by the prosecutor in court (Stanland, 2021: 69):

> From approximately October 2012 to the current date, Mr. Stanland committed fraud against the victim, using his position and vast knowledge of the company's policies to his illicit gain. Specifically, Mr. Stanland operated a service contract fraud scheme in which he purchased or controlled approximately eighteen service contracts for the victim's networking parts. Pursuant to these service contracts, Mr. Stanland – using aliases "Alan Johnston" of Opex Solutions, "Kyle Booker" of KLB Networks, "Steve Jones" of SHO Networks, "Robert Johnson" of Adaptations, "Paul Smith" of PS Solutions, among others – made hundreds of false service requests to the victim to replace purportedly defective computer networking parts. Based on these requests, the victim shipped replacement parts to various addresses at Mr. Stanland's direction, including to his home in Stamford; to his wife's business in Brookly, New York; and to two post office boxes in Greenwich, Connecticut. Mr. Stanland sold the new parts to third parties to enrich himself. Through this scheme, Mr. Stanland fraudulently obtained nearly 600 parts from the victim. In one month alone, Mr. Stanland profited $28,000.

The main convenience theme in the willingness dimension was neutralization of guilt as he felt he did not really harm his employer. The company was a large business, while his minor fraud had no real financial impact on his employer. He refused damage from crime, as there was no visible harm from the action. As an offender, he attempted to minimize the harm done. Denial of injury involves justifying an action by minimizing the harm it causes. The misbehavior is not very serious because no party suffers directly or visibly because of it. The common expression – no harm, no foul – appropriately represents denial of injury (Sims and Barreto, 2021).

Maybe he also felt entitled since he thought he was good at his job (Stanland, 2021: 229)

> I was good at my job. Very good. Always in the top three. Plaques, accolades, trips to Hawaii, the whole nine yards. A few times a year, the company held sales meetings and every meeting began the same way. One by one, each account executive would state their name, the office they worked in, and their client demographic. "Craig Stanland. Stamford, Connecticut. My client base is compromised of the largest financial institutions in the world".

How He Reinvented Himself

The book title claimed that he would describe in his autobiography "how I reinvented my life after prison". It is not easy to detect from reading the book if or how he reinvented his life despite the back cover suggesting a new life for him:

> Today, Craig is an author, speaker, and reinvention architect. He specializes in working with people whose lives have fallen apart, helping them reinvent themselves by showing them how to rebuild their self-worth and create the extraordinary lives they have always wanted.

He was asked if his crime was worth it. He was asked if the money was buried in the backyard. A few people liked to play the game of asking: Would you go back to prison for 30 days for a million dollars? Free and clear, no taxes. He would be an instant millionaire. But his response was no, he would not do it for a billion. Not one day. There is not enough money in the world.

Maybe this is the reinvention. That money does not matter. He went to the seaside where there is no money charge for swimming. He went to the forest where the trails are free to use. He sat on the bench in a park for free to watch people passing by (Stanland, 2021: 282): "I'm exactly where I am meant to be at this moment. I'm at peace. Every lesson learned; every moment led me here."

He concludes his book saying that it has been an incredible journey, the hardest of his life so far. He knew there were still more obstacles. He knew the past would catch up with him. He knew he would once again lock himself in the prison cells of shame, not being enough, unworthiness, and fear. The difference, he claims, is that now he has the keys.

White-Collar Support Group

Progressive Prison Ministries is the name of the white-collar support group. The community members of individuals, families, and groups with white-collar criminal justice issues have a desire to take responsibility for their actions and the wreckage they have caused. They want to make amends, change their lives, and move forward in a new way of life centered on hope, care, compassion, tolerance, and empathy (White Collar Support Group, 2021):

> Our experience shows us that many of us are suffering in silence with shame, remorse, and deep regret. Many of us have been stigmatized by our own families, friends and communities, and the business community. Our goal is to learn and evolve into a new spiritual way of life and then to reach out to offer all those suffering from these issues. In so doing, we will share our experiences, feelings, and resources to help make the quality of each other's lives more manageable.

One of the testimonials for Jeff Grant at Progressive Prison Ministries is posted on the website www.prisonist.org:

> Three months or so into dealing with a federal indictment for conspiracy (and wire fraud) in my wife's Ponzi scheme, I was confused at what I was facing, and scared at the thought of what this would do to my family, especially my youngest children then aged 9 and 11 who were soon to lose both their parents to prison. I remember the first time I spoke to Jeff. I had just dropped off my two at school and was sitting in my car in the Walmart parking lot where I wouldn't be disturbed. Jeff answered my call, and I nervously introduced myself. I realized fairly quickly that this would be someone who could help me find some of the answers I was seeking. We talked for at least 90 minutes that morning, and never once did he rush me off or make me feel I was an inconvenience, or my issues were not important.

When downloading from the open website www.prisonist.org in August 2021, the community is presented by Jeff Grant in the following way:

> Progressive Prison Ministries, Inc. is the world's first ministry supporting the white collar justice community. Founded by husband and wife, Jeff Grant and Lynn Springer in Greenwich CT in 2012, we incorporated as a nonprofit in Connecticut in 2014, and received 501(c) (3) status in 2015. Jeff has over three decades of experience in crisis management, business, law (former), reentry, recovery (clean & sober 17+ years), and executive and religious leadership. As Jeff was incarcerated for a white-collar crime he committed in 2001, he and Lynn have a first-hand perspective on the trials and tribulations that white-collar families have to endure as they navigate the criminal justice system and life beyond.

> Progressive Prison Ministries, Inc. is nonsectarian, serving those of all faiths, or no faith whatsoever. To date we have helped over three hundred fifty (350) individuals, and their families, to accept responsibility for their actions and to acknowledge the pain they have caused to others. In accordance with our commitment to restorative justice, we counsel our members to make amends as a first step in changing their lives and moving towards a new spiritual way of living centered on hope, care, compassion, tolerance, empathy and service to others. Our team has grown to over ten people, most with advanced degrees, all of whom are currently volunteering their time and resources.
>
> Progressive Prison Ministries' goal is to provide spiritual solutions and emotional support to those who are feeling alone, isolated, and hopeless. We have found that these individuals are suffering from a void but are stuck, and don't know what to do about it. Our objective is to help them find a path to a healthy, spirit-filled place on the other side of what may seem like insurmountable problems. Many of those we counsel are in a place where their previous lives have come to an end due to their transgressions. In many cases their legal problems have led to divorce, estrangement from their children, families, friends and support communities, and loss of a career. The toll this takes on individuals and families is emotionally devastating. White-collar crimes are often precipitated by other issues in the offenders' lives such as alcohol or drug abuse, and/or a physical or mental illness that lead to financial issues that overwhelms their ability to be present for themselves and their families and cause poor decision making. We recognize that life often presents us with such circumstances, sometimes which lead us to make mistakes in violation of the law.
>
> All conversations and communications between our ordained ministry and licensed clinical staff/partners and those we serve fall under state privilege laws. This is one reason that attorneys often allow and encourage their clients to maintain relationships with us while in active prosecution or litigation situations.
>
> If you, a friend, family member, colleague or client are suffering from a white collar criminal justice issue or are experiencing some other traumatic or life-altering event, and would like to find a path to a healthy, spirit-filled place on the other side of what seems like insurmountable problems, please contact us to schedule an initial call or appointment.
>
> Our ministry, as a 501(c) (3), accepts reasonable donations that are deductible to the extent permitted by law. For our Contact Us page to arrange an initial call, video chat, or in-person appointment, click here. For Jeff Grant's bio, click here. For Lynn Springer's bio, click here. For team member bios, click here.

Lynn Springer presented herself as the founding advocate of the innocent spouse and children project. As the innocent partner of a white-collar criminal, and a mother, "Lynn is called to this ministry with a heart of compassion and understanding". The team consisted of Chloe Coppola (organizing online meetings), Iyabo Onipede (supporting mission minded folks), Joshua Cagney (facilitating outpatient programs), Jacqueline Polverari (mentoring people), Tom Hardin (training anti-fraud), Babz Rawls Ivy (hosting criminal justice insider), Basia Skudrzyk (managing projects), Joseph Ciccone (supervising minister), Steve Bonenberger (writing), and Matt Lockwood (digitizing marketing).

The community started its white-collar crime weeks with the podcasts at prisonist.org in the fall of 2020 as listed in Table 10.1.

The list in Table 10.1 indicates the variety of topics and issues relevant to a community of white-collar offenders.

On Christmas day December 25, 2020, Jeff Grant emailed the following holiday message:

> In these most difficult times of personal and community trauma, I feel especially called to reach out to you with a message of hope and optimistic vision for the future. Whether God be everything, or God be nothing, I have chosen to accept God in all things. I have chosen to be one with God, and to open my heart and life – and my will – to this Higher Power to do with me in ways far beyond my imagination. This is a commitment I make every single day through spiritual practice, right action and by putting one step ahead of the other. Through this, I have been led out of the despair of my addictions, legal issues, self-sabotage, and poor choices.
>
> I know now that I have been blessed with a new and better life, although I certainly didn't know or understand this when things looked most bleak. For this, I am humbled and grateful beyond measure. I offer this to you in this holiday season as a gift of comfort and hope. You are not alone. We love you and are there for you. Knock on the door – it will be opened. Prayers and blessings my friends to you and those you love for happy & healthy holidays.
>
> With great love and admiration, Blessings, Jeff. Rev. Jeff Grant, J.D., M. Div. (he, him, his). Co-founder, Progressive Prison Ministries, Inc., Greenwich CT & Nationwide. Co-host, The Criminal Justice Insider Podcast. Host, White Collar Week.

The slogan for the community is the following statement: "It's the isolation that destroys us. The solution is in community". The mission of the community is as follows:

> Our mission is to introduce you to other members of the white collar justice community, to hear their very personal stories, and hopefully gain a broader perspective of what this is really all about. Maybe this will inspire some deeper thoughts and introspection? Maybe it will inspire some empathy and compassion for people you might otherwise resent or dismiss? And maybe it will help lift us all out of our own isolation and into community, so we can learn to live again in the sunshine of the spirit.

Table 10.1 List of podcast episodes in the first year of white-collar crime week

Episode	*Podcast for White-Collar Crime Week by Progressive Prison Ministries*
0	White-collar crime week with Jeff Grant: What is white-collar crime week?
1	Prison and reentry in the age of Covid-19: An evening without white-collar support group.
2	Substance abuse and recovery during Covid-19: Guests Trevor Shevin and Joshua Cagney.
3	Compassionate lawyering: Guests Chris Poulos, Corey Brinson, Bob Herbst, and George Hritz. Compassionate lawyering is defined as giving something more than just a case solution to clients. It is putting in that extra mile to help clients find a better, more productive life during and after their issues.
4	One-on-one with Tipper X: Tom Hardin. On this episode of the podcast the community had Tom Hardin, best known in the financial and legal world as "Tipper X". He spent much of his career as a hedge fund stock analyst. In 2008, as part of a cooperation agreement with the Department of Justice, Hardin assisted the U.S. government in understanding how insider trading occurred in the investment management industry. He became one of the most prolific informants in securities fraud history, helping to build over 20 of the 80+ individual criminal cases in "Operation Perfect Hedge", a Wall Street house cleaning campaign that morphed into the largest insider trading investigation of a generation.
5	Trauma and healing when mom goes to prison: Guests Jacqueline Polverari and her daughters Alexa and Maria. Polverari is presented in a previous chapter as a trusted female offender in this book.
6	Madoff talks: Guest Jim Campbell.
7	White-collar wives: Guests Lynn Springer, Cassie Monaco, Julie Bennett, and special guest Skylar Cluett.
8	The academics: Guests Cathryn Lavery, Jessica Henry, Jay Kennedy, and Erin Harbinson.
9	Small business edition: Guest tax girl Kelly Phillips Erb.
10	The ministers: Guests father Joe Ciccone and father Rix Thorsell.
11	The blank canvas – How I reinvented my life after prison: Guest Craig Stanland who wrote the book with the same title.
12	The truth tellers: Guests Holli Coulman and Larry Levine.
13	Everything but bridge gate: Guest Bill Baroni.
14	Recovery and neighborhood: Guest Tom Scott. Thomas W. Scott was an American entrepreneur and co-founder of Nantucket Nectars, a beverage company he founded with Tom First. The company reached national prominence as one of the fastest growing U.S. companies five years in a row. The success of Tom & Tom, as the business duo became known, has been documented in a Harvard Business School case study written by Biotti, Lassiter, and Sahlman. Eventually Tom & Tom sold Nantucket Nectars to Cadbury Schweppes. Tom Scott then started the Nantucket Project, a thought and ideas festival each fall on the island of Nantucket. He also founded the Neighborhood Project that brings films about what matters most to discussion groups in people's homes all over the country and the world. This is where Jeff Grant got to know him. The power of neighborhoods can bring justice-impacted families out of isolation and into communities.

Episode	*Podcast for White-Collar Crime Week by Progressive Prison Ministries*
15	A brave talk about suicide: Guests Bob Flanagan, Elizabeth Kelley, and Meredith Atwood.
16	Politicians, prison and penitence: Guest mayor Joseph Ganim in Bridgeport, Connecticut.
17	Truth heals: Systemic abuse and institutional reform with Vanessa Osage featuring guest co-host Chloe Coppola. Vanessa Osage tells her story of reporting sexual abuse at one of the United States' elite boarding schools, retribution, cover-up, engaging, and then abandoning the legal system, attention in some of the nation's most respected newspapers and media, starting a non-profit to serve others going through these kinds of issues, and writing her memoir "Can't stop the sunrise: Adventures in healing, confronting corruption, and the journey to institutional reform". Joining as co-host is Chloe Coppola, an advocate with the Progressive Prison Ministries, who shares the story of her sexual abuse and institutional response while she was a student at her own prep school.
18	Is your life a movie? The producers with guests Lydia B. Smith, Bethany Jones, and Will Nix. Many in the white-collar justice community tell that they are writing books about their experiences, or that someone should make a movie about them.
19	Insider trading charges dismissed: Guest Richard Lee. He was a trader at Steve Cohen's hedge fund, SAC Capital, and had insider trading charges against him dismissed after a 7 year fight to clear his name. Lee initially pleaded guilty to insider trading charges in 2013, and upon discovery of new evidence in 2017, he moved to withdraw his original plea. On June 21, 2019, a federal court judge for the Southern District of New York granted Lee's motion to vacate his guilty plea, and then on November 27, 2019, federal prosecutors dismissed all charges against him.
20	Reinventing yourself after prison: Guests Glenn E. Martin and Richard Bronson. Martin talks about his journey from armed robber, to prison, to nonprofit executive, to founding JustLeadershipUSA, to entrepreneur, executive coach and investor. Bronson talks about his Wall Street life, including at Stratton Oakmont (made famous in the movie 'The Wolf of Wall Street'), federal prison, and then founding two companies to lift up returning citizens. The main character at Stratton Oakmont and in the movie was Jordan Belfort (played by Leonardo DiCaprio), who is presented in a previous chapter on chair of the board in this book.
21	Hanna Smolinski providing small businesses with financial clarity as they grow.
22	The goddess Babz Rawls Ivy: In this episode, the podcast goes into her story of childhood abuse and trafficking. She served time in Danbury federal prison.
23	Robert Katzberg who has seen it all as a federal prosecutor and as a criminal defense trial lawyer.
24	Seth Williams became a federal inmate serving 5 months of his 60 months sentence in solitary confinement. Seth describes his fall from grace from being elected the first African-American district attorney of Philadelphia, America's fifth largest city, to being tried for corruption charges and incarcerated for five years.
25	Seth Williams in the second episode of a two-part interview. Seth describes his fall from grace becoming a federal inmate.

Episode	*Podcast for White-Collar Crime Week by Progressive Prison Ministries*
26	Jaco and Leslie Theron on oppression and identity. They are two ministers in South Africa serving the poor and marginalized people in the bush.
27	Bryan Cuban wrote the book "The Addicted Lawyer, Tales of the Bar, Booze, Blow and Redemption".
28	Kelly Paxton and Brian Willingham are two private investigators who work in the world of fraud, embezzlement, and other forms of white-collar crime.
29	David Israel and Spencer Oberg, two successful entrepreneurs who both served time in prison.
30	Barry Bekkedam was a real estate investor, a multi-billion dollar investment manager, and then some of his clients lost money in the Rothstein Ponzi scheme.
31	The confessional: Nadia Bolz-Weber wrote books entitled "The Cranky, Beautiful Faith Of A Sinner & Saint" and "Accidental Saints: Finding God in All The Wrong People".
32	The blank canvas – How I reinvented my life after prison: Guest Craig Stanland who wrote the book with the same title. Same as podcast 11, but now his book was out.as well as his blog quoted earlier.
33	The outlaw-insider takes on criminal justice: Chandra Bozelko is a fellow traveler with the white-collar support group. She was the 2020 Sigma Delta Chi Award winner from the Society of Professional Journalists.
34	Drifting between liminal communities: Bobby Jagdev is of Sikh heritage. He and his family found themselves strangers in a strange land, refugees living in liminality between their old world and the new, between traditional and contemporary values, navigating prejudice and distrust. Similarly, people prosecuted for white-collar crime and their families often find themselves stigmatized by their former friends and families, and the business community – people without a country, mourning the past and afraid of the future, struggling to find acceptance of the reality of their new and very difficult situations. It is the isolation that destroys you, while the solution is in community.
35	The great women of fraud podcast with Kelly Paxton. She is the workplace dishonesty expert. "I am an expert on dishonesty in the workplace. I want to talk to you about how good people can make bad choices. For over 20 years, I've worked all types of investigations: money laundering, embezzlement, conflict of interest, and criminal defense work. I have worked in the public and private sector. My clients have been government agencies, publicly traded companies, non-profits, medical offices and gaming. They all hired me because they needed to uncover the truth and take action to fix the problem".

So, we invite you to come along with us as we experience something new, and bold, and different – a podcast that serves the entire white collar justice community. I hope you will join us.

Then following this mission statement come requests for donations: Thank you for your support! Thank you for your generous donation! We have no dues or fees, but we do have expenses!

References

Belfort, J. (2008). *The Wolf of Wall Street: How Money Destroyed a Wall Street Superman*, London, UK: Hodder & Stoughton.

Benulic, B. (2018). *Inte mitt krig (Not my war)*, Sweden: Cultura Aetatis publishing.

Kerik, B.B. (2015). *From jailer to jailed: My journey from correction and police commissioner to inmate #84888–054*, New York, NY: Threshold Editions.

Middelhoff, T. (2017). *Der Sturz: Die Autobiografie von Thomas Middelhoff (The Fall: The autobiography of Thomas Middelhoff)*, Stuttgart, Germany: LangenMuller in der F.A. Herbig Verlagsbuchhandlung.

Olav, H.E. (2014). *Det store selvbedraget: Hvordan statsmakt ødelegger menneskeverd og velferd (The grand self-deception: How state power harms human dignity and welfare)*, Oslo, Norway: Kolofon publishing.

Olav, H.E. (2015). *The Grand Self-Deception: A Libertarian Manifesto Against the Deep State – The Failed Welfare-Taxation Model of Norway*, Kindle Edition, printed in Great Britain by Amazon.

Sims, R.L. and Barreto, T.S. (2021). In defense of leader misconduct: The use of neutralization techniques by ingroup members, *The Journal of Social Psychology*, published online doi:10.1080/00224545.2021.1944033.

Stanland, C. (2021). *Blank Canvas – How I Reinvented My Life After Prison*, Lioncrest Publishing.

White Collar Support Group (2021). Meets online on Zoom Monday evenings 7 pm ET, 6 pm CT, 5 pm MT, 4 pm PT, 2 pm HST, *Progressive Prison Ministries*, www.prisonist.org.

Conclusion

In the Norwegian Business School in Oslo, Norway, students in the elective class on financial crime have recently evaluated a number of investigation reports similar to what is presented in this book. Their evaluations are interesting in the perspective of assessing work by investigating firms such as Ernst & Young, PwC, Deloitte, and KPMG. Students were asked to grade investigation reports on a scale from 1 (grade A) to 6 (grade F). In the sample from the last two years, there were 23 student grades for Ernst & Young work, 41 student grades for PwC work, 22 student grades for Deloitte work, six student grades for BDO work, and one student grade for KPMG work.

The average score for Ernst & Young was 2.8, for PwC 3.4, for Deloitte 2.5, for BDO 3.7, and for KPMG 4.0. Thus, business school students found the best work among Deloitte reports, followed by reports from Ernst & Young and PwC, ending with KPMG at the bottom. Of course, this is by no means sufficient material to judge the various auditing firms when they conduct fraud examinations for their clients. Nevertheless, it is an interesting avenue for future research.

The largest grade samples for Ernst & Young (23 student grades) and PwC (41 student grades) was sufficient for a statistical test of difference. The statistical test was concerned with the issue of whether the distributions of grades for the two firms were significantly different with averages of 2.8 and 3.4. T-statistic resulted in a significance of .064, which is not satisfactory. When the same test included Deloitte and PwC with averages of 2.5 and 3.4 respectively, the difference was indeed significant at .002. Thus, from a statistical point of view, students consider work by Deloitte fraud examiners to be significantly better than work by PwC fraud examiners.

As documented in this book, most fraud examiners have a long way to go before their work can be considered an investment at the highest maturity level in the stages of growth model for internal investigations. One of the problems is the treatment of suspects who become the subjects of investigations. Therefore, I have provided the following 18 pieces of advice to individuals who become subjected to fact-finding investigations published by Khrono:

1 Find yourself a lawyer and require that your employer pays for the lawyer, who will assist you before, during, and after the fact-finding.

DOI: 10.4324/9781003305071-12

2 Require access to documentation of the investigator's competence within organizational behavior and management.
3 Require that the examiner be certified by a public authority or professional association.
4 Require that the client for the fact-finding is included as a topic in the mandate.
5 Demand openness and transparency in the investigation process as an examination is never about a personnel matter.
6 Check that the fraud examiner never presents information that can be confirmed by only one source of information.
7 Take your time when you are given the opportunity for a defense (contradiction), where you counter claims about yourself.
8 Check that the inquiry is limited to misconduct and never takes a position to potential violations of the law.
9 Expect that the inquiry be completed at the expense of the investigator if the financial funding has been spent.
10 Contact the police if you experience unreasonable treatment or if the private investigator obstructs the work of the police.
11 Report to the police if the examiner assumes all three roles of investigator, prosecutor, and judge.
12 If you do not understand the text of the report from the investigation, you should demand that the report be rewritten.
13 Any objection (contradiction) from you should be included in its entirety in the investigation report.
14 Require time for your own review of the draft report to make sure that examiners have understood and reflected your contradiction in the report before the examiners submit the report to their client.
15 Reject lawyers' secrecy and client-attorney privilege for fraud examiners, because lawyers as consultants in factual investigations do not have a duty of confidentiality.
16 Reject a conclusion that is based on the preponderance of probability, because it must be documented that the conclusion is valid beyond any reasonable doubt.
17 In the event of unreasonable treatment by the examiner, you should demand compensation and reversal payment from the examiner and the examiner's firm.
18 In the event of an unfounded initiative for the fact-finding that has placed an unreasonable burden on you, you should demand that your employer pay you compensation and cover reversal needs.

The market for internal investigations might be classified into the following three categories:

(A) Clients who pay whatever it takes to get a clean bill: Swedish bank Swedbank paid law firm Clifford Chance to reduce the bank's responsibility for money laundering in Eastern Europe, Danish bank Danske Bank paid similarly law firm Bruun Hjejle to reduce the bank's responsibility for money laundering in Eastern Europe, Icelandic seafood company Samherji paid law firm Wikborg Rein to distance the headquarters from corruption incidents in Namibia, and Wirecard paid audit firm KPMG as presented in this book.

(B) Clients who pay as little as possible to demonstrate that they have investigated the matter: FIFA world cup corruption was investigated by the ethics committee headed by Garcia, and IMDi paid audit firm Ernst & Young to investigate Born Free as presented in this book.

(C) Clients who are negative to investigations: Oceanteam disliked being investigated for management fraud by law firm Sands, and Stange forests disliked being investigated for owner dispute by Ernst & Yong. However, court orders required and requested these investigations.

Swedbank allegedly paid USD 190 million for the Clifford Chance investigation. That seems to be a record-high price to pay for an internal investigation. Bruun Hjejle allegedly received USD 20 million from Danske Bank. In contrast, IMDi paid USD 15,000 to Ernst & Young for their investigation into Shabana Rehman's Born Free. In the final category C, Oceanteam was forced by the court to pay USD 900,000 to Sands. As emphasized by Gottschalk and Tcherni-Buzzeo (2017), there is secrecy that dominates internal investigations by fraud examiners, especially when it comes to what clients have paid examiners; so obtaining market prices for various private investigations is extremely difficult.

There are a substantial number of lessons that can be drawn out of the case studies in this book, which represent recommendations for fraud investigators. These lessons relate to mandate, strategy, and outcome. The lessons can help future examiners climb to a higher maturity level in their next internal investigation assignments. First, the mandate is the contract between examiner and client regarding the substance of work. Too often, clients tend to have an opinion about the money side of an examination in terms of the price they have to pay, and then leave it to examiners to identify what has to be investigated. Clients may claim that this is new to them, and that examiners know what to do. However, clients have the problems, not examiners. Therefore, examiners should work with clients to improve the mandate ahead of investigations, so that everyone can see after investigations are closed whether or not assignments were successfully completed.

This leads to the second lesson concerning strategy, as strategy should be considered and possibly included in the mandate. It is not solely for the examiner to decide what knowledge categories, information sources, value configuration, computer systems, and inquiry approach should be applied to a specific investigation. Rather, the client should be asked to have an opinion about relevant choices concerning these strategic themes. Too often, examiners mainly offer and apply legal knowledge by attorneys. They should discuss with clients in advance whether other categories are more appropriate in addition or instead of legal knowledge. For example, if the investigative challenge starts by identifying potential offenders and victims, then organizational management knowledge combined with psychology and sociology is most relevant to apply to the examination. It is not the firm – whether audit firm, law firm, or other kind of consulting firm – that is conducting the investigation. Rather, it is individuals who currently have time – and who are not necessarily most relevant or qualified – that are assigned to investigative tasks by the supplier of forensic services.

Knowledge categories are linked to the second strategic theme concerning information sources. Typically, an investigation starts by exploring human information sources such as whistleblowers and other observers, potential victims and offenders, and stakeholders. Interviewing skills are crucial at this stage of the investigation. Cooperative rather than confrontational interviewing styles have proven to be most efficient, since the purpose of interviews is to obtain as much information as possible about relevant circumstances. Interviews tend to point and guide examiners in the direction of relevant written materials to be studied, which typically include emails and reports, minutes of meetings, accounting and financial statements, and bank transactions. Content analysis skills are crucial at this stage of the investigation, as examiners have to interpret text and number in a relevant context. Visiting potential crime scenes can be of relevance, as peoples' behaviors and office spaces might indicate structural and cultural aspects in the client organization that can provide new inquiry leads.

New inquiry leads impact the third strategic theme of value configuration. A choice exists between the sequential approach of a value chain and the iterative approach of a value shop. New inquiry leads require the value shop approach where examiners return to the first primary activity of defining and redefining the client's problem. Examiners have to ask themselves whether they have somehow misunderstood what the client problem is all about. They have to question their own inquiry approach, which is the fifth strategic theme. Often, examiners need to rephrase their information needs that can only be satisfied by digital tools, which is the fourth strategic theme. Now computer skills are needed to search for digital evidence. Too often, examiners are passive receivers of information from clients, and they are reactive in their inquiry approach. Examiners have to be active inquirers who access client computer systems, social media, and other digital sources to explore and exploit inquiry leads.

The final lesson from this book is concerned with outcome. Typically, the outcome is a report of investigation that can range from 30 to 3,000 pages. While a report of 30 pages seldom covers the need to explain how examiners reached their conclusions, a report of 3,000 pages is a hopeless endeavor to dive into. A summary of some pages does not compensate for a very long report, since most examiners fail in writing a summary as an abstract of the complete report. The report should convince the reader of the relevance and justification of examination conclusions. The outcome of an examination should be a clear answer to questions in the mandate. Examiners should never blame others when they fail in answering the mandate. For example, if some information sources were unwilling to be questioned in interviews, examiners should blame themselves for failing in gaining the confidence of potential interviewees.

There is a desperate and acute need for developing an academic program concerned with educating fraud examiners for internal investigations. Crime investigations are mainly taught in criminal justice departments at universities in some countries such as the United Kingdom and the United States, and mainly taught at police academies in some countries such as Norway and Germany. There is a need for business schools at universities to develop courses on fraud investigations that move beyond the traditional topics of business ethics. Business school students need to learn how to conduct inquiries when there are suspicions of misconduct and crime related to financial matters in the organization.

References

Gottschalk, P. and Tcherni-Buzzeo, M. (2017). Reasons for gaps in crime reporting: The case of white-collar criminals investigated by private fraud examiners in Norway, *Deviant Behavior*, 38 (3), 267–281.

Index